'*The KM Cookbook* fulfils many of the needs of knowledge management professionals in the sense that it provides an applied deliberation on the new KM standard, ISO 30401. Collison, Corney and Eng continue by explicating the interpretation of ISO 30401, preparing for an audit and the actual audit process. However, *The KM Cookbook* proceeds by applying the key principles of the ISO 30401 as several leading use cases of KM are discussed from within the framework of the KM standard.'
Dr Deonie Botha, Associate Director, Deloitte & Touche

'A book on knowledge management which not only sets new standards for this discipline but is actually fun to read. The enthusiasm and passion of the authors – who live and breathe KM – is reflected on every page of their cookbook.'
Dr. Raffael Büchi, Owner of OWLegal, a consulting company focusing on legal KM, and Chair of the conference KM Legal Europe (since 2014)

'Collison, Corney and Eng have taken a would-be dry subject and delved into it in a creative manner, weaving fact and guidance into a narrative that simultaneously informs and entertains. What they have done with this book is a demonstration of a key aspect of knowledge management itself: the use of storytelling to make important knowledge accessible to the average person. Certify that, ISO 30401.'
Larry Campbell, Partner, KPMG China

'Make no mistake – this book is worth its weight in salt. While it prepares you for the ISO Standards, it has some of the finest current case studies globally. Anyone reading this book will come away truly enriched and motivated. It is crafted in simple but elegant language devoid of jargon. For me, this book serves a higher purpose. I am constantly asked to 'simplify' KM to a level where a lay person can understand. I have found an answer to that in the form of *The KM Cookbook*.'
Rudolf D'Souza, Chief Knowledge Officer, Afcons Infrastructure and Chair 2019, KM Global Network

'Chris Collison, Paul Corney, and Patricia Eng have written a practical and easy-to-understand guide to knowledge management. *The KM Cookbook* combines a helpful explanation of ISO 30401 – the first international KM standard – with methods, tools, and stories to support successfully implementing KM. It uses the clever metaphor of a restaurant to describe the KM standard, tools, and stakeholders. The KM Chef's Canvas is included as a useful tool to assess KM programmes applying the new standard.'
Stan Garfield, Knowledge Management Author, Speaker, and Community Leader

'*The KM Cookbook* is aptly named, as it draws from global perspectives, global solutions and is patterned together through extensive, detailed experience. Both the immediate and the practical as well as the introspective, and strategic are offered as recipes. This is a book that will help to connect leadership within organizations with the insights and methods to enact their vision.'
Eric Hunter, Managing Director of Spherical Models, LLC and Chief Technology Officer of Bradford & Barthel, LLP

T0322976

'This is a wise, practical and very accessible book, spiced with examples from knowledge managers in the field, to illustrate how the ISO 30401 KM standard can be applied in practice. It captures the variety and context sensitivity of KM, as well as its focus on excellence. Metaphors can be distracting or overly abstract, but in this book, the restaurant metaphor is a winner!'
Patrick Lambe, Partner, Straits Knowledge

'Being a committed KM sponsor, or "Restaurateur" as *The KM Cookbook* would define me, I recommend the book as mandatory reading for all leaders and experts in KM roles. Not only does it explain the international standard on Knowledge Management, the new ISO30401, it also shares 16 very interesting stories on how different businesses, government organisations and NGOs deal with KM and exercise best practice.'
Aku Sorainen, Senior Partner, Sorainen

'Much more than a recipe book. *The KM Cookbook* goes beyond the 'what' to the 'how'. Part I offers a wealth of practical insight into the knowledge, tools and strategies that enable KM Masterchefs to reliably deliver great food, day after day. The rich diversity of KM is beautifully illustrated in Part II, with its global showcase of stories of KM in practice. Chris, Paul and Patricia show how getting the basics right can professionalise KM without compromising its wide range of flavours.'
Dr Sharon Varney, The Henley Forum at Henley Business School

'I'm one of the first to raise my hand as a skeptic of certifications and standards, feeling they are unnecessary boxes for emergent or complex practices. So I was gratified to read a pragmatic examination of the new KM standards and examples of how they might manifest through extensive case "stories" in *The KM Cookbook*. Standards aside, any organizational KM person can learn many things from this book - things they could implement tomorrow. So this is a win win, regardless of your view on the ISO standards! Dig into the "meal" that Chris, Paul and Patricia have prepared for us.'
Nancy White, Founder, Full Circle Associates

The KM Cookbook

Every purchase of a Facet book helps to fund CILIP's advocacy, awareness and accreditation programmes for information professionals.

The KM Cookbook

Stories and strategies for organisations
exploring Knowledge Management Standard
ISO 30401

Chris J. Collison, Paul J. Corney
and Patricia Lee Eng

facet
publishing

Published by Facet Publishing
c/o British Library, 96 Euston Road, London NW1 2DB
www.facetpublishing.co.uk

Facet Publishing is wholly owned by CILIP: the Library and Information Association.

British Library Cataloguing in Publication Data
A catalogue record for this book is available from the British Library.
ISBN 978-1-78330-431-8 (paperback)
ISBN 978-1-78330-432-5 (hardback)
ISBN 978-1-78330-433-2 (PDF)
ISBN 978-1-78330-434-9 (EPUB)

First published 2019
Reprinted with corrections 2023

Cover design by Kathryn Beecroft

Typeset from authors' files by Flagholme Publishing Services in 10/13pt University Old Style and Futura
Printed and made in Great Britain by CPI Group (UK) Ltd, Croydon, CR0 4YY.

Contents

List of illustrations

Appendices

Introduction

Everybody loves a cookbook. A real cookbook, that is.

You see them on coffee tables, kitchen tables, ready to be idly thumbed through - or meticulously followed through.

For many people, they are a source of inspiration to dip into for that perfect main course or hard-to-think-of dessert. For others, they spark new ideas for twists and variations on somebody else's theme. For a few people, cooking through the entire book becomes a goal in its own right . . .

The 2009 film *Julie and Julia* was the first major motion picture to be written about a blog. In the film, based on a true story, Meryl Streep plays Julia Child, chef and author of the 1961 classic *Mastering the Art of French Cooking*, and Amy Adams plays Julie Powell, a young, frustrated New York writer and blogger with a passion for food. Julie decides to cook all 524 recipes from Child's book in 365 days and blog her experiences. As she progresses towards this impossible goal, her blog gathers momentum and Julie gathers followers (and some heated relationship challenges) as she ticks every recipe and shares her experience of 'cooking out loud' with an ever-growing community.

ISO 30401 is widely seen as the first international standard to be written for Knowledge Management. Based on the experiences of regional practitioners and consultants around the world, it set out to define a measurable framework to describe Knowledge Management from the perspective of a management system. The process gathered momentum, and numerous followers and commentators (and some heated philosophical differences), working out loud to enable public comment. The first version of the standard was published in November 2018.

When the three of us met in the summer of 2018 for the first time to discuss this new development in KM, there was already plenty of debate and some angst amongst the KM cognoscenti regarding the new standard. Some welcomed it, some feared it, and some just didn't know what to think about it!

We wanted to help dispel some of the myths, misunderstanding and misconceptions.

We wanted to find a way to explain and unpack the standard which would move it beyond a 'ticking every recipe' experience but make it an enriching experience for organisations considering the merits of accreditation.

Finally, we wanted to position it as an opportunity for inspiration for those starting out in KM, and for established practitioners, a framework to review strengths and discover what might have been missing in their own programmes.

Chris and Paul have over 35 years' experience of KM consulting between them, working with around 200 organisations. Combined with Patricia's background as a long-time auditor, writer of regulations and KM programme lead, we felt that we were uniquely positioned to provide insight into the ISO audit process, what the standard does and how KM practices in the real world could be mapped or evaluated against it.

Patricia set out on the path to become a certified ISO KM, passed the ISO Lead Auditor exam, and became the world's first certified ISO KM Auditor in April 2019. Chris and Paul began interviewing experienced 'KMers' from around the globe to learn how they succeeded in their KM programmes and approaches – and to map their experiences and strengths back to the KM Standard.

All three of us worked on a one-page framework (the 'KM Chef's Canvas') for organisations to use as an internal audit tool for assessing the health and maturity of their KM programmes through the lens of the new standard.

We have learned a huge amount through writing this book together and hope that you find our efforts helpful and the stories from fellow practitioners in 16 organisations to be inspirational. Above all, we hope that *The KM Cookbook* appears on your table – ready to be thumbed through or meticulously followed. *Bon Appetit!*

Chris, Paul, and Patricia. July 2019

About the book

After many years of committee meetings and discussions, the International Standards Organization (ISO) published a standard for Knowledge Management systems (that's systems with a small 's') in November 2018. Adoption of the standard is voluntary. However, if used wisely, it provides a very helpful list of 'ingredients' for organisations to consider and gives professional credibility to a discipline which has been accused by some of being poorly defined or even 'fluffy'!

As experienced practitioners and authors, Paul Corney, Chris Collison and Patricia Eng feel strongly that this international recognition of Knowledge Management at an organisational level provides an important moment for KM to receive strategic attention. At this writing, there is also work under way to provide 'Chartered Knowledge Manager' status for individuals working in the field - hence it is a key time for professionalising Knowledge Management.

We believe that this is the moment to share and celebrate the work of successful organisations, and to include these stories into a practical and inspirational guidebook for leaders.

Conversely, it would be disappointing if the new standard resulted in a compliance or box-ticking exercise when it's actually a golden opportunity to 'prepare the perfect dish' of strategy, process, methods and leadership.

We want the book to stand out and be accessible, so we will be employing the cooking metaphor and finding parallels for the cook book: ingredients, recipes, menu, decorations, kitchen staff, chefs, hygiene inspectors - relating these to strategy, measurement, methods and tools, policy, communication, engagement, implementation, roles, leadership, external advice and governance.

Patricia's experience as a certified quality management programme inspector and creator of an award-winning KM programme brings a unique perspective. Her input will provide key insights into the ISO KM standard and the auditing process to help organisations prepare for an ISO KM audit.

The remainder of the book will be dedicated to a selection of 'menus' from organisations that have a particular strength in the way they have implemented their KM approach.

Explaining the metaphor

Throughout *The KM Cookbook* we have used the metaphor of a restaurant to describe the relationship between the KM Standard, tools and stakeholders. The table below will help you navigate through the book.

The New Kitchen	The fresh opportunity that ISO 30401 provides to establish or to review and improve your KM programme (Chapter 1)
The Restaurant	The KM programme or plan of activity (Chapter 2)
The Customers	KM Programme stakeholders and beneficiaries in your organisation and beyond
The Restaurateur	The sponsor ('investor') or champion who supports the KM programme at a senior level (Chapter 3)
The Chef	The KM programme leader (Chapter 4)
The Staff	KM team members, local enthusiasts and external consultants (Chapter 5)
The Ingredients	KM tools, methods, processes and activities (Chapter 6)
The Restaurant Critic	The ISO KM Auditor (Chapter 7)
The Menus	The KM approaches taken by other organisations (Chapters 10–25)

Part I

A new way to cook?

1
A new kitchen

We love cooking. Especially other people's cooking!

Food is such a versatile and varied commodity. For some, eating is a functional activity; energy-in-energy-out. For others, it's an experience to be savoured: full of subtlety and flavour. Eating can be a solitary experience, or a social expression of community and family.

Eating *out* can be a reassuringly consistent visit to a favourite restaurant chain, where you know precisely what you want, and you know that it will be delivered exactly as you like it. Alternatively, it can be an adventure, perusing an array of street-food vendors in search of new and distinctive tastes.

Food – a functional necessity or a taste adventure?

Food fads, movements and cuisines

Food movements have been with us for years, evolving from a focus on 'convenience' (satisfying hunger between time commitments), to 'diversity' (satisfying a curiosity for new, global flavours), to 'sustainable and environmental' (satisfying a desire for ethical and social responsibility).

Examples of this include organic food, and the Slow Food Movement, created as a protest against fast food and to promote locally grown, sustainable food.

As consumers share their experiences over time and begin to vote with their feet and wallets, some food movements give rise to recognised cuisines, served in many countries around the world – Turkish, Italian, Chinese and Indian cuisines serve as examples.

Management fads, movements and disciplines

Knowledge Management isn't a new movement. In one flavour or another, it has existed as a management discipline for 25 years as a set of business improvement tools and approaches. As a discipline, it has always been a bit 'fluid' – encompassing everything from building people-networks, ensuring that organisations learn lessons and reuse good practices, dealing with the issues of retiring experts 'walking out of the door with their knowledge', and developing and implementing processes and technologies to help groups connect, collaborate, curate and navigate.

'Attending a KM conference can be a bit like visiting an international street-food market!'

Much has been written, presented, and tried by tens of thousands of practitioners, including in-company specialists, hybrid HR, OD and IT professionals and external consultants. KM has often been accused of being 'just another management fad', yet whilst other methodologies have come of age, defined boundaries, declared methodologies and developed franchises – Knowledge Management (KM) has never had an agreed set of tools, a commercial accreditation, or a standard. Attending a KM conference can be a bit like visiting an international street-food market.

So, is KM ready to move from being a 'movement' to establishing itself as the equivalent of a 'recognised cuisine'?

For a potential restaurateur who has moved beyond casual street-food and is looking to sell an experience to customers, the challenge – and the opportunity – is to provide a distinctive offering with consistency and professionalism. Here, success requires a number of elements: credible reputation, premises, staff, tasty and appealing menus and recipes, compliance with relevant food hygiene standards, and, of course, blood, sweat and tears. At the heart of it all, with its appliances, utensils, and food stocks, is the restaurant kitchen.

In many ways, the arrival of an internationally agreed standard and vocabulary provides knowledge managers with a brand-new kitchen, and an opportunity to pause for a moment and consider what they provide to the organisations.

In writing this book, we want to catch the excitement of the arrival of this 'new kitchen' and demonstrate how the arrival of the ISO Knowledge Management System Standard (ISO 30401) provides so much more than an opportunity to certify a KM programme.

It provides a moment to re-evaluate, to return to first principles, and to learn from others. Imagine you had the opportunity, not just to enjoy a new, well-equipped and fully inspected kitchen, but also the chance to sit down with KM 'chefs' from around the world, across different industry sectors and listen to their stories. That's exactly what we have set out to do with *The KM Cookbook*.

Draw up a chair – we hope you're hungry!

Exploring the kitchen metaphor for a KM programme

Every profession and industry has its own ideals, its own processes, and its own jargon. ISO audits and KM programmes are no exception. To explore how an ISO standard and the accompanying audits function, we have expanded the restaurant metaphor to explain how ISO 30401 would be used to audit a KM programme and determine its effectiveness.

There are many different ways to deliver the same cuisine. Some restaurants are fancy, some are casual, some are mobile – but all of them buy raw ingredients which they prepare for a variety of dishes. Chefs in all restaurants use a variety of tools to prepare the food; knives, chopping boards, whisks, pots and pans, and griddles. Different cultures use different utensils – hence the saucepan, wok and tagine shown on the cover of this book – but all strive to produce the best food they can and hope for rave reviews by their patrons. Using the restaurant analogy, let's deconstruct a KM programme.

KM raw ingredients – knowledge, insights, ideas, expertise and experience.

KM utensils – techniques, tools and approaches.

The raw ingredients for a KM programme represent the knowledge, insights, ideas, expertise and experience which we seek to combine and present in the best way to satisfy (and occasionally educate) a customer's appetite.

The cooking tools and utensils are the selection of techniques and approaches in use; for example: communities of practice, expertise locators, artificial intelligence, knowledge packages and assets, archives, the recognition and reward system, and any other initiatives and processes used by the organisation to accomplish the goals and objectives of the KM programme.

Skilled staff are key to the success of a restaurant. A talented and experienced chef knows how to best use their tools to prepare the raw ingredients into something delicious, nutritious and appealing; skilled and experience wait staff know how best to serve and present the food as well as how to charm the customers. Similarly, skilled KM staff can use their skills to design and implement tactics to produce a vibrant and effective KM programme and also to engage, coach and encourage staff to participate in KM-related activities.

Restaurant chef and staff – KM programme lead, team and partners.

Just as chefs and kitchen staff need to develop and hone specific culinary skills, so KM programme staff should be ready to investigate, navigate, negotiate, facilitate, collaborate, communicate, curate and celebrate. Each of these skills are useful in creating, developing and managing an effective KM programme. We refer to these skills in Chapter 4, and a detailed discussion of these eight 'ates' and their contributions to a successful KM programme can be found in Paul and Patricia's book *Navigating the Minefield* (2017).

Restaurant evaluation standards – ISO 30401.

If KM programmes are our 'restaurants', then the ISO Standard 30401 could be likened to the evaluation factors used to rate restaurants. Where TripAdvisor offers the rating categories of food, service, value and atmosphere, readers also consider the quality, quantity and currency of reviews to judge the merits of a given restaurant. The ISO standard was written by an international committee and provides evaluation guidance in the areas of organisational context, leadership, planning, support, operations, performance evaluation, and improvement.

Restaurant critic – the ISO assessor.

Continuing the analogy, the ISO auditor may be likened to a restaurant critic, in that they assess each programme against consistent, defined rating criteria. The good news is that in this case, the rating criteria are published and readily available.

Standards for knowledge? How does that work?

How could anyone standardise KM?

As experienced practitioners, all three of us had a similar instinctive reaction when we encountered the idea of a KM standard. Patricia expresses it well:

> When I first heard that ISO was going to issue a KM standard, I couldn't believe it! How could anyone standardise KM? As a quality inspector for the US government for almost 30 years, I have written national and international standards and applied them to real-life situations. Having created the KM programme for the US Nuclear Regulatory Commission (USNRC), I knew how complicated a KM programme could be and how it was specifically designed for our organisation and our specific culture.
>
> People get nervous and defensive when a new program is proposed which takes resources from other existing programs. KM was such a program. So, I decided to do some research about ISO, its standards and ISO audits. Although I have decades of inspection and audit experience with the US government, I took the ISO Quality Lead Auditor Class to learn about the ISO philosophy and its basic tenets, and to find out what ISO auditors focus on when doing an audit. I got all that and more. I also learned what auditors could and could not do. After passing the Lead Auditor exam, I took another look at the ISO KM standard. I now saw value in the standard. Working with Chris and Paul on this book has given us the chance to help dispel some of the misconceptions, and to help others to see the opportunity it presents.

Each organisation has its own unique context.

Just as a restaurant menu is designed based on the premise of the restaurant and the preferences of its customers, KM programmes must be designed for the organisations in which they operate. Each organisation has its own unique context, culture, mission and structure. What works in one organisation can't be blindly copied and pasted into another organisation – just as you probably won't find spaghetti in an Ethiopian restaurant!

Given that a KM programme is uniquely designed for each organisation, why then should anyone consider adopting a KM standard?

Most KM professionals and enthusiasts attend conferences to hear about other KM programmes, hoping to come away with a new approach or initiative to bolster or improve their programmes – a 'secret sauce' perhaps? Sometimes they learn a technique that worked well elsewhere which they decide to adapt for their own organisation, and sometimes they learn what to avoid. Either way, they usually return to their organisations determined to renew, experiment and reinvigorate their efforts.

In the restaurant business, there are obvious commonalities between successful businesses: well-conceived and well-prepared food, congenial and attentive staff, a pleasant ambience.

In the less obvious and more nuanced world of Knowledge Management it's harder to derive patterns or examples for such questions as:

> 'What makes a successful KM programme so successful?'
> 'Is there an underlying basis for these successful programmes?'
> 'What should each person newly assigned to work in KM know?'

These are the precisely the questions that the ISO KM Committee has tried to answer and document in the ISO Standard 30401.

Identifying patterns of success.

Requirements and recommendations.

An overview of ISO 30401

The stated intent of ISO 30401 is to 'set sound Knowledge Management principles and requirements as guidance . . .'.

The standard is best summarised as a set of *requirements* and *recommendations* which have been drawn up by an international committee of experts, with additional input and review from national 'chapters' and interested members of the general public.

The ISO KM standard follows the templated format and the overall structure of ISO 9001, *Quality Management Systems*, by defining requirements in seven general areas: organisational context, leadership, planning, support, operations, performance evaluation and improvement. Requirements in these areas are written in statements containing the phrase 'the organisation shall', which designate those practices which the ISO KM Committee believed *must be present and functioning* in a KM programme. ISO 30401 contains over 50 such statements.

For example, 4.1:

Requirements are clearly stated as 'the organisation shall . . .'

> The organisation shall determine external and internal issues that are
> relevant to its purpose and that affect its ability to achieve the intended
> outcome(s) of its Knowledge Management system.

Recommendations are
stated using the word
'should'.
The standard also contains *recommendations* as non-mandatory
statements, often in the form of guiding principles, containing the
word 'should', e.g.

> Knowledge Management should be phased, incorporating learning and
> feedback cycles.

Organisational context

This section refers to the scope of the Knowledge Management system
or programme and how it connects with the organisational strategy
and culture. It also identifies several dimensions of a Knowledge
Management system including:

- knowledge development: acquiring, applying, retaining and
  refreshing knowledge
- knowledge conveyance and transformation: human interaction,
  representation (codification), combination (curation),
  internalisation and learning
- Knowledge Management enablers: human capital, processes,
  technology and infrastructure, governance and culture.

Leadership

This part addresses how leadership and management commitment can
be demonstrated through lived values, communication, effective
change leadership, measurement and improvement – all expected
behaviours of effective sponsor champions. Also included in this
section are the impacts of policy, governance and expectations on staff,
together with the assignment and communication of specific roles and
responsibilities for the KM management system.

Planning and operation

These short sections specify the requirement to reflect the
organisational needs in planning processes, programming objectives
and managing risks and opportunities. Requirements for reviewing
and controlling changes (planned and unplanned) are also defined.

Support

This is one of the longer sections of the standard. It sets out requirements for resourcing, ensuring competence, education and training, effective communication, and the creation and update of documentation.

Performance evaluation

In this section, the requirements for monitoring and measuring effectiveness are outlined, together with the role of internal audits and management reviews.

Improvement

This final section looks at KM through the lens of 'quality management' and ways of dealing with non-conformance, together with approaches for continuous improvement.

'What', but not 'how'

Note that the standard defines *what* should be done but is silent on *how* to do it. This is the case with all ISO standards, since ISO recognises that each organisation has its own mission, environment and culture. The standard provides a framework for KM programmes which each organisation can use to design a KM programme uniquely suited to its own needs. It would be highly unusual for a Mediterranean restaurant to cook a Peking Duck in a tagine!

> ISO defines the 'what'. The 'how' is left to the organisation to craft its own approach.

Each organisation's KM programme must meet its company-specific needs while making sure that it addresses the ISO standard requirements within the organisation's context and culture.

Whilst a first look at ISO 30401 can be intimidating, it's important to bear in mind that the methodology, processes and tools used to accomplish the requirements are left to the organisation's discretion. The standard underlines this in its introduction: 'Each organisation will craft a Knowledge Management approach, with respect to its own business and operational environment, reflecting their specific needs and desired outcomes.' For example, Section 4.2 of the standard states:

> Understanding the needs and expectations of interested parties (stake-holders)
> The organisation shall determine:
> – the interested parties that are relevant to the Knowledge Management system;

– the relevant requirements of these interested parties.

These requirements shall be analysed, prioritising the main areas and contexts relevant to the organisation and the Knowledge Management system.

So Section 4.2 defines an activity that must be done (the *what* – in this case, a stakeholder needs analysis) but it does not dictate *how* to do the analysis – simply that it must be done. Every KM programme manager must first determine who the KM programme will serve and identify the needs of these stakeholders before developing the actual KM programme. The ISO standard leaves *how* this activity is done to the organisation. ISO fully understands that the question of choosing and implementing the most effective and efficient process is one for the organisation to address.

The stakeholder analysis in question could be as simple as having a meeting of managers to identify the interested parties and their interests, or as complex as conducting a comprehensive multi-level survey of employees and customers.

Later in this book, in Chapter 11, Dan Ranta at General Electric explains how he successfully assessed stakeholder needs through an engaging and intensive day-long workshop, whilst Margot Brown at the World Bank (Chapter 10) describes a six-month long process of continuous engagement and listening.

Naturally, a restaurateur will be interested in the online reviews written about their restaurant – and also other restaurants in the area. They may even pay a visit to the other restaurants to sample their food and customer service and learn from the experience. It is important to remain curious, to avoid complacency and to seek ideas and adapt good practices from others.

Stories told first-hand by 15 'KM chefs'.

In this book, we interviewed 16 different organisations at different stages of KM programme maturity, sustaining the impact and benefits of recent or long-lived KM initiatives. As you dip into *The KM Cookbook*, you will get to hear their stories told first-hand – just as though you were sitting down to dinner together with a fellow chef or restaurateur. We hope that their examples will inspire and energise you and that they will stimulate your appetite for excellence in Knowledge Management.

How might the standard be used?

This is a question which we asked ourselves continually as we wrote *The KM Cookbook*.

For some knowledge managers, the very existence of an international standard will give credibility to the field they have spent their careers working on, whilst looking enviously over the shoulders of other more 'official' disciplines. Others will doubtless see it as a useful framework around which to develop, refine, test or internally audit a KM strategy and action plan.

During the course of our interviews, we were surprised by the level of interest in pursuing formal accreditation, particularly from those who are already standards-oriented and also from organisations who see it as a source of competitive advantage or a unique selling point to clients. Clearly there is value in any of these applications of the standard — and each organisation must determine where the maximum value lies for them.

Whatever the rationale for referring to or adopting the standard, it's our heartfelt belief that it shouldn't become burdensome to an organisation, as this cautionary tale taken from *The Guardian* illustrates:

> **Acclaimed French chef asks to be stripped of three Michelin stars**
> One of France's most celebrated chefs, whose restaurant has been honoured with three stars in the Michelin guide for almost 20 years, has pleaded to be stripped of the prestigious ranking because of the huge pressure of being judged on every dish he serves.
> Sébastien Bras, 46, who runs the acclaimed Le Suquet restaurant in Laguiole where diners look over sweeping views of the Aubrac plateau in the Aveyron while tasting local produce, announced on Wednesday that he wanted to be dropped from the rankings of France's gastronomic bible.
> Michelin said it was the first time a French chef had asked to be dropped from its restaurant guide in this way, without a major change of positioning or business model.
> Bras said he wanted to be allowed to cook excellent food away from the frenzy of star ratings and the anxiety over Michelin's anonymous food judges, who could arrive at his restaurant at any moment. Le Suquet had been consistently described by the Michelin guide's restaurant judges as so good it was 'spellbinding'. Bras, dressed in his chef's whites, announced his decision in a Facebook video with the local landscape rolling out behind him, saying: 'Today, at 46 years old, I want to give a new meaning to my life . . . and redefine what is essential.'
> (*The Guardian*, 20 September 2017)

As we continue to explore how to use the new kitchen which ISO 30401 provides, let's be sure not to lose sight of what is 'essential'!

Margin notes:

Credibility to generate leadership support.

Developing and reviewing strategy.

Competitive advantage from accreditation.

The potential burden of measurable reputation, and the importance of knowing 'what is essential'.

2

What kind of restaurant?

What is Knowledge Management?

Just as the owner of a restaurant will decide what kind of restaurant they want to establish and what cuisine they want to serve before they start designing the menu, so we need to be clear about what we want 'Knowledge Management' to mean to our organisation.

We could have included the Wikipedia definition of Knowledge Management in the book, but it will probably have been altered several times before *The KM Cookbook* appears on bookshelves!

ISO 30401 acknowledges that Knowledge Management has no single accepted definition and opts for the somewhat generic statement that it is 'management with regard to knowledge'.

Footnotes in the standard detail a familiar shopping list of 'identification, creation, analysis, representation, distribution and application', and remind readers that KM is holistic and systematic, and the focus is on learning, improved results and value creation. It is not unusual for ISO standards to issue a separate terminology document with clearer definitions. At the time of writing this is under active consideration for ISO 30401.

An international standard or a Wikipedia entry are very unlikely to provide perfect definitions for an organisation; far better to take the opportunity to tailor the definition to the strategic needs of your organisation.

'Management with regard to knowledge.'

Cook up your own definition, for your own context – you are unlikely to find the perfect one already prepared.

What kind of restaurant do you want to create?

Our recommendation is to start with your organisation's strategic goals, objectives and priorities and consider the definition and approaches which will best align with and satisfy those needs. If growth by merger or acquisition is on the radar, then you might define Knowledge

Management in a way which illuminates connections and synergies. If success is predicated on business expansion, and the replication of operational processes to new countries, then your perspective on KM will have a different flavour.

Take the taste challenge!

Here's a 'taste challenge' for you! Consider these three KM definitions from three different organisations:

Three tailored definitions of KM.

1 Knowledge Management is a set of processes, tools and behaviours which connect and motivate people to share expertise, good practices and learning.
2 Knowledge Management includes the capabilities by which an organisation captures the knowledge that is critical to it, constantly improves it and makes it available in the most effective manner to those who need it, so that they can exploit it creatively to add value as a normal part of their work.
3 Knowledge Management is a set of principles, tools and practices that enable people to create knowledge, and to share, translate and apply what they know to create value and improve effectiveness.

One of the definitions is from pharmaceutical giant, GSK, who described their strategic priority at that time as: 'looking to deliver shareholder value through growth of a diversified and global business, by delivering more products of value, simplifying our operating model and by running our business responsibly'.

One is from the World Health Organization, which describes a number of strategic directions, including 'improve the culture for and practice of research evidence creation, adaptation and use' and 'catalyse knowledge translation at the global level'.

Three strategic directions.

Finally, one of them is from Agri-chemicals Syngenta, formed from the merger of parts of Novartis and Zeneca (see Chapter 18). At the time this definition was written, Syngenta was in the middle of a major cultural transformation programme which had a strong behavioural element. Concurrently they were also embarking on a major operational improvement project focused on learning from experience and accelerating performance by sharing good practices.

Can you match the definition to the organisation (answers on the next page).

The point is that the definitions differ because the organisations, their histories, customers and strategic priorities differ. The way Knowledge Management is defined and implemented, the selection of tools and approaches, and the way KM effectiveness is measured and reported, should be aligned with the organisation's strategy and mission.

Framing Knowledge Management – is there more than 'connect' and 'collect'?

In 1999, *Harvard Business Review* (March–April 1999) published Hansen and Nohria's much-read article 'What's your Strategy for Managing Knowledge?', which set out alternative approaches to KM in professional services firms and drew distinctions between 'codification' and 'personalisation' strategies. In later years, these alternatives, often represented as opposite ends of a spectrum, have become commonly known to the KM community as 'collect and connect'.

Collect is used to refer to the KM activities closest to document management and information management. It invokes thoughts of explicit knowledge, knowledge capture, intranets, portals, libraries, knowledge assets, FAQs, wikis, folksonomies, taxonomies – and more recently, aspects of rudimentary artificial intelligence.

Connect takes us into the areas of people-oriented KM – implicit knowledge, networks, communities, social networking, expertise profiling and discovery, conversations, cafés and randomised coffee trials.

There's nothing wrong with either of these domains, but it is restrictive to limit our thinking to these two dimensions, aligning our methods and tools along a continuum solely between these two. It is also important to consider how we support and enable knowledge *creation*.

There's more to KM than collect and connect: creation.

Considering knowledge creation

Knowledge *creation* is a helpful third dimension to consider when defining and planning strategic KM activities. Which of our ingredients (KM tools and approaches) supports the generation of new knowledge and insights? We could consider any offerings which support organisational learning and reflection (The IOC, TfL and PDO demonstrate this in their stories, found in Chapters 15, 17 and 22). Other organisations discuss tools which could be helpful in recognising new patterns in large data sets (see the use of organisational network analysis by GE, Chapter 11 and machine learning in the World Bank, Chapter 10). Still other organisations use facilitated workflows to support ideation and the process of innovation (see the 'think, do, shout' example from Linklaters in Chapter 19).

Knowledge creation approaches from our 'KM chefs'.

The addition of knowledge creation as a third dimension expands the connect–collect continuum into a triangle against which our various tools and methods can be positioned. Many of these tools and methods will lie between these three corners.

Mapping your KM activities to your strategic objectives

Here's a simple way to use these three dimensions to ensure that your KM approach and methods are where you need them to be.

In a workshop setting, consider your organisation's strategic objectives, and use sticky notes to position them (where possible) on the connect-collect-create triangle (see Figure 2.1).

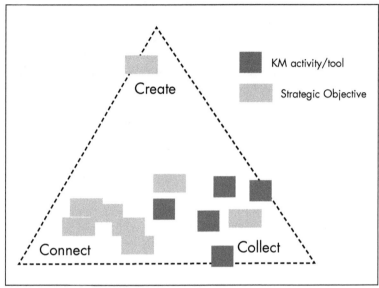

Figure 2.1 *The connect–collect–create triangle*

Consider each one in turn — is the objective best addressed through improved connections (integrating an acquisition for example), or through the creation of new knowledge (increased innovation or new market entry perhaps)? Some of them will have no obvious collection — you can place these in the centre.

Then, using a different colour note, consider your main KM methods and tools (the ones which consume the most time or budget) and map them on the same triangle.

Knowing where your centre of gravity lies.

Most organisations will have a weighting, or a centre of gravity somewhere on this triangle which reflects their strategic needs, and it is critical that the KM tools and methods align with this.

If your organisation's strategic centre of gravity requires an emphasis on generating connections following a recent major acquisition, but your KM toolkit and efforts focused on 'collections', it's probably time to consider realigning your programme. You don't want to open a steak restaurant in the middle of the vegetarian quarter of town!

Ensuring strategic alignment.

If there is a mismatch of focus between what you offer and what your organisation needs, you will hopefully find some inspiration for new 'ingredients' in the chapters and stories which follow.

Naturally, organisational strategies and objectives will change as markets and policies change – so it's valuable to revisit this alignment, or even to partition your strategy so that you deliver what is required for 'today' whilst leaving space to test and experiment with what might be needed for 'tomorrow'.

In Chapter 10, you'll meet Margot Brown, Director of Knowledge Management at the World Bank. Her approach serves as an excellent example of a *partitioned* knowledge strategy:

> We decided to have another stream of activity because we knew that a lot of the foundational stuff was going to take time to put in place. The other stream was much more responsive, much more tactical and really would show operations that we are making a difference. This was our experimental stream. So, there we really focused on the pain-points that operations were experiencing in knowledge.

We have now established how Knowledge Management can be defined for your organisation and discussed how you can determine if you are attempting to open the right kind of restaurant (with that brand-new kitchen) – in the right part of town.

The next step is to look at the role of the restaurateur and the skills of the chef – or to put it another way, the characteristics of a KM sponsor and the capabilities and soft-skills of a KM leader.

3
The role of the restaurateur

If you've ever had the chance to speak with a restaurateur, or an entrepreneur who owns a national chain of restaurants, you'll be struck by a couple of things. First, an obsession with the customer experience; secondly, an insatiable appetite to embed and replicate what is working well into a successful business model. They listen very attentively as you talk about your experiences and views on customer service, from the moment you enter the restaurant, to the moment you leave – or the moment you leave a review on TripAdvisor. We have all been asked to complete surveys which gather information on customer service at a variety of businesses. Reputation, brand values, improvement and ultimately the impact of these factors on profitability are where they focus.

Excellence, replicability, and continuous improvement have an impact on the bottom line.

In our metaphor, the restaurateur is the senior person who sponsors or champions your KM programme – they feel a sense of ownership for the approach you are taking, and value it. They'll pay for and promote your restaurant – but don't expect them to rush into the kitchen to chop the onions or taste-test the sauce. They are interested in results, but not necessarily in how you got there.

Knowledge Management sponsorship usually, but not always, originates in the same area as the reporting relationship for the KM programme. This means that your KM sponsor or senior champion might be found in a wide range of functional areas: Strategy, IT, HR, Organisational Development, R&D, Operations, Project Management, Quality and Business Excellence, Customer Management, or sometimes directly from the Executive team or CEO.

We have seen successful programmes involving all of these – and in many respects, *it's the enthusiasm, credibility, and active support* of the sponsor which matters more than their specific functional home. It's also true to say that the more senior your sponsor, the greater the

Sponsor enthusiasm and credibility matter the most.

likelihood that they can connect you with opportunities and synergies *beyond* their specific domain, as they have greater exposure to the strategic initiatives in other functions.

Ten characteristics of effective sponsors

Change management insights from academics and business gurus.

Sponsors and champions are cited in most change management frameworks as being critical to the success of any transformation. The ten characteristics below are common to many change models, and are drawn specifically from the work of Darryl Connor, author of *Managing at the Speed of Change* (1993) and Professor John Kotter's bestselling book *Leading Change* (2012). As we step through these ten principles for effective sponsorship from celebrated academics, we will highlight where they match the requirements listed in ISO 30401 Section 5.1, which discusses how top management 'shall demonstrate leadership and commitment with respect to the Knowledge Management system'.

1 Positive dissatisfaction

Heartfelt frustration, with a belief that things can be improved.

You want your sponsor to be sufficiently dissatisfied with the current state of knowledge sharing in your organisation such that they want to see action to improve sharing effectiveness. These sponsors need to be frustrated at the loss of value, the inefficiency, the lack of collective wisdom, the missed innovations and the embarrassment of wheel reinvention or unwarranted duplication. In Chapter 10 Vivek Sharma recounts the words of a senior manager at the World Bank who inspired him to take a KM role. It's easy to detect the 'positive dissatisfaction' in his words:

> This is what the challenge is at the Bank. When people are doing new projects at the Bank, they end up doing everything from scratch, because it's really difficult for them to identify whether the Bank has something similar in the past, whether there are learnings from the past that we can borrow, can we be sure that we're not making the same mistakes over and over; and whether we are learning from our successes?

Senior leaders (sponsors) with their own executive support teams can become insulated from the day-to-day frustrations felt by less senior employees, so it's important to expose your sponsor to the feelings of the broader workforce, perhaps using the results of a survey, focus group, or best of all, through 'management by walking around'.

A sponsor who thinks 'everything is generally OK, and this KM stuff – well, it's just the icing on the cake!' is unlikely to be able to defend or promote your work with any authenticity.

2 Making resources available

There's little point in firing up a sponsor who lacks the wherewithal to help you take action. If they don't have the budget or resource available themselves, can they help you through their connections and relationships? The KM Standard articulates this clearly:

> Top managers shall demonstrate leadership and commitment with respect to the Knowledge Management system by ensuring that the resources needed for the Knowledge Management system are available.

Top managers shall demonstrate commitment by making resources available.

In Chapter 17, Liz Hobbs of TfL describes how she used examples of successful KM practices from other organisations in a board presentation on KM. As a result, she was able to request and get resource to support her future work programme.

3 Understanding the impact on people

This is particularly critical for Knowledge Management sponsors, because KM is fundamentally a people-based approach.

An organisational development expert once asked the following question to illustrate the importance of a human perspective in relation to change programmes: 'What's the difference between a frog and a bicycle?' The answer was: 'You can take a bicycle apart and put it back together again, and it still works'. Sadly, some leaders have a mechanical mindset when they consider organisations, and people really are thought of as 'human resources', rather than individuals with valuable knowledge. Does your sponsor perceive the organisation as a frog or a bicycle?

Understanding the difference between a frog and a bicycle!

How would you rate your sponsor's emotional intelligence and empathy? You will need to be able to engage them in discussions about the culture of the organisation and the behaviours of leaders. They should be sufficiently self-aware that they know how their own personal behaviours impact on and reinforce your programme.

4 Public support

Naturally you will want a sponsor to be willing and able to speak on behalf of your 'programme' at every opportunity. You may well need to equip them with briefing materials and an 'elevator speech', some visual materials and some compelling success stories – as well as reminding them of the reasons for their dissatisfaction.

Equipping your sponsor with compelling success stories.

ISO 30401 states a requirement that senior management 'communicates the importance of effective Knowledge Management and of conforming to, or exceeding, the Knowledge Management system requirements'.

Nic Thomson from Syngenta (Chapter 18) describes the sponsor for their KM programme:

> He was a passionate advocate for what we're trying to do. He really believed in developing people. He really believed in connecting and collaboration. He was a great sponsor and took every opportunity he could to either give us words, or give us a video interview; to be there when we were making presentations – wherever he could make his presence felt. Whenever he could talk to people about what we were doing, he would do it.

Quotes from CEOs who understood the value of knowledge management.

A quote (or even better, a 'talking heads' video) from the *very* top of your organisation will be a huge asset to any programme. Consider the power of these two quotes from former CEOs:

> An organisation's ability to learn and translate that learning into action is the ultimate competitive business advantage. The operative assumption is that someone, somewhere, has a better idea; and the operative compulsion is to find out who has that better idea, learn it, and put it into action – fast.
>
> (Jack Welch, GE)

> The way we see it, anyone in the organisation who is not directly accountable for making a profit should be involved in creating and distributing knowledge that the company can use to make a profit.
>
> (Lord Brown, BP)

5 Private support

Walking the talk.

This is the authenticity test. Will your sponsor speak with the same level of passion and heartfelt credibility in a private conversation with their peers – or is it just a mask they wear when they're wheeled out to make positive speeches? You need a believer who will say the same off-mic as they will when the microphone is on. If their *dissatisfaction* with the current state is genuine, then they are far more likely to pass that authenticity test in private conversation.

Hank Malik of Petroleum Development of Oman (Chapter 22) noted:

> I launched the KM programme in a half day through an Envisioning Workshop with some of the directors and leads and we had a photograph taken at the end. Dr Suleiman Al Tobi, the former Operations South Director, had it blown up, put on his wall, and placed in our internal PDO Magazine.

When your sponsor decides to put your photo on his wall, then you know they're privately supporting you! Everyone who enters his office — from the cleaning staff to the CEO — knows he values the KM programme.

6 Good networkers

Your sponsor needs to be adept at spanning boundaries, spotting synergies and sneaking around the back door of silos. To the extent practicable, their network needs to become your network. ISO 30401 expresses this requirement as:

> supporting other relevant management roles to demonstrate their leadership as it applies to their areas of responsibility.

Influencing laterally.

> ensuring the integration of the Knowledge Management system requirements into the organisation's business and project processes.

7 Tracking performance

This is one of the acid tests of sponsor interest and commitment. Is sponsorship of your activity something which is on their agenda, or is your programme just a medal that they wear on special occasions? Agree what 'good' looks like, agree the immediate steps and agree on the indicators and measures you need to focus on. Book meetings in their diary, preferably on a quarterly basis. If they're dashboard-oriented, then build one for them, but remember the quote from sociologist William Bruce Cameron (sometimes inaccurately attributed to Albert Einstein): 'Not everything that can be counted counts, and not everything that counts can be counted.'

The KM Standard is vocal on leadership involvement, with two related requirements of top managers:

> ensure that the Knowledge Management policy and Knowledge Management objectives are established, are compatible and are aligned with the strategic direction of the organisation and can be evaluated

and

> promote continual improvement of the Knowledge Management system

8 Reinforcement when needed

Sometimes a political issue can mean that you might need to 'send for reinforcements'. Select a sponsor who is willing to encourage collaboration, broker a negotiation, challenge, knock heads together, unblock the corporate drains and generally provide you with air cover when you want it.

9 Focus on the future

Understand the big picture.

The most effective sponsors fully understand the 'big picture' – and can communicate it compellingly. What is their personal vision for the organisation three years from now? Is your KM strategy aligned with the big picture? Is your governance structure such that it will support the sponsor's vision?

Work to ensure that briefings of the sponsor focus on the long-term vision and the organisation's strategic goals and objectives. You don't want your sponsor bogged down in details such as how many page views occurred in a given week. But you do want them to know that people are saving time by finding things on those web pages and that staff are finding the KM initiatives helpful in doing their jobs.

10 Behavioural modelling

KM is people-oriented, so people will notice if what you say is not what you do.

Finally, your sponsor needs to walk the walk, as well as talk the talk. When you champion knowledge sharing, you become vulnerable to accusations of hypocrisy to a greater degree than if you were the sponsor of a systems implementation programme. It's behavioural and relational; and people notice what you do.

You might want to equip your sponsor with some simple questions to ask others that will get people thinking about KM and its successes. Syngenta (Chapter 18) are good at this. They provided a number of 'leading questions' on a pocket card to help their senior champions to verbalise their commitment and to invite others to get involved:

> 'Who could you share this with?' 'Who did you learn from?' 'Who might have done this before?' 'Who could you ask for help and advice?'

ISO 30401 includes two requirements which relate to behaviours and values, namely:

> foster organisational values which enhance trust as a key element for Knowledge Management

> manage the process of change towards adoption and application of the Knowledge Management system, and towards the cultivation of a culture that values, supports and enables Knowledge Management

It is unlikely that any sponsor will possess or demonstrate all of these capabilities and attributes, but they represent a helpful list if he or she ever asks you the question: 'What can I do for you to support your programme?'

Having explored the characteristics of an effective KM sponsor, who in our metaphor is the restaurateur, we now turn our attention in the next chapter to the person with responsibility for making things happen: the skilled chef.

4
The skilled chef

As we continue with our gastronomic metaphor, we arrive in the restaurant kitchen itself. And if the kitchen is where the magic happens then it's the chef who is the magician. In our world, it's the person responsible for leading KM in your organisation. There are a number of titles for this person that are often influenced by the size of the team and the importance to the organisation. For example, in restaurants, there can be an Executive Chef, a Head Chef, one or more Sous-Chefs, a Chef de Partie or Commis Chef. For KM it can be Chief Knowledge Officer, Director/ Head Knowledge Management, Knowledge Manager, Knowledge Management Specialist, and Knowledge Management Assistant.

In this chapter, we will take a look at the skills and capabilities which these busy, talented people require in order to meet the demands of their customers and sponsors alike.

Naturally, there is no cookie-cutter approach to leading and sustaining a Knowledge Management programme. KM leaders will match their implementation approach to the culture of the organisation, and the nature of the 'change landscape' at the time. Selecting the right approach or combination of approaches requires political instinct and awareness, an understanding of what is already on the 'initiative radar' and an understanding of how to make change stick.

'There is no cookie-cutter approach.'

We will look first at eight different *implementation approaches* and tactics which a KM leader might adopt or adapt, before exploring eight *capabilities* or '*soft-skills*' which successful KM leaders demonstrate.

Eight implementation approaches and eight key capabilities.

Eight different implementation approaches for Knowledge Management
1 Top-down, Big Bang
This is the traditional 'someone-at-the-top-has-said-this-needs-to-

Getting people's
attention . . .

'happen' approach; often accompanied by a project management office, communications and engagement plan, mugs, mouse mats and posters in the lifts!

In some organisations, they can be the only way to get people's attention. The challenge is to find ways to *keep* people's attention and

. . . keeping people's
attention.

to get them involved – particularly when the board or senior sponsors have moved onto their next management fad.

You might consider setting up a programme board or steering group with some of the senior players, which will keep them collectively on the hook for your programme. It's much more difficult for the whole group to shift their energy away than it is for a single sponsor to become preoccupied by the next big idea. It's this challenge of *sustainability*, which leads us neatly to the second approach:

2 Top-down, bottom-up

This approach is a sophistication of the Big Bang approach, using the same level of visible senior support to send a clear message across the organisation. The critical difference is that there is a deliberate effort to harness the energy, passion and good practices of workers at the front line, and to involve them in the programme, perhaps as a group of advisors or a community of practice. These people are key in helping to

Engaging the front line
and finding out what
they already do well.

translate the messages from the top and set them in the right context locally.

An approach which reaches further and deeper into the organisation is more likely to discover where there are already 'pockets of excellence' or local good practices. This in turn will deepen engagement with a sense that you are listening, as Dan Ranta outlines in his reflections on KM in GE, Chapter 11:

> You have the mentality that even if you know you are smart, the best ideas generally come from other people and it's your role to combine them – that's just a key piece of the change management process.

Creating a community of
KM champions.

One way to orchestrate the 'bottom-up' part of this approach is to form a community of practice for any existing KM enthusiasts. They will feel valued and are likely to reciprocate by acting as willing local champions when needed.

3 Pilot

A pilot approach will often take a subset of KM methods and apply them locally – in contrast to the Big Bang, which usually takes KM as a whole and attempts to apply it globally.

A pilot enables you to try the aspects of KM most likely to make a difference quickly, to build credibility locally, and to learn from each implementation. That could mean launching a community of practice for one part of the organisation, closing the learning loop on major projects, working on knowledge retention for retiring experts and experimenting with augmented reality in an operational team – all as parallel, focused activities. The deliberate intention to experiment and learn is what shifts these pilots from isolated successes to scalable successes.

What might the selection criteria be for a successful pilot?

Selection criteria for a successful KM pilot.

- manageable and capable of showing results (measurable value would be ideal) within six months
- involves a core process which is repeatable elsewhere
- involves strategic areas of knowledge
- close to the heart of any key sponsor or stakeholder
- resources are available
- carries an acceptable risk to the business
- and ideally a recognisable part of the organisation (not too esoteric) which will make their story easy to understand.

4 Slipstream

Use the momentum of other initiatives to advance your programme.

Slipstreaming is about working in partnership with other initiatives or 'transformation projects', and looking for ways in which you can feed off each others' momentum. If you're familiar with competitive cycling, you'll relate to the idea of a peloton formation, where different cyclists take turns to lead the pack forward, taking their share of the headwind whilst others tuck in behind them.

The beauty of KM is that it's a broad discipline. That means it is easy to find ways to complement and support other programmes and functions. We have seen KM effectively slipstream behind many different initiatives, including: business improvement and Six Sigma projects, operational excellence, new project management methodologies, enterprise software deployments, acquisition integration activities, 'culture change' movements and the introduction of new corporate values.

One thing to be wary of, which affects competitive cyclists and runners who slipstream – is the danger of getting 'boxed in'. If you're slipstreaming the roll-out of Office365 with a view to sharing a broader set of knowledge-sharing behaviours and methods, then watch out that the technology doesn't grab all the headlines and rob you of impact. It's always best to agree these things up front as part of the partnership,

The risks of getting 'boxed in'.

rather than emerge unexpectedly and assume that you can push KM to the forefront whenever you like.

5 Stealth

Sometimes labels get in the way. Sometimes you have to find ways to build up your organisation's capability to manage and share knowledge without them realising what your master plan actually is. You need to get smart at making small adjustments to processes, spotting political opportunities and allies, tweaking the configuration of information-sharing platforms, encouraging knowledge-sharing networks and facilitating conversations to improve performance and learning.

Approaching KM as your secret mission!

After a few years, you'll be able to look back and say to yourself 'You know what, we're pretty good at managing and sharing knowledge!' – but you probably won't get much praise or a bonus. Your reward will be the satisfaction of having helped to build a knowledge-friendly environment which may be more sustainable than a managed programme would have achieved.

From the examples in *The KM Cookbook*, the Médecins Sans Frontières story comes closest to operating by stealth. In Chapter 16, you'll find Robin Vincent-Smith describing an opportunistic, almost guerrilla-style, approach to making what we might recognise as KM interventions, without using the label – or even the job title:

> I've just chucked away my job title. My e-mail signature now reads: "My name is Robin. I'm here to help. My agenda is up to date. Book me!"

6 Copycat

This is more of a tactic than an implementation strategy *per se* – but it's often successful to point to examples of successful KM tactics and initiatives from other organisations (competitors and customers are particular effective) to create some 'us too' or 'us better' demand. Find a good example and invite them in to tell their story in a way which gets heard at a senior level. Check whether your board members have strong connections with or recent prior experience of other companies who have powerful stories to tell. They might be politically good choices to pursue, and can also be used to create that sense of dissatisfaction in your sponsor.

Play positively to the senior leadership egos.

Some of the longest-running KM programmes can trace their roots back to a 'copycat' moment with an influential leader. Schlumberger's Eureka programme in Chapter 13 is an excellent example:

In 1997 our CEO, Euan Baird went to an event and started hearing about Knowledge Management. He returned from the meeting and said, 'We need to do Knowledge Management! We need to start sharing knowledge across the company.' That's why it started.

7 The buffet menu

Providing an empowering range of options, rather than a prescription.

The success of a buffet approach depends on a high level of demand for knowledge. Rather than investing effort in creating an appetite or a willingness to experiment, this approach works with the demand already present, and provides an array of tools and techniques from which the organisation chooses to implement.

The International Olympic Committee (Chapter 15) is a great example of this. They set out a veritable smorgasbord of learning processes, observer visits, secondments, extranet platforms, access to experts, databases, distilled recommendations and lessons learned. This creates a veritable knowledge feast for a future Olympic organising committee, which, once awarded the Olympic Games, enters a seven-year preparation and planning process with a tremendous appetite for knowledge.

Demand-led programmes are most likely to be sustainable, as there is no need to persuade people to seek out or apply knowledge – they want to learn from the past and make their Games even better!

8 Phoenix-from-the-ashes

Reawakening a passion for KM.

For many organisations, Knowledge Management is not a new idea. For some, there have been several historical Big Bangs, pilots and copycat initiatives.

Talk with people about what has happened in the past and learn from it. At times, just talking to these KM 'old-timers' can rekindle enthusiasm, tinged with nostalgia. It is quite possible for KM to rise, phoenix-like, from the ashes and fly even higher than it did before:

> Why didn't we make more of that? What did we lose in momentum then? Perhaps now the timing is better? Perhaps now, with a new sponsor? Perhaps, now that there is a new international ISO standard, and KM has come of age, we should take a fresh look?

In practice, organisations often combine approaches, or transition from one to another. For example, a bottom-up approach might identify a practice so effective that it is made visible to the organisation through a 'buffet table' of KM good practices and use-cases.

Skills for Knowledge Management leaders

In their previous book, *Navigating the Minefield*, Patricia and Paul identified eight critical soft-skill capabilities for knowledge managers based on their research interviews. The discussion of these eight '-ates' have become a popular feature in their presentations and workshops.

Different approaches require different skills.

The necessary capabilities of our skilled chef – the person leading a KM programme – will vary, depending of the type of implementation approach or approaches which have been chosen. A stealth approach will require a very different level of communication skills when compared with a top-down initiative.

The eight '-ates'

1 Investigate

Take time to fully understand the nature of your challenge or opportunity.

It's important to take time to understand the context you're working in. Are you putting out a fire? Solving an immediate business need? Addressing a risk? This could be described as 'Operational KM'. Alternatively, is this 'Strategic KM', driven by the vision from the top consistent with the organisation's business direction? Margot Brown articulates this perfectly in her experience immediately after joining the World Bank (Chapter 10):

> I had to resist the call to just start doing something. There was a lot of pent-up demand for something to happen. Coming in new to the organisation and new to development, I had to do my due diligence and understand the ground realities in which I was to operate and add value.

Be prepared to adapt your role.

Christine Astaniou at the Financial Conduct Authority (Chapter 21), found that her 'investigation' led to a change in her role:

> . . . when I got here, I realised they didn't need someone to keep up to date with legislation and disseminate information about the latest case law. They needed someone to effect mindset change, behavioural change and develop Knowledge Management strategies.
> I quickly adapted, as having been recruited to do one thing I realised that what they needed was quite different.

2 Navigate

As KM professionals, we help our organisations to navigate their way through information overload and complexity and to discover and use the most critical knowledge resources. In order to act as navigators and guides, we need to map the critical knowledge areas of our organisation. This might include helping to create and promote a directory of the organisation's knowledge assets and experts.

MAPNA (Chapter 24) describe the intent of their KM programme as: 'the intention of identifying, protecting, measuring and reporting the organisation's knowledge assets'.

3 Negotiate

Knowledge Management touches a large number of related disciplines (ISO 30401 lists many of them). These multiple boundaries are beneficial when we come to consider opportunities to collaborate, but it's equally important that you manage the expectations of your sponsor and negotiate clear boundaries and deliverables. Agree the scope of your role with your sponsor and be prepared to negotiate what success will look like and how your objectives will be measured.

Know what you're committing to and negotiate the scope.

Your chosen implementation approach will impact how critical this skill is. A 'Big Bang' will require clearer negotiation of scope than a series of learning pilots.

4 Facilitate

So much of what a KM manager does involves facilitation. This has come through as clearly in our interviews for *The KM Cookbook* as it did for *Navigating the Minefield*. As a KM leader, you will become a hub knowing who the go-to people are for a whole range of questions. You have to facilitate connections, meetings, interactions, events, reviews and communities. This requires resilience, boundless energy, adaptability, emotional and social intelligence, matchmaking skills and a real understanding of cultural nuances.

As the demands for his facilitation skills have grown Robin Vincent-Smith at MSF (Chapter 16) has set mechanisms in place to build facilitation capability in others:

> I spend quite some time coaching others in facilitation – because I think this is a basic business skill – to run magic and meaningful meetings through structured freedom. Meetings are about transferring knowledge: people's opinions, people's ideas and people's expertise. If you frame this correctly, then knowledge transfer happens happily; but if you don't, it doesn't.

Facilitation – a valued KM capability.

Some of the most personal disclosures from our interviews related to breakthroughs in facilitated meetings. This is illustrated best by Liz Hobbs at Transport for London (TfL), who witnessed a turning point with a cynical manager seeing the value of her work during a challenging 'project lessons learned' meeting (Chapter 17):

> I left the meeting and went outside in the pouring rain – and I'm going up and down dancing – such was my delight to have someone who was cynical now 'gets it'.

5 Collaborate

You will find yourself working in alliances with other business areas, such as IT or HR, and occasionally with external suppliers or partners. You need to be adept at recognising dependencies, synergies and finding the win:win in these situations.

Synergies, dependencies and finding a win:win scenario.

This is particularly important if your implementation approach involves working through others via stealth, or 'slipstreaming' behind other programmes and initiatives.

We often see collaborative alliances with the IT function, with KM involved in definition of requirements, and in the positioning and willing exploitation of new digital capabilities. Dom Davies at Dstl (Chapter 20) described the importance of the interface of his knowledge and information management team with the IT function:

Collaborating to positively impact the physical workspace.

> These people might know what to do and how to do it, but you need to ensure that there is time in their day to do it and that it is in their interest to do it. Policy and process only get people to do what you tell them to, not to do it well.

One, often overlooked, collaborative alliance relates to the design of the physical workspace. Several of our interviewees described the collaborative nature of their office space, and importance of the common areas of 'liminal space' such as coffee areas and hallways between meeting rooms. In some cases, KM teams have partnered with others to experiment with the creation of new spaces to support new behaviours. The Innovation Lab at Linklaters (Chapter 19) is one such example, as Rachel Manser explains:

The importance of virtual facilitation and collaboration skills.

> The Innovation Lab started off being more virtual. Then we realised people would like to have a place that they could come and collaborate and think differently. We have an area in the London Office for this. It's a place which is different, where you can draw on the walls and where you are encouraged to think in a different way.

Listening for feedback – 'two ears, but only one mouth'.

Increasingly, organisations are encouraging their employees to 'work out loud', i.e. to make use of their social enterprise tools to share in a highly visible manner what they are working on. It is unrealistic, for example, to expect colleagues to blog and use tools such as Twitter if KM professionals don't use these tools themselves. Effective collaboration is not merely about making use of social tools – it is also about demonstrating leadership by doing.

6 Communicate

Senior KMers tell you to devote 30% of your time to communicating what you do and getting as much feedback as you can get. Have your KM 'elevator pitch' always with you but ensure that it invites dialogue. Ask open-ended questions and develop marketing materials for your programme. Try to make sure that these materials invite curiosity.

In PDO (Chapter 22), Hank Malik's KM Steering Group co-created their 'Connect, Collaborate, Succeed' mantra and created four simple icons for the building blocks of connecting, knowledge transfer, skills and collaboration. These were turned into posters that people readily embraced and a set of eight knowledge business cards with a famous quote or saying from a philosopher on the reverse:

> We'd go out to the field with the knowledge cards and put them on tables and leave them in the coffee shops and people started to talk about that and say, 'but what is this thing, KM?'

7 Curate

So much of what passes for Knowledge Management is about creating and storing content and making it available for reuse. Knowledge curation is more than the role formerly undertaken by Information professionals and librarians; it involves being a *proactive* custodian of organisational knowledge and organisational knowledge bases – seeking out, collecting, refining, combining, updating and managing the content which comprises the organisation's critical knowledge assets.

Be a proactive custodian.

The IOC's approach to creating and cyclically refreshing the Games reference materials (Chapter 15) enables future host cities to immediately access current recommended practices and examples around such topics as 'Ceremonies', 'Operational Readiness' and 'Olympic Villages'.

Curation using collective wisdom and artificial intelligence.

The World Bank (Chapter 10) has introduced machine learning to great effect to provide real-time curation of 'knowledge packages' tailored for a specific project:

> We now have an algorithm which is able to take your project description, break it down into separate queries, query external data sources and

curate the top 50 results, all without human intervention – and the results are really good!

8 Celebrate

Success stories and use-cases are important for gaining and keeping people's attention. Recognition awards are a wonderful way to surface these stories and to build up a network of engaged champions and advocates. We recommend that celebration and recognition schemes are symbolic and desirable rather than of significant material value. The glow from peer recognition and senior acknowledgement will outlast the gratification of a cash bonus. It is far better to reinforce the belief that KM activities and behaviours are contributors to organisational success and personal objectives, rather than something which merits additional financial reward.

Syngenta's TREE awards (Chapter 18) illustrate this principle and demonstrate that the right kind of recognition approach can be a long-term success. They have accumulated hundreds of KM-related success stories which have had a significant positive impact on the business over an eight-year period.

A good 'chef' will cultivate all these skills. The personal development is well worth the time and effort. Our experience is that the KM community are generous when it comes to sharing their experience. Don't be afraid to seek out experienced KMers and ask them for tips on how to develop and apply these skills.

Having explored the role of the chef, in the next chapter we turn our attention to the people who support the chef: the kitchen staff.

Awards as a feedstock of valuable stories for your programme.

Provide the right kind of recognition.

5
Getting some help: the staff

In every restaurant, the chef is surrounded by a team of staff. This team can include waiting staff, sous-chefs, a sauté cook, bartenders, the maître d'hôtel, and perhaps a dedicated sommelier . . .

Through our interviews it has been fascinating to see the spread of different structures and roles which different KM programmes and teams have assembled. Some have technical roles – taxonomists and wiki experts; some have content managers, others have access to facilitators, community of practice coaches and workflow experts.

In many cases, we see a combination of formal, central roles and a wider, distributed group of champions. These local champions are KM enthusiasts and advocates who can serve as change agents, participants in pilots, a conduit for communications and for obtaining feedback, and providers of success stories. In many of the organisations we interviewed, the leaders/co-ordinators/facilitators of communities of practice played a *de facto* role of knowledge manager and champion for their specific domain or work unit.

Working with KM champions throughout the business.

Dan Ranta at General Electric (Chapter 11) sums this up well:

75% of our best ideas have come from the business – across all generations.

Law firm Linklaters (Chapter 19) describe the senior role of 'Knowledge and Learning Partners' as a senior group of influential champions around the world:

In a way, they're our key communication channel – because the most effective communication is always partner-to-partner. We encourage them to talk to other partners about what we're doing in the knowledge and learning world.

Getting extra help – the role of external consultants

Restaurants have to cope with the peaks and troughs of demand. A major corporate event or a wedding party can generate a requirement to increase *capacity* substantially. A change in customer demand or desire to follow a new food trend can also require new skills and *capabilities* in the kitchen, resulting in the temporary appointment of a specialist chef, or a training course for established staff. Even experienced chefs might need additional support or skills to meet the demand for an intricate new dish.

In a similar way, a KM programme manager will often encounter moments when they need to add capacity, build capability, or both. These are the moments when they might reach out for the help of an external consultant.

Identifying, selecting, and working with consultants can be challenging and rewarding, from both sides of the relationship. A poor consultant might tell you what they think you want to hear instead of working with you to developing the best solution for your needs. A good consultant will have worked with a number of organisations and previously seen issues similar to yours. They might have different thoughts about how the assignment or task could be done and may challenge your way of thinking. Ultimately, they will develop or deliver a solution considering your organisation's context – and explain it in terms that your organisation can understand.

A great consultant will give you an honest opinion irrespective of the impact on their future business. Sometimes a consultant is posed with what is known as the 'consultant's dilemma', when they don't believe that the assignment that they have been given will provide the most beneficial outcome. The dilemma is framed with the question 'Do you give them what they want, or do you give them what they need?'

The authors of *The KM Cookbook* have had experience in consulting with around 200 organisations, as well as having procured consultancy from within our previous corporate roles. We'd like to present our recipe for a successful relationship with a KM consultant.

Top 10 tips for the client

1   When selecting your consultant, ask yourself 'Can I work with them?' Cultural fit is important. Ask them what makes the best client-consultant relationship from their perspective.

2   Be clear about what you are asking the consultant to do, and why you are asking them to do it. Explain both the what and the why and ask them if they have any questions.

Consultants can temporarily build capacity, capability, or both.

Recipes for a productive client–consultant relationship.

Recommendations for the client.

3   Ask the consultant for examples of where they have addressed similar challenges, and what they think might be different about your context. That will help avoid them being tempted to copy-and-paste into your situation. Copy-and-paste solutions rarely exist, and you're paying a consultant to be insightful, flexible, responsive and adaptive.

4   Be open about related work which has been done previously, by you, or other consultants in the past, which might affect the success of the current work. Tell them about past successes – and failures. Don't leave it to them to discover skeletons in the cupboard!

5   Produce a scope that is specific on outcome and outputs but not overly constraining on inputs and methods. Include milestones and deliverables.

6   Include break clauses in the agreement to permit evaluation of the work done and allow the client to determine whether to continue, change consultants, change direction or issue a follow-on contract.

7   Beware when hiring software consultants that they don't over-engineer the solution. When you ask them the time, make sure they don't build you an atomic clock.

8   Assemble a steering group to oversee and evaluate the deliverables and act as champions for the work.

9   Be prepared to own and co-develop the outputs – don't subcontract your thinking.

'Don't subcontract your thinking'.

10 And finally, don't be too ambitious and expect the consultant to solve every issue with one assignment.

Top 10 tips for the consultant

1   Do your homework. Be interested. Read, follow, Google, research and network your way into a better understanding of the organisation – as though you were going for a permanent job!

A good client organis-ation is one where you have contacts at three levels of the organisation.

2   Ask the client what will delight them, and what would frustrate them. See if they can describe what a successful outcome will look like and what it would mean to them and their organisation.

3   Include a risk register describing how you will deal with setbacks (e.g. changes in scope of work, unavailability of key personnel, unforeseen delays) in your proposal.

4   Suggest the creation of a short inception report or informal statement of work on starting the assignment. This clarifies client expectations and provides an opportunity to discuss any changes following the initial contracting phase.

5   Don't be afraid to say what you can't do, or what others would do better. Your client will respect your integrity more than your attempt to bluff your way through.

6   Accredit and acknowledge others with frameworks and models when you use them. You client is employing you for your connections as well as your collections.

7   Encourage your client to consider how you might build up their capability or coach a team member to leave new skills behind. Aim to leave a legacy rather than create a dependency.

8   Seek to co-create frameworks, models, tools and methodologies rather than produce your own from your back pocket. It's very rare to be confronted with an 'obvious' or 'simple' problem for which you have a 'best practice' solution. If it was that obvious, they probably wouldn't be hiring you!

9   Avoid the temptation to criticise the work of previous consultants. You don't know the context or conditions that they were working under.

10 Be a giver, not a taker. The KM world is relatively small, and good natured – you'll find that what goes around, comes around!

Aim to leave a legacy rather than create a dependency.

Professional accreditation

Professional chartership in knowledge management.

The arrival of the KM Standard isn't the only significant 'coming of age' activity for Knowledge Management.

As we write *The KM Cookbook*, CILIP, the UK library and information association, is working with a group of leading international Knowledge Management practitioners to pilot and launch the first Professional Registration in Knowledge Management backed by Royal Charter. This important professional accreditation work fits with a wider inclusive International Knowledge Professional Society (IKPS) which is forming as an umbrella network for connecting these initiatives and KM sub-communities around the world.

We believe that professional accreditation (chartership) will become an increasingly important option for corporate KM staff and consultants alike which will provide a common approach to assuring competency and bring KM one more step towards corporate legitimacy.

Now that you have the staff or know-how to get the help, and you are aware of future routes to professional development, it's time to open up the kitchen cupboards and the fridge and start to understand and combine your ingredients.

6
Understanding the ingredients

Taking stock

Many readers of *The KM Cookbook* will have already created or inherited a KM programme, including action plans, knowledge products, project workstreams, methods, tools and solutions. Before we move into our new KM kitchen, it makes sense to open up the cupboards and conduct an inventory of what we have to work with.

Opening up the kitchen cupboards.

In this chapter, we're going to define the ingredients as a combination of:

- Knowledge assets – critical, strategic content and expert insight which is valued, refreshed and maintained. You can think of these as the 'centrepiece' of a meal – the sizzling steak, freshly prepared fish or the spicy tofu.
- Tools and processes – the combination of solutions and methods which you use to enhance and connect, capture or create your knowledge. These are the accompaniments – the rice, vegetables, dressing and sauces which provide a tasty and balanced meal.

As a KM Chef, you'll probably be responsible for many of these. We will have to keep aware of the 'use-by' dates on our knowledge assets; knowledge has a shelf-life, too!

Understanding your critical knowledge assets

If you have ever been asked 'What's the difference between information and knowledge?' during a workshop or by a senior stakeholder, your heart probably sank as you braced yourself for a somewhat academic and semantically fruitless conversation. One simple way of distinguishing between the two is to ask:

Nobody ever complains about knowledge overload.

It's very common to hear people say they are suffering from information overload, but when was the last time you heard anyone say that they had too much knowledge?

Even though we probably don't have too *much* knowledge individually, it is definitely helpful for our organisations to identify, map and manage knowledge deemed as *critical*.

In their article 'Managing Your Mission-critical Knowledge', Martin Ihrig and Ian Macmillan set out an iterative process for this:

> We generally start by assembling a multifunctional team – at the organizational, divisional, or business unit level – to articulate what the members consider to be key dimensions of the company's competitive performance and the knowledge that underpins them. It can be useful to shape this conversation by giving individuals assignments in advance.
>
> Senior managers might be asked to outline the business model and high-level critical knowledge, such as areas of advanced expertise, intellectual property, and the relationships with customers, suppliers, and distributors that make that model successful.
>
> Market researchers and sales managers might be asked to delineate the attributes of new products and services that customers will need in the near future.
>
> Technical and operations managers might describe organizational routines that support needed areas of expertise.
>
> (*Harvard Business Review*, January–February 2015)

The article continues to describe a way of ranking these various assets on the basis of how structured the knowledge is, and how diffused it is within or outside the organisation. Finally, Ihrig and Macmillan explain how to consider each critical area and discuss how it could increase in value to the organisation by being dispersed or being more structured.

This approach is one example of a process used in a knowledge audit.

Knowledge audits and knowledge mapping

Generally, a knowledge audit encompasses a systematic review of your knowledge assets and how they contribute to your organisation's key activities. It covers explicit knowledge (documents and data) and tacit knowledge (deep, hard-to-articulate expertise, skills and experience) and provides a chance to identify knowledge flows and gaps.

A knowledge audit can use a variety of methods and approaches, including one-to-one interviews, workshops, surveys, network analysis, content analysis, focus groups, story collection and observation studies. Typical steps in a knowledge audit include:

Conducting a knowledge audit.

1 Communicate the intent to your leadership team and secure their buy-in.
2 Invite nominees from each department: two to four people. These people should be familiar with the key activities of the department and how knowledge and information are used.
3 Brief the participants on the process and schedule knowledge mapping sessions.
4 Conduct group knowledge mapping sessions (see below).
5 Ask departments to validate and add to the draft maps.
6 Share maps between departments to see where assets can be re-used and shared.
7 Analyse and identify actions and recommendations.

For the knowledge mapping activity, ask the group to identify their key activities and map them out on the wall. If you have them, you can use business process maps as input to this.

For each key activity, consider what kind of knowledge assets are required to make them happen (inputs). Categorise them using coloured sticky notes against the following: documents/data; methods and shared routines; skills and competencies; experience; relation-ships; natural talent (skills that cannot be readily taught). Finally, for each knowledge asset, identify actions based upon:

Categorising the knowledge assets.

Getting into action.

- knowledge **risks** (e.g. rare skills in older staff members)
- knowledge **gaps** (e.g. missing methods or documents)
- knowledge **access** problems (e.g. documents are not shared).

These processes of auditing and mapping key areas will provide you with an inventory of your critical knowledge assets. The rest of your ingredients are the methods and tools, apps and processes which you provide to the organisation.

We wish to acknowledge Patrick Lambe as a reference source for this section (*Knowledge Audits and Knowledge Mapping* (2015)).

Ingredients from KM programmes

A quick internet search will yield 'top 10', 'top 20' and even 'top 100' lists of favourite KM tools, methods and approaches. Some lists appear to be focused on specific technology vendors, and other lists seem to be all-encompassing, arguably reaching across into other adjacent disciplines such as information management, organisational develop-ment, operational excellence and innovation management.

We have elected not to sit in judgement as to whether or not, for

'If it adds flavour – then it's worth including in the recipe!'

Ingredients from later chapters in *The KM Cookbook*.

example; 'positive deviance' belongs in the KM cupboard. It seems as pointless as arguing whether a bay leaf is defined as 'food' when it is added to a casserole. As far as we're concerned, if it adds flavour – then it's worth including in the recipe.

Listed below are the KM ingredients which you will discover in the 'menu chapters' from each organisation, bearing in mind that most of the interviewees shared just a part of their KM story. There are doubtless many more ingredients in their cupboards but we're sure you'll find something in the following chapters to your taste!

- project debriefs and retrospects, lessons portals, after-action reviews, baton-passing, peer assists, learning visits
- communities of practice, expertise locators, network analysis, discussion forums, enterprise social media, collaboration
- positive deviance, river diagrams, self-assessment
- taxonomies, document repositories, periodical circulation, internal search tools, machine learning/analytics, wikis/knowledge packages, knowledge guides/cards, animated videos
- on-boarding/induction, recognition/reward processes, alumni, knowledge transfer/retention, open learning
- meeting facilitation, knowledge cafés, fishbowls, lunchtime seminar/webinar, personas, storytelling, ideation
- virtual/augmented reality, gamification.

Some of these require the involvement of a trained facilitator or may even require the help of an external expert. Others are intuitive or easily learned.

In Chapter 14, Luciana Menezes from PROCERGS describes a deliberate phased approach to the way they have provided and introduced their KM tools – Practices 1.0, 2.0 and 3.0:

> Practices 1.0 are already fully internalised and happen throughout the company without the need for intervention by the KM team: intranet, institutional site, methodology, processes, information security, circulation of periodicals, document repository, normative documentation (see Fig 14.1, training, physical and virtual library.
>
> Practices 2.0 is the current focus of KM actions: Knowledge Quest, Blogs, Idea Portal (see Fig 14.2), Corporate Social Networking, Practice Communities, Discussion Forums, Agile Methods, Design Thinking, Storytelling, Coaching, Fishbowl and Animated Videos.
>
> In addition, there is a set of 3.0 practices under way, characterised by the generation of knowledge artefacts and lessons learned in discussion groups and work groups that work on new approaches, methods and tools of Innovation.

Organising and replenishing your kitchen cupboards

Finally, with such a wide array of content, assets, tools, techniques, pilots and experiments to manage, it's easy to lose a sense of the overall perspective or forget an ingredient. You might even question whether the ingredients you have are sufficient to satisfy the future appetite of your organisation – tastes can and do change!

Getting organised for the future.

One useful workshop approach which we would advocate is the creation of a 'transformation map'. This is a facilitated, collaborative approach which enables the group to set out an inventory of activities, tools, processes and initiatives against a timeline, which usually leads from the current position to a future state. This future state is often described as a vision statement, a picture or 'day-in-the-life' for a set of personas.

Creating a transformation map.

As part of the workshop process, a large space is prepared on a wall, with a summary of current position bottom-left, and a description of the future 'vision' placed top-right. Radiating out the from the vision, along the timeline, are a number of segments against which the tools, methods and initiatives can be mapped.

Visualising the vision!

In the example shown in Figure 6.1, the five segments are: *Culture & Leadership, People Capability, Process, Technology* and *Content.*

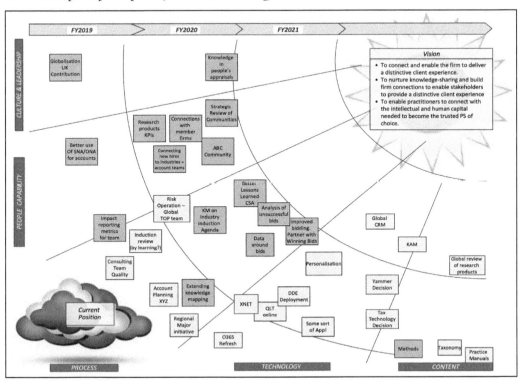

Figure 6.1 *Example of a transformation map*

Ensuring a balanced diet.

In the first stage, a group captures the activities and methods which are currently known (in place or in plans). The segmentation provides a perspective on how balanced the overall programme is, and whether any areas have been overlooked. In nutritional terms, you might say it illustrates whether the restaurant menu provides the recommended 'five-a-day'!

Looking backwards to inform the future.

In the second stage, the group proposes changes or additions to the tools and initiatives on the transformation map which increase the likelihood of that vision being achieved.

In this chapter, we have taken stock of our ingredients, ensuring that they map well to the strategic needs and objectives of the organisation, and looked at ways to classify what you have and plan to fill any gaps – spaces in your cupboard!

At this stage in *The KM Cookbook*, we have reviewed the cuisine, restaurant type, restaurateur, chef, staff and now the Ingredients. Your kitchen is ready to go – and the restaurant critic is ready to call!

7

The restaurant critic: what to expect in an audit

As a restaurateur, when you see a recognised food critic coming through the doors of your restaurant, it's likely that you heart rate will increase. But what if a food critic invited you to join them for dinner? Relax! That's a very different proposition. What questions would you love to ask them? What inside stories would you enjoy hearing?

In writing *The KM Cookbook*, we wanted to explore the new standard and illustrate 'what's possible' with some inspirational stories and examples – and we had another secret ingredient. We wanted to provide the reader with the opportunity to gain insights from an experienced auditor who has led a KM programme, has undergone the ISO 9001 Lead Auditor training and is a certified ISO KM Auditor; a rare combination. The remainder of this chapter is that opportunity; take your seat at the dining table with Patricia.

> The secret ingredient that makes *The KM Cookbook* unique.

To achieve certification, organisations will have to undergo a certification audit. These audits will be conducted by ISO auditors, who themselves should be appropriately trained and certified. Auditors must have experience in the areas that they audit, so that auditors conducting audits of KM programmes will have to have personal experience of KM. For example, persons auditing environmental management systems must have significant personal experience in designing or operating environmental management systems and be certified by an independent accrediting body as an auditor against the ISO Standard 14001 in order to audit environmental management systems.

The auditor's role

The ISO KM Auditor's job is to examine the organisation's programme and determine whether the organisation has developed processes to effectively address the ISO standard requirements. The ISO auditor is also tasked with determining if the organisation has put appropriate processes in place to actually do the things the organisation says that the KM programme is supposed to do. That is: 'Does the KM programme help the organisation meet its stated strategic objectives and goals?' Just as restaurant critics do not tell the restaurateur or chef how to do things, the auditor does not tell the organisation how to meet its objectives and goals – they simply assess the ability of the organisation to do so.

'It is not an auditor's job to fix or criticise the programme'.

Also like restaurant critics, auditors must be independent and impartial. ISO auditors are not allowed to provide consultancy to the organisations they audit. Similarly, consultants are not permitted to audit the organisations for whom they have worked; to do so would be considered a conflict of interest and unacceptable. To be clear, if a person helped company A develop their goals and objectives or developed an implementing initiative for company A, that person would be prohibited from auditing company A's KM programme.

'Auditors must be independent and impartial'

Although the role of the ISO auditor is clear, some people have expressed concerns about audit consistency. Auditors are subjective human beings – hence, what is acceptable to one auditor may not be acceptable to another. This is a valid concern and organisations have a means of recourse, should this happen.

Anyone who has used TripAdvisor knows that there are some reviews that just don't seem right. All of us have seen great restaurants get one- or two-star reviews based on what may have been an isolated incident. TripAdvisor readers have the option of believing these outlier reviews or not. While it is not quite the same for ISO audits, if an organisation believes that an auditor has gone beyond the ISO standard, or if the audit findings seem unreasonable, the organisation can discuss its views with the audit team leader during the audit. If, after discussion with the audit team leader, the matter is not resolved and the organisation still believes that the auditor has gone too far, the finding may be appealed to the certifying body. There is no stigma attached to an appeal and some audit findings have been overturned in the past.

Organisations can appeal auditor findings.

What is it like to go through an audit?

The average audit generally takes between one to two weeks depending on the organisation and its structure. So how will the audit team conduct the audit in this short amount of time?

ISO QMS (Quality Management Systems) audits are usually conducted by a team which can range from two to five people. Auditors must be trained and certified to conduct audits by the proper accreditation body. Ask whether or not the auditors are certified. Auditors should have been trained and demonstrated their knowledge of how to audit by passing an exam given by a certifying body. In the USA, Exemplar Global, UTMB-HMI, Deka, BSI group and ASQ provide auditor certification training. In the UK, the United Kingdom Accreditation Service (UKAS) is the sole UK national accreditation body, which has accredited some organisations such as Lloyds Register to provide ISO auditor certification training.

Make sure the auditors are properly trained and certified.

Make sure that the persons who audit your programmes are properly certified. Experienced auditors will most likely be more efficient in conducting an audit. A certified auditor will have no problem in providing a copy of their certificate.

Normally, audit dates are known well ahead of time so that the organisation can prepare for the audit. This would include gathering the KM programme documents and getting staff ready for interviews by the audit team. Detailed tips on preparing for the audit are found in the Appendices pp. 245-61.

Given the limited amount of time for most audits, the audit team will evaluate programme effectiveness by using a sampling process. The team will request copies of the programme documentation, including governance documents, programme descriptions or charters, pertinent meeting minutes, archives, summaries of electronic databases, etc., to identify the processes, practices and procedures used to implement the KM programme.

They may also request job descriptions, on-boarding and training materials and annual reports. Often this request comes before the actual on-site audit, so the team can familiarise themselves with the KM programme and minimise the amount of time on site. When you are contacted, ask the audit team leader if there is anything in particular that he or she would like to know before they arrive or if they have any needs that you can arrange to make their visit efficient. Your willingness to help the team do their job will be noted.

When the team arrives on site, they will request an 'entrance meeting', to meet the organisational representatives and managers and present their audit plan. The audit team will then explain how they will proceed and most likely will ask to interview a number of staff and their managers. If possible, make key KM staff available during the audit to answer questions and provide clarification as requested. Often team members will split up so that they can cover as much ground as possible in the allotted time. Individual auditors will observe processes in progress and interview staff to assess staff awareness and understanding of the KM programme. While managers and persons

Auditors will look both horizontally and vertically.

overseeing the KM programme are well versed in KM programme goals and objectives, other staff may be less so; often interviews of workers reveal communications weaknesses.

Auditors will ask questions to determine whether staff know, understand and are fulfilling their KM responsibilities. For example, if the programme states that employees are encouraged to identify areas for improvement, and the interviewed staff don't know that they can provide input to the KM programme, that would reveal a weakness in communications. Auditors will also examine KM programme tools to determine whether the technology and process tools meet the needs of the people using them. If a junior staff member says that they don't know about the KM tools available to them, that also reveals a weakness in KM programme execution. The audit goal is to answer the following questions: 'Does the KM programme align with and support the organisation's mission and goals? Do the KM tools, e.g. the expert locator, really help staff? Do the people who are responsible for accomplishing the goals and objectives of the KM programme know their KM roles and responsibilities? Is the KM programme designed to work within the organisational context? Does the organisation encourage a learning, sharing culture? Is there an effort to identify weaknesses and improve the KM programme?'

To answer these questions, auditors will look for objective evidence, such as blogs, meeting minutes, programme revision requests and documents on any or all KM tactics and initiatives. Note that this is all based on the KM programme description and may include posters, company-wide announcements, etc.

It is important that interviewees are open with the auditors. If they do not know something, they should say so. Auditors will look for objective evidence so if there is anecdotal evidence, interviewees should make sure that the auditors are aware of such evidence if it exists.

The audit team will present its findings at an 'exit meeting'. Some auditors will not accept questions or additional information during the exit meeting, so it is important that the organisation provide information as requested during the audit before the exit meeting.

Insider tips on how to prepare for an on-site audit are found in the Appendices.

Pre-audit internal assessment

The three of us have first-hand experience with KM programmes and so as we discussed the premise for this book we developed a tool for organisations to use when assessing their own KM programme. If used correctly, this tool will simulate a KM programme audit and could be used to conduct a mock or internal audit. This tool, the 'KM Chef's Canvas', is explained in the next chapter. Better to find your programme weaknesses before the audit team arrives than have the auditors find them.

The KM Chef's Canvas contains questions an auditor might ask.

Now, knowing what the ISO standard does, what an auditor does, and how an auditor would go about conducting an audit, perhaps you can go look through the following chapters and ask the questions in the KM Chef's Canvas as you read through the interviews. With all this information, you may now be able to look at your own KM programme with a more critical eye.

What evidence would be needed to demonstrate that a programme initiative is really working? How would you get that evidence? How many examples would you need to justify your findings to your peers or to the certifying body? More importantly, what evidence would demonstrate that the processes are *not* working? Using a 'reverse brainstorming' method like this may be helpful in identifying areas for improvement.

Finally, here are some questions you could ask yourself, regardless of whether you choose to pursue certification under ISO 30401 or not:

- How would your programme fare under such scrutiny?
- Are your KM governance and programme description documents current?
- Do the right people know and follow these documents?
- Are the roles and responsibilities clearly defined?
- Have you effectively communicated expectations to the appropriate staff?
- Where are the weaknesses? What could be improved? Are you open to changes?

That, in a nutshell, is the essence of an audit.

Still hungry?

Having had the opportunity to enjoy a discussion over dinner with Patricia, the next chapter explores the 'KM Chef's Canvas' planning tool – with its '57 varieties' of further questions – in much more detail.

8
Planning the menu: the KM Chef's Canvas

In 1896, whilst riding an elevated train in New York City, Henry Heinz noticed a sign advertising '21 styles of shoes' which he appreciated as clever advertising. He combined his and his wife's lucky numbers, 5 and 7 respectively, and began using the slogan '57 Varieties of Pickles' in his advertising later that year.

The origin of the 'Heinz 57 varieties'.

In 1934, Heinz published their own cookbook with 57 products listed. Today the company has more than 5700 products around the globe, but still uses the magic number of 57.

In *The KM Cookbook*, we felt that it was important to provide a simple one-page set of prompting questions for anyone who was thinking about ISO 30401 accreditation.

Inspiration for the 'KM Chef's Canvas'.

In this chapter, we present the KM Chef's Canvas. It is a tool to stimulate dialogue, and help a KM leader, their sponsor and their team to explore their KM programme and help in understanding the ISO KM standard. The Canvas could be used to simulate a KM programme audit, or as a lens through which to view your existing KM programme and to test its robustness and effectiveness, regardless of whether or not you pursue ISO 30401 accreditation.

As we have discussed in Chapter 1, the KM standard does not address the 'how' of your KM programme, just the 'what'. We wanted to go beyond the scope of the KM standard and offer some additional 'how' questions to explore. These are primarily in the areas in the centre of the Canvas: interaction and internalisation; codification and curation; and culture.

Going beyond the requirements of the KM standard.

The KM Chef's Canvas contains 57 (yes, really!) questions which will help prepare you, but we don't claim to condense 28 pages of the official ISO document into a single sheet. Whilst we can't guarantee you will sail through a future ISO audit – you will definitely sail further and faster!

57 questions to ask yourself.

How to use the KM Chef's Canvas

If you are using it as a pre-assessment or a 'mock audit', we suggest the following steps:

Running a workshop
using the KM Chef's
Canvas.

- Schedule a meeting for 2–3 hours with your KM sponsor, KM team and a few KM champions representing different parts of the organisation.
- Nominate a person to play the role of the assessor. This role can be rotated during the workshop.
- Ask the assessor to read Chapter 7, 'The restaurant critic', and 'Preparing for an audit' in the Appendices.
- Provide everyone with a copy of the KM Chef's Canvas (Figure 8.1) before the workshop.
- Ask the 'assessor' to choose a section – we suggest that they work left-to-right across the canvas.
- The assessor should play the role as a 'naïve questioner' – as though they have no prior knowledge of the KM programme. Encourage them to press for objective evidence and examples and to challenge assumptions.
- Capture answers as you go, using a blank copy of the template, or a set of flipcharts.
- Identify the areas which are priorities to address.
- Use the 'menu' chapters in Part II of *The KM Cookbook* to find examples from other organisations which you can learn from.

KM Chef's Canvas and its 57 questions in detail

The notes in the margin in subsequent pages refer to the reference points in ISO 30401 addressed by this section. Remember that the best objective evidence is a combination of documents and interviews.

Strategic context

Strategic context
4.1, 4.2 and 4.3

1   How well is KM aligned with the organisation's strategy and objectives?
2   Do we know who our internal stakeholders are?
3   Do we know who our external stakeholders are?
4   Do we know what the key knowledge areas for the organisation are?
5   Does the scope of our KM system address our knowledge lifecycle and consider the appropriate elements of our organisation?

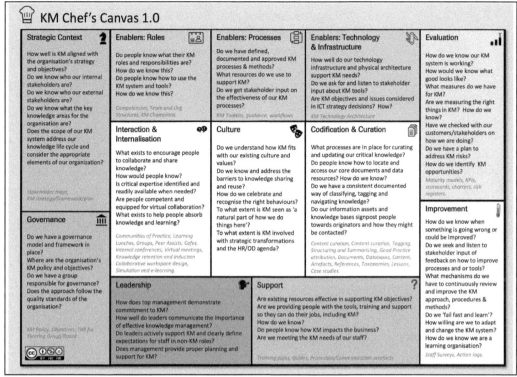

Figure 8.1 *The KM Chef's Canvas in more detail*

Potential evidence includes: stakeholder maps, KM strategy/framework/plan.

This maps to sections 4.1, 4.2 and 4.3 of ISO 30401.

Governance

6 Do we have a governance model and framework in place?
7 Where are the organisation's KM policy and objectives?
8 Do we have a group responsible for governance?
9 Does the approach follow the quality standards of the organisation?

Governance
4.4.4d

Potential evidence includes: KM policy, objectives, ToR for steering group/board.

Support

10 Are existing resources effective in supporting KM objectives?
11 Are we providing people with the tools, training and support so they can do their jobs, including KM?

Support
7.1, 7.2, 7.3 and 7.4

12 How do we know?
13 Do people know how KM impacts the business?
14 Are we meeting the KM needs of our staff?

Potential evidence includes: training plans, guides, promotion/communication artefacts.

Leadership

Leadership
5.1

15 How does top management demonstrate commitment to KM?
16 How well do leaders communicate the importance of effective Knowledge Management?
17 Do leaders actively support KM and clearly define expectations for staff in non-KM roles?
18 Does management provide proper planning and support for KM?

Enablers: roles

Enablers: roles
4.4.4a

19 Do people know what their KM roles and responsibilities are?
20 How do we know this?
21 Do people know how to use the KM system and tools?
22 How do we know this?

Potential evidence includes: Competencies, team and organisational structures, KM champions.

Enablers: processes

Enablers: processes
4.4.4b

23 Do we have defined, documented and approved KM processes and methods?
24 What resources do we use to support KM?
25 Do we get stakeholder input on the effectiveness of our KM processes?

Potential evidence includes: KM toolkits, guidance, workflows.

Enablers: technology and infrastructure

Enablers: technology and
infrastructure
4.4.4c

26 How well do our technology infrastructure and physical architecture support KM needs?
27 Do we ask for and listen to stakeholder input about KM tools?
28 How are KM objectives and issues considered in ICT strategy decisions?

Potential evidence includes: KM technology architecture.

Evaluation

29 How do we know our KM system is working?
30 How would we know what 'good' looks like?
31 What measures do we have for KM?
32 Are we measuring the right things in KM?
33 How do we know?
34 Have we checked with our customers/stakeholders on how we
    are doing?
35 Do we have a plan to address KM risks?
36 How do we identify KM opportunities?

Evaluation
9.1, 9.2 and 9.3

Potential evidence includes: maturity models, KPIs, scorecards, charters, risk registers.

Improvement

37 How do we know when something is going wrong or could be
    improved?
38 Do we seek and listen to stakeholder input of feedback on how
    to improve processes and/or tools?
39 What mechanisms do we have to continuously review and
    improve the KM approach, procedures and methods?
40 Do we 'fail fast and learn'?
41 How willing are we to adapt and change the KM system?
42 How do we know we are a learning organisation?

Improvement
10.1 and 10.2

Potential evidence includes: staff surveys, action logs.

Interaction and internalisation

43 What exists to encourage people to collaborate and share
    knowledge?
44 How would people become aware of this?
45 Are people competent and equipped for virtual collaboration?
46 Is critical expertise identified and readily available when
    needed?
47 What exists to help people absorb knowledge and learning?

Interaction and
internalisation
4.4.3a and 4.4.3d

Potential evidence includes: communities of practice, learning lunches, groups, peer assists, cafés, internal conferences, virtual meetings, knowledge retention and induction activities, collaborative workspace design, simulation, e-learning and on-boarding.

Codification and curation

Codification and curation
4.4.3b and 4.4.3c

48 What processes are in place for curating and updating our critical knowledge?
49 Do people know how to locate and access our core documents and data resources?
50 How do we know?
51 Do we have a consistent documented way of classifying, tagging and navigating knowledge?
52 Do our information assets and knowledge bases signpost people towards originators and how they might be contacted?

Potential evidence includes: content curation, tagging, structuring and summarising, good practice attribution, documents, databases, content, artefacts, references, taxonomies, lessons, case studies.

Culture

Culture
Annex C

53 Do we understand how KM fits with our existing culture and values?
54 Do we know and address the barriers to knowledge sharing and reuse?
55 How do we celebrate and recognise the right behaviours?
56 To what extent is KM seen as 'a natural part of how we do things here'?
57 To what extent is KM involved with strategic transformations and the HR/OD agenda?

Food for thought

The Chef's Canvas provides you with some questions and potential action points. It can be used to shape your strategy, assist in designing an internal audit, or prepare you for an ISO KM audit. For the remainder of *The KM Cookbook*, we want to inspire with some real stories from actual 'KM chefs' around the world.

From the Canvas to real life.

Each story will end with our observations on how initiatives from these KM programmes align with the KM Chef's Canvas. While several of these stories describe many initiatives and have many strengths, we have limited ourselves to three canvas areas for each story.

Before we open up these 16 menus, though, we want to introduce you to our highlights: the chef's specials.

9

The KM chef's specials: taster menu

In a few moments (if you've resisted the temptation thus far) you will see how leading organisations have arranged their KM kitchens and produced an array of mouth-watering menus.

A smorgasbord of tasty bites.

Like good Knowledge and Information Management professionals, we wanted to help you navigate these menus by creating a taster menu that features courses, ingredients and approaches that appealed to us from the 16 chapters that follow. At the end of those chapters we mapped aspects of their KM programme against the KM Chef's Canvas, selecting three areas we thought particularly strong. We treated all of the chapters in the same way, limiting ourselves to three highlights. What follows is a summation (**in bold**) of the areas we found compelling.

Of course, no self-respecting menu would be complete without a 'dish of the day'. It's our way of featuring a compelling story that illustrates the ingenuity of Knowledge Management professionals.

This will not be the perfect menu; we have different tastes, preferences and capacities. Nor we will be attempting to answer the 57 KM Chef's Canvas questions – we encourage you to have a go at that as you read through the chapters that follow and to come up with your favourites.

Strategic context

Most KM programmes begin in response to a burning platform issue or as a solution to an operational problem. Our examples bear this out. We were able to identify strategic intent and a direct link to strategy. Here's a couple: PROCERGS of Brazil and The International Olympic Committee (IOC), based in Lausanne, Switzerland.

Headquartered in Porte Alegre, with over 1,000 employees

spread across the Brazilian state of Rio Grande do Sul, PROCERGS provides information, technology and communication (ICT) solutions and infrastructure for the state to keep it running. It took a strategic decision over a decade ago to set up a Knowledge Management and Innovation Unit to support its drive to make government more efficient.

Using innovation and KM to transform public and citizen services.

The Knowledge and Innovation team's goals are totally aligned with those of the organisation's. The output of their work informs policy and is mapped to strategic guidelines.

The International Olympic Committee facilitates the successful delivery of the most famous global sporting event. Knowledge, learning and experience gained from previous editions of the Games are consolidated and transferred from one host city to the next.

A successful Olympic Games relies on effective knowledge transfer from one host city to the next.

The work of the Olympic Games KM Team (OGKM) is 100% aligned with the successful and efficient delivery of the Olympic Games. Knowledge products and learning processes are linked directly to the strategic goal and plans of a host city's organising committee. All stakeholders are understood and engaged with. This is enhanced through the provision of targeted executive coaching to address strategic knowledge gaps.

Governance

We anticipate that organisations with quality assurance/quality management functions will see ISO 30401 as an opportunity to align the KM programme with a recognised international standard. Many will have effective governance structures already in place. Here are two examples we found compelling: MAPNA of Iran and USAID of the USA.

MAPNA is a multi-division, multi-layered industrial firm employing more than 15,000 people. It is involved in thermal and renewable energy, oil and gas, railway transportation and other industrial projects, and manufactures the major equipment required for these businesses.

KM is part of MAPNA's quality management systems.

MAPNA is a process-oriented firm. It has a governance model approved by the board.

The company processes are underpinned by a quality management system that adheres to International Organization for Standardization (ISO) standards. All of its processes, procedures, tools and techniques are audited twice a year, one internal and one external. This requires documentation of all aspects of KM, frequent review and improvement. Each KM-related job and the tasks that are associated with it are documented, reviewed and periodically improved.

The United States Agency for International Development (USAID) is an independent agency of the US Federal Government primarily responsible for administering civilian foreign aid and development assistance.

> **Collaborating, Learning and Adapting (CLA) is clearly embedded in the programme lifecycle and is 'on the radar' for both the programme teams and central teams. Application of the techniques is measured, and it is clear that USAID staff see it as strategic and valuable, such that they voluntarily participate well beyond the mandatory aspects of the programme.**

CLA is USAID's approach to supporting effective development by becoming a more collaborative, learning and adaptive organisation.

Support

Here we looked for evidence that the KM team provides the support needed for people to meet their objectives, and a training curriculum that encourages the development of staff. We liked that both the Financial Conduct Authority (FCA) of UK and Schlumberger of US illustrate the importance of aligning individual learning with KM.

The Financial Conduct Authority (FCA) is a regulator for the financial markets in the UK. It aims to make markets work well – for individuals, for business, large and small, and for the economy as a whole.

Effective regulation requires an informed investigation team supported by the latest knowledge of legislation and sharing of knowledge gained in the field.

> **The establishment of an Investigation Academy reflects FCA's emphasis on knowledge sharing and learning. It provides a learning pathway for staff in the Investigation Department and is especially valuable for new entrants. By monitoring people's progress through the curriculum and how they use the mentoring facility FCA are able to target future training where there is most need.**

Investigation Academy allows FCA to identify and plug knowledge gaps.

Schlumberger is the world's largest oilfield services company. It employs roughly 100,000 people across 85 countries with four principal executive offices, in Paris, Houston, London and The Hague. Their Eureka programme bears witness to the company's website incentive for prospective employees that 'You will always be encouraged to grow and you will never stop learning.'

> **The Eureka programme has documented all underlying processes and principles, and provides dedicated training and mentoring for Eureka leaders, who are asked for feedback through surveys and regular conversations with the central**

Eureka: supporting online communities of practice to facilitate knowledge sharing.

team. The programme is fully integrated with professional development and is well known to staff.

Leadership

One of the key enablers of any KM programme is the extent to which leaders show active and energetic support. Every KM presenter will tell you that without it the programme is doomed to fail and those that have it will be able to look back to a time when the sands shifted and 'C Suite' focus changed. In both examples selected, PDO and Saudi Aramco, the support from the top has been tangible and ongoing.

Petroleum Development Oman (PDO) is the leading exploration and production company in the Sultanate of Oman, delivering the majority of the country's crude oil production and natural gas supply.

The KM programme was initiated by senior management, who, with a succession of major projects on the horizon, believed there was much to be gained from identifying and applying lessons from previous projects.

An official approved code of practice stipulates that every business should have a resource committed to KM.

PDO's leaders have consistently demonstrated support for the KM programme: from the clear mandate to the early 'picture on the wall', to the various awards and to making clear what's expected of KM across the organisation.

Saudi Aramco is the national petroleum and natural gas company of Saudi Arabia, based in Dhahran. Its operations and 65,000 employees span the globe and include exploration, production, refining, chemicals, distribution and marketing. It is one of the largest companies in the world by revenue.

With a relatively young workforce it has the luxury to plan for a time when key knowledge leaves the business, which is why a decade ago it set up a knowledge transfer programme to mitigate knowledge loss. This became a key part of the corporate knowledge policy.

The corporate policy is a powerful tool for gaining support.

Saudi Aramco's CEO signed the Knowledge Management Policy, which is one of only 41 corporate policies. This was a major milestone and a major enabler/door-opener. KM is stated within the training and development vision and objectives, and is a natural enabler in activities such as e-learning, social collaboration and gamification.

Enablers: roles

Irrespective of where the KM function is located in the organisation – and many will have been through multiple reporting lines – a recurring success factor is the extent to which people know the KM roles and responsibilities and how to use the KM system and tools.

The examples selected are from different industries: Linklaters is an international law firm, Syngenta an international agrochemicals business. There is much to admire in both.

Linklaters LLP is a multinational law firm headquartered in London. It is a member of the 'Magic Circle' of elite British law firms, employing over 2000 lawyers across 20 countries.

Knowledge is the firm's core asset and so it is imperative that everyone knows their role in the identification and delivery of legal advice.

'Special Forces crack units of the knowledge and learning world.'

The KM programme benefits greatly from the global presence of senior 'Knowledge and Partners' at strategic levels in the firm and the large team of professional support lawyers providing knowledge updates to legal teams, described as 'the Special Forces crack units of the knowledge and learning world!' KM roles and responsibilities now have an external client-facing dimension, with KM capability recognised as value-added service.

Syngenta is a Swiss-based global company that produces agrochemicals and seeds. It is a business that aspires to helps humanity face its toughest challenge: how to feed a rising population, sustainably.

Sharing what it knows across the global business and collaborating with external partners are key to its success. LEAP — 'learning from experience and accelerating performance' is where this comes together for Syngenta's global supply operations.

The LEAP programme is rooted in the creation and support of collaborative networks, with direct encouragement to share knowledge through the TREE award recognition scheme.

Roles for network leaders are well defined, and supported with training programmes and maturity assessments. Sponsor, topic lead and core team roles are also fully documented.

Enablers: processes

Creating KM processes is not for the faint-hearted! It is an essential element for those with quality systems in place (see Governance, above). As a KM programme becomes established, so it's important to build the resilience which processes, methods and toolkits bring. These examples from TechnipFMC and IOC stood out.

TechnipFMC is a global leader in oil and gas, in subsea, onshore, offshore and surface technologies, whose aim is to enhance performance of the world's energy industry. Headquartered in London, with operational HQs in Houston and Paris, it has a global workforce of 37,000.

Accelerating Integration:
. . . defined, docu-
mented and approved
KM processes and
methods.

Creating a team with resources from merging organisations can be difficult, especially when two-thirds of the business has a different view of what KM is and can do. The week-long team retreat to assess KM & Social Learning's products and techniques resulted in a long list of valuable services packaged as Accelerating Integration. In itself that was impressive. What struck us was that those 34 services were then transformed into documented organisational processes.

In IOC's case, knowledge is at the heart of its activities and the Olympic Games KM team is responsible for ensuring that the organising committees of host cities get the full benefit from tailored knowledge transfer and learning processes and play their part in updating knowledge resources and guides for future games.

Passing the knowledge
and learning baton from
one host city to the next.

OGKM's processes, methods and 'learning pathways' are well documented and communicated. Stakeholder input is frequently sought from KM staff in organising committees, many of whom continue to meet and work collaboratively with the central IOC team to enhance KM and learning for years after the delivery of the Games in their host city.

Enablers: technology and infrastructure

KM is often viewed exclusively through a technology lens and many times the authors have heard, 'We do KM, we have SharePoint or a document management system.' It's often the case that the most successful KM programmes are underpinned by what Hank Malik of PDO described as 'the killer app'. While that might be true of some programmes, of equal importance is how that killer app fits into an infrastructure that recognises the value of data and information as well as knowledge.

The two examples selected, from Defence Science & Technology Laboratory (Dstl) of the UK and the World Bank, headquartered in Washington, DC, are great illustrations of how to present critical knowledge and information in a way that stakeholders find useful and relevant.

Dstl is an executive agency of the UK Ministry of Defence. It delivers science and technology research and advice to the Ministry of Defence and other parts of government. Dstl believes that effective Knowledge and Information Management requires infrastructure, both physical and electronic.

The development of a Knowledge Ecosystem underpinned by an Information Architecture designed to augment search is at the core of Dstl's efforts to provide scientists with access to relevant

content. That Dstl has defined four information types and makes clear the distinction between Knowledge and Information, we found compelling.

Dstl's four information types: Technical; Organisational; Project; and Personal.

The World Bank has 189 member countries as its stakeholders; 10,000+ staff from more than 170 countries; and offices in over 130 locations.

As a knowledge institution, its knowledge work spans multiple themes and regions, allowing the institution to harness multi-sectoral, integrated research that reflects the strategic priorities of countries, the Bank, and the wider development community. This harnessing of knowledge is supported by the creation of 'knowledge packages'.

The Bank's activities with machine learning and artificial intelligence to create 'knowledge packages' is distinctive and has been very well received internally. There is evidence that the successful application of helpful, proactive technology is changing the way staff relate to information and the value they attribute to tagging and managing it as an asset.

Knowledge packages: a snapshot of critical knowledge and expertise combined with external research.

Evaluation

Few KM programmes survive if they are unable to pass the 'value test'. As KM becomes a more accepted corporate discipline we believe there will be less of a need to produce statistical justification in terms of hours saved – such as dollars not spent, ideas generated or reduced time to produce a product. (Nobody ever asked the Finance function to justify their value-add!)

Evaluation is both a curse and a blessing, as our examples from TechnipFMC and USAID show.

Few organisations that practice KM and Social Learning have found an accepted mechanism to evaluate their activities. TechnipFMC's Net Promoter Score (NPS) is an innovative measure that builds on Return On Expectations and reflects their approach to providing value to the business through engagement, connection and facilitated collaboration.

Informal Net Promoter Score: would you recommend, would you use us again?

USAID uses a traditional approach to value the impact of its KM activities. The annual CLA Case Competition sources examples from USAID staff and implementing partners. More than 100 stories showcasing CLA in practice are available on the USAID Learning Lab website and can be searched by sector and region. They are also analysed to study the impact of CLA on organisational effectiveness and development outcomes.

Using self-assessment to
identify material impact.

The Collaborate, Learn and Adapt framework itself, and the self-assessment process, demonstrate a mature level of evaluation. Material impacts are identified, celebrated through a 'Case Competition', captured and shared in an evidence base of successful CLA cases which is publicly searchable.

Improvement

Increasingly organisations see KM as delivering process improvements and helping it make better decisions. The KM system needs a periodic review to ensure that it continues to be fit for its purpose. The examples from TfL of the UK and Saudi Aramco of Saudi Arabia demonstrate how operational process is informed by knowledge of, and a review of the KM system informed by ISO KM Standards.

As the integrated transport authority, responsible for meeting the Mayor of London's strategy and commitments on transport in London, Transport for London (TfL) runs the day-to-day operation of the capital's public transport network and manages London's main roads.

Facing massive investment on a huge infrastructure project, TfL recognised the importance of drawing on lessons from previous projects.

Building knowledge into
process to improve
project performance.

As reporting lines changed and KM was located in Continuous Improvement, so the emphasis moved to process improvement: embedding lessons into TfL's Stage-Gate® New Product/Project Development process to ensure that knowledge supports investment decision. They have been able to measure progress by the quality of the lessons input to their lessons-learned portal.

Although KM in Saudi Aramco is a relatively recent practice, the KM team are constantly reviewing the KM system.

Using ISO 30401 to
remodel a KM
consultancy offering.

Saudi Aramco is using the new ISO KM Standard to remodel its KM consultancy offering: specifically, the knowledge assessment (KM audit and maturity). The assessment is shaping up to be in line with the standard's tacit/explicit operational dimensions. The rationale is to be able to benchmark their activity with other organisations.

Interaction and internalisation

If you ask ten knowledge managers to name the most important component of a KM system, the majority will say 'people'. In many of the interviews where knowledge sharing, knowledge transfer, lessons learned and collaboration were cited as drivers for the KM programme, the talk was of how to run communities, how to train, how to stimulate ideas. People are the fulcrum of KM, and the way human interaction is managed is critical to success, as these examples, from GE of the USA, PROCERGS of Brazil and Médecins Sans Frontières (MSF) of Belgium, show:

GE's Knowledge Management strategy and story are built upon the success of their communities of practice, executed at a scale well beyond most other organisations. 'This may be the biggest, fastest implementation in the history of Knowledge Management, anywhere'. Virtual collaboration is a natural competency within the firm, with a well-developed collaborative infrastructure. Interactions are characterised and analysed through dynamic organisational network analysis.

Using virtual collaboration techniques to run successful communities of practice.

There are many examples of PROCERGS' KM team engaging with its stakeholders: Fourth of Knowledge, Knowledge Wednesdays, Innovation Hackathons and Seminars. We were impressed by their approach to a major project, Big Data & Data Science, which seeks to understand how government services and products are used during the life of the citizen. The use in expert group sessions of storytelling to map the lifecycle of a student surfaced issues that might otherwise have remained hidden.

Using storytelling to help inform future state policy.

Robin, who heads up KM at MSF, describes himself as 'always findable'. There is a significant focus on the quality and effectiveness of collaboration and facilitation in meetings. Learning and training resources are very human-centred, immersing staff in an authentic and emotionally engaging process, through gamification and virtual reality. Organisational design is an area which falls under the responsibility of the KM team.

Using gamification and virtual reality to prepare for and learn from critical incidents.

Codification and curation

In a world of 'fake news' veracity of source is critical. The role of KM in codifying and curating organisational knowledge is often under-estimated. It's not enough to collect information and knowledge: how it's organised and presented, when and for whom, are key.

These examples, from PDO Oman and GE of the USA, illustrate how critical knowledge is captured and presented in a compelling way to those for whom it will be of value.

Turn lessons identified into lessons learned.

PDO's Learnings Knowledge Base is a great example of how an organisation turns lessons identified into lessons learned that have tangible business impact. The Featured Learning Cards are an imaginative approach to sharing critical knowledge that can be applied across the business, as well as identifying the source so that others can approach the originator.

Using a wiki build on an
organisational taxonomy.

One particular strength in this area is the underlying taxonomy, which GE describes as its 'circulatory system'. Other strengths include the streaming and channelling of external sources into community spaces and the curation of knowledge products through 'wiki-as-a-service'.

Culture

Organisational culture is often cited as being a barrier to effective KM. When KM programmes are successful, the 'what's in it for me?' is addressed on an individual basis, as well as what's in it for the team and the organisation.

Motivation, hence culture, is likely to differ in each organisation. Would a public-sector organisation in Brazil have the same motivation, culture and values as a multinational oilfield services company with an executive office in France? It's unlikely. The examples selected, Médecins Sans Frontières (MSF) and Syngenta, recognise the importance of tailoring the KM programme to the prevailing culture, behaviours and values.

MSF is an international humanitarian medical non-governmental organisation best known for its projects in conflict zones and in countries affected by endemic diseases. People who work for MSF are attracted by the organisation's values and direct humanitarian impact.

Creative, culturally aware
methods of on-boarding
and off-boarding.

KM is deeply linked with MSF's quality principles, which in turn build upon the organisation's values and principles. Robin is frequently adapting his range of services in order to address cultural challenges – for example through the improvement of meeting facilitation. KM is intertwined with on-boarding and off-boarding of staff with the creative approach to engagement, even extending to the use of chocolate!

Syngenta have many enthusiastic KM practitioners and advocates. Here's one reason why:

Using a recognition
scheme to acknowledge
good knowledge-sharing
behaviours.

Syngenta pays particular attention to knowledge-sharing behaviours and has a very well established recognition scheme (the TREE awards) in place to acknowledge where the right behaviours have been demonstrated. The LEAP programme has been positioned as a cultural transformation programme, making use of established models of change management.

Dish of the day

This, from Iran, highlights many good attributes we'd look for in a KM system: interaction and internalisation, culture and improvement. This is Firoozeh's story:

> We invited a blind professor to a KM tools and techniques workshop in order to discuss his experience in preparing blind children to get into society and teaching them how to survive in the outside world.
>
> The reason for this invitation was the similarities between a blind person's challenges of getting out in the world with the situation of project managers and their team in progressing their projects in challenging situations.
>
> The professor explained how he teaches children to get familiar with their surroundings by gathering a wide range of information before stepping into society. This familiarisation includes identifying different flooring materials such as asphalt, mosaic, wood, etc., recognising the dimensions of their environment by speed of reflection of sound, estimating the number of people present around them, and so on.
>
> The children share their experiences with the environment, challenging situations and new technologies. The professor also teaches them to work with a variety of new technologies, such as smartphones or tablets, audio taping and using websites for blind people.
>
> The fact that tools such as Peer Assist, Brainstorm, and After Action Review proved beneficial and effective for people with physical limitations motivated the attendees of this workshop to start using these types of tools to help solve unexpected issues in their projects.

Drawing on the experiences of blind teachers to demonstrate the potential value of KM tools and techniques

A health warning

The chefs' specials are a consolidation of KM practices we believe meet and exceed the requirements of ISO KM Standard 30401.

However, a restaurant run by people who've read a catering manual yet have no culinary expertise, use incompatible ingredients and possess a limited understanding of what their customers want to eat is surely doomed to fail! The analogy applies equally well to the world of KM.

It is not enough to just read and follow the standards. While they provide a framework, they are no panacea – no recipe for success, without the right people, processes and technology in place and a good understanding of the organisational context in which Knowledge Management is operating.

Part II
Menus to savour

Introduction: How to read the menus

We wanted to capture the story from each organisation *as told by* the KM leader (and in some cases, by other team members too). Each chapter is heavily narrative-based — just as though you were sitting down for dinner with each person and asked them to describe their KM approach from a personal perspective.

As you proceed through the chapters which follow, you will see a similar structure, which reflects the common approach which we took to conducting the interviews.

Section	Icon

Chef(s): personal context/introduction to the narrator(s)

Starter: business context

Main course: details of the KM programme

Dessert: reflection from the narrator

Coffee: Brief analysis from *The KM Cookbook* team, mapping the story to the KM Chef's Canvas

The annotated KM Chef's Canvas below indicates which three aspects of the KM Standard we have highlighted for each organisation. Note that we limited ourselves to just three areas in each case to provide balance; many of the organisations had further areas of strength.

Use it as an index to help you navigate the examples, using the chapter numbers indicated in parentheses.

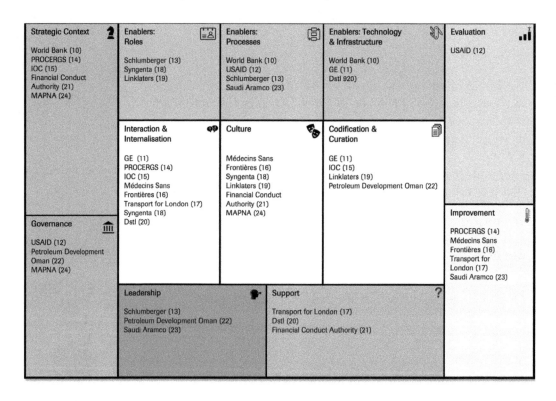

10

The World Bank: Knowledge Management and machine learning

NARRATED BY MARGOT BROWN (DIRECTOR OF KNOWLEDGE MANAGEMENT) AND VIVEK SHARMA (SENIOR IT OFFICER)

The World Bank is no stranger to Knowledge Management, having been known publicly for its knowledge activities since the late 90s. Managing knowledge as an asset has always been part of the Bank's *raison d'être*, as Margot Brown, who joined as Director of Knowledge Management in 2016, noted:

> It's a prolific, producing organisation – thousands and thousands of works of development information and reports and incredible output that forms the basis for a lot of other work. In that position, the Bank is unparalleled, but where it has always had difficulties is in fully getting its arm around that asset, utilising it efficiently and effectively. It's a challenge of scale.

Previous Directors of Knowledge had been drawn from Operations, and had deep expertise in their own domain (e.g. economics). Whilst they had an appreciation of KM and realised the importance of it, they didn't have the professional backgrounds in information or Knowledge Management to design and direct a holistic KM programme. One result of this was that in practice, the main focus had been primarily on knowledge creation activities. Margot explains how she addressed this:

> That was one of the big distinctions that we made:
> 'We are in Knowledge Management, we don't get involved on the knowledge creation side.'
> We leave that to the subject-matter specialists in Operations who are experts in their domain. We don't comment on quality. We don't comment on relevancy. Where we get involved is that once something is actually explicit, then we make sure that it's structured properly in the architecture; it's been tagged, it's able to be used collaboratively; in fact, that it's getting used at all.
> That distinction started to get picked up in the Bank and people started to get a better understanding of how the work that we are doing and the

'Our job is to make the job of operations easier.'

approach that we're taking is different from the approaches that were used before. We continue to reiterate and deliver that message across our key stakeholders so that it is fully understood. We are seeing appreciation from our operational colleagues as we offer them solutions to address the gaps that they experience in their daily work. We're very much positioned as a support function; as facilitators. Our job is to make the job of operations easier.

The first 100 days as Director of Knowledge Management

Margot recounted how she oriented herself to the organisation, working her way carefully back through the layers of Knowledge Management initiatives in a manner almost similar to an archaeological dig.

'I had to resist the call to just start doing something!'

I had to resist the call to just start doing something. There was a lot of pent-up demand for something to happen. The Bank had reached the point of becoming weary of talking about this. It was just so ready for change and for a new approach. Coming in new to the organisation and new to development, I had to do my due diligence and understand the ground realities in which I was to operate and add value. There was a lot of really good work done prior to my arrival – many, many reports and diagnostics and analysis. I took the time to go through all of that, way back to the first report done I think in 1999 by Steve Denning. I started with that and then I worked my way forward. There was certainly a lot of really useful work that was done when the Bank reorganised in 2014 into the Global Practices. There has also been a lot of work done around incentives and change management, which was really quite helpful to the work we were doing.

The other thing that I undertook quite quickly was to just get out and talk to people and listen to what they were telling us. So, the consultation was at all levels of the organisation. We started with the Task Team Leaders (TTLs), who are the undisputed 'kings of the organisation'. These are the individuals who are running the projects – anything from $100,000 projects to $100,000,000 projects – these individuals are so important to the organisation. I started there, and then all of the key stakeholder groups identified a number of individuals across all of the global practices to have consultations with; hundreds of interviews and many, many focus groups.

Concurrently with internal due diligence, Margot undertook external research as well, learning from other organisations in the development sphere, their KM strategies and plans.

Using perspectives from outside the Bank.

I was already bringing my own external experience from the consulting industry and I was using a lot of that and used it in structuring what we would do differently at the Bank. I liked the work that IFAD (International

Fund for Agriculture Development) had done. Their approach was very pragmatic and that was what was needed. The Bank had a lot of great reports and plans which had provided input to the KM situation – but they were still high level. Our action plan had to be really tangible, very practical, very pragmatic – so that's what we went for.

Developing a vision, a plan and a team

Margot spent six months gathering information, socialising her ideas across the Bank and seeking input from management teams as she iterated her plan.

Six months of information gathering and socialisation to ensure buy-in.

You can't go away and do this in a vacuum and then bring it into operations and have people accept it. It was really, really key to make sure that people were being brought along as we went.

After the consultation, there was a period of time where we had to put all of this together into an understandable story to provide a strategic vision. That process took a month – sitting down with all of the interview material from the focus group, all of my observations, pulling all of this together. The next step was to figure out how it would best resonate with the Bank. How does what we're doing fit in with the Bank's strategy, where it's going and all the other initiatives that are under way? Making sure that you're connected and plugged into all of the other initiatives and campaigns that are going on across the institution was so important – those connections and linkages emerged as a result of the socialisation.

Connecting the objectives to the organisational strategy

At the time Margot joined the Bank, the context within which the organisation was operating and the nature of international development was changing. Many other players are emerging in the development landscape who are offering both technical and financial assistance in this rapidly evolving landscape. It is critical that in line with the Bank's organisational strategy the KM strategy would bring added value to help the Bank leverage all that it knows and generates through its operations. By doing so, the institution is able to provide maximum value to clients.

It was becoming increasingly obvious that the Bank needed to address this challenge of managing and leveraging its knowledge and assets so that they are fully tapped into and utilised. Given that clients have always valued this know-how and 70-plus years of development experience that the Bank has (sometimes more than lending), this placed an even higher emphasis on the need to capitalise on it. This meant addressing some of the foundational components that were critical to establishing an effective knowledge-sharing ecosystem.

Capitalising on 70-plus years of development experience.

How Knowledge Management impacts the World Bank's work

Finding pockets of
excellence.

In serving the organisational strategy, the KM action plan aims to:

> . . . incorporate better management of what the Bank knows within the operational workflow, providing faster and more effective access to relevant knowledge, which can help staff work more efficiently, effectively, and with agility.

The Knowledge Management Action Plan operates under a set of principles or 'components':

- ensuring that processes and new ways of working add value without adding administrative burden
- leadership for accountability around knowledge sharing
- ensuring that roles and responsibilities are clear

Essential components
and strategic principles.

- working to get the right mix of tools and technology
- awareness-building about Knowledge Management work across the Bank; getting the right mix of incentives to encourage knowledge sharing; building a culture of knowledge sharing
- and increasing connectivity among staff, clients and partners.

Knowledge Management is now also delivered through a number of teams and initiatives, including:

- The Global Delivery Initiative. This is a collaborative effort with 40 partners across the development field aimed at creating a world-class evidence base of delivery know-how.

Initiatives with
development impact.

- The South-South Experience Exchange Facility, which facilitates knowledge exchange directly between countries who share similar development challenges. An example of this, following the 2010 earthquake in Haiti, was a learning visit of Haitian officials to provinces in Indonesia to learn directly from reconstruction experts and government officials, drawing out lessons and developing co-ordination skills.
- The Geospatial Operational Support Team, who provide innovative services around the use of imagery and data and the application of new technologies, including satellites and drones.
- The Open Learning Campus provides 'a unique ecosystem of customisable and just-in-time curricula, lessons, tools, conversations, and communities to help World Bank clients, partners and staff update their knowledge and co-create solutions'.
- Finally, as part of the KM team, the Text and Data Analytics Unit

helps practitioners to navigate and use the huge wealth of unstructured and structured data – including project documentation and insights from the terabytes of data generated from World Bank operations.

Dual streams – rebuilding the foundations, whilst experimenting with the future

Margot described the Bank as having many pockets of excellence in Knowledge Management, and that her role was to adapt and scale up these across the Bank. Examples of these *'pockets of excellence'* include:

- The Water Global Practice's 'Ask Water Helpdesk' – a process for answering staff enquiries by combining designated experts, SkillFinder, collaboration sites, curated libraries and databases.
- The 'Knowbel Awards' and the 'Community Management Appreciation Day', which celebrate knowledge-sharing behaviours: Share, Create, Reflect and Explore, and successful communities of practice respectively. These events attract hundreds of submissions from across the Bank each year.

This foundational work, however, was only half of the story.

We decided to have another stream of activity because we knew that a lot of the foundational stuff was going to take time to put in place. The other stream was much more responsive, much more tactical and really would show Operations that we are making a difference. This was our experimental stream. So there we really focused on the pain-points that Operations were experiencing in knowledge. That's where knowledge packages fit in.

Vivek and the team within our Text and Data Analytics Unit had developed a machine learning algorithm which was born out of the engagement that they had been having with operations. As we were looking at some of this work, and in the light of our experimental streams, we said, 'Well, you know, we think we could probably not do it just for the occasional leader who asks for it because they know that the team can produce it. Why don't we just do it for every single project?'

We started to work with some teams to fine-tune the algorithm. The teams that we started showing it to started to get really excited because they had never received anything like this before. Somebody said to me, which I thought was amazing – 'This would take the work of a short-term consultant about two months to put together and you can do it within 24 hours using machine learning.' So, to me that was just, Wow!

Foundational and tactical, experimental streams running in parallel.

Condensing two months' work into 24 hours.

Vivek Sharma, Senior IT Officer at the World Bank, takes up the narration

Vivek Sharma is an economist by training (former senior economist at Ford Motor Company in Asia Pacific). He is now a Senior IT Officer, but originally he wanted to join the World Bank to pursue a career as an economist. Instead, he was first approached for an internal role in Knowledge Management.

'This is what the challenge is at the Bank. When people are doing new projects at the Bank, they often end up reinventing the wheel.'

I told them 'I don't think I'm the guy you're looking for!' I wanted to be an economist, but the Director who hired me said 'You can do this for a couple of years. Have a few years in the Bank doing something critical – you should pursue that.'

When the manager who hired us came to India, he explained the Knowledge Management problem to us practically. He said: 'This is what the challenge is at the Bank. When people are doing new projects at the Bank, they often end up reinventing the wheel, because it's really difficult for them to identify whether the Bank has done something similar in the past, whether there are learnings from the past that we can borrow, can we be sure that we're not making the same mistakes over and over; and are we learning from our successes?'

We identified that it's really important that we are able to go and match and identify projects on multiple dimensions rather than one. That was essentially the problem – to identify similarities between different projects.

We presumed that all of this would sit in one place; when we made ourselves more familiar with the Bank's systems we found that it wasn't really like that!

Vivek explained how he came to develop an algorithm which used a statistical technique, clustering the text from publications, and how that algorithm is still the core of what have come to be known as 'knowledge packages'. Interestingly, it was an experience from his previous work at Ford Motor Company which had sparked the idea. Clustering is commonly used to identify customer segments. The challenge at the World Bank though, was to identify the *projects*.

We now have 560 knowledge packages and we have automated the end-to-end collection of the data that goes into the knowledge package, to spitting out the final output as a set of results in your browser. As a recipient of the knowledge package, you practically do nothing. You just select your project ID and boom! The system takes a few seconds and just throws at you all the knowledge in a package.

Creating knowledge packages

As Vivek and the team dug deeper into the information resources at the World Bank, they saw the complexity of the challenge growing.

We looked at all the metadata that we have for projects – the Bank tags everything by sector, country and theme. We thought it would be very simple – take the metadata around countries that we know are similar, for example. We first had an algorithm that identified similar countries, then we thought that we could take something based on project-level metadata and cluster based on that, beside the financial commitment, sector and theme to give us something fairly similar. But then we understood that every sector (sanitation, for example) has major differences. It's a big jigsaw. If you look at the taxonomy which identifies the nuances in our interventions, there are 65 sectors, 176 teams and over 5300 topics that you can potentially tag a project to!

'It's a big jigsaw!'

In addition to the complexity of categorisation, Vivek went on to describe additional sources that also yield the content of a 'knowledge package'.

The challenge is that if I can take the text of your project, and an equivalent text from all the other projects – the Bank so far has done over 18,000 lending operations, and 25,000 analytical reports – then you have to add databases that are relevant. Apart from that, you also need to identify internal experts, and beyond that there's the knowledge which sits outside the World Bank – some very strategic pieces of work that a project needs in order to operate – all knowledge that you hope to have available for the project in that country.
These are the components of the knowledge package.

Adding external research sources with the library team.

While the machine learning algorithm could produce knowledge packages from internal materials almost instantaneously, there was a desire to include external research, which initially brought a greater degree of human judgement into the process.

We started working with the library team inside the Bank. We had to take the project description and give it to them, and then a research assistant, a librarian, would read that description and identify key concepts that she would then search in a subscription-based resource of millions of publications, and give us the 20 most relevant results.
The challenge was that this was time-consuming – a human step in the process made the 24-hour anticipated turnaround time difficult to achieve. We did this for around 300 requests, but did not have the capacity to deliver based on the increasing demand. Even though the team was doing a phenomenal job – they just didn't have the time.
We now have an algorithm which is able to take your project description, break it down into separate queries, query external data sources and curate the top 50 results, all without human intervention – and the results are really good!

Package delivery.

Delivering knowledge packages

Knowledge packages represent a snapshot of all the critical knowledge and expertise derived via the machine algorithm, combined with external research. The knowledge package is delivered online via the browser (see Figure 10.1). Vivek was enthusiastic about the way in which knowledge packages are integrated with the day-to-day project reporting activities of staff.

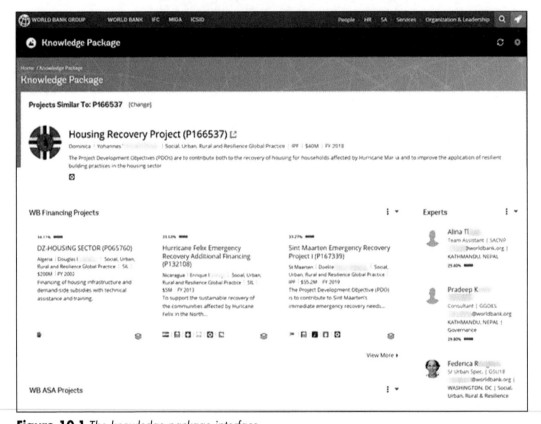

Figure 10.1 *The knowledge package interface*

This is one of the things that people really liked. Like most organisations, we have complex enterprise systems that come together. SAP is a common one; Task Team Leaders refer to their interaction with these massive Bank systems as 'feeding them'.

When a project is initiated, they put in a project description and make a project ID – that's where they are saying 'this is what I'm going to do'. This is where they feed the system the first time.

'No one likes feeding the system. The system never gives anything back.'

No one likes feeding the system. It's a requirement; you are measured on it. Before implementing a project, you need to provide all of this information – but the problem is that the system never gives anything back.

So, what we thought was – when they are putting in the first description, if we can take it from there – you're just doing your job – we never ask you to do anything different, all you do is put in a description and get an automatically generated PID (Project Initiation Document). We pick up the description from there, we run it through our algorithms, we pick up all the knowledge and then – boom! The next day in your inbox is a knowledge package saying, 'You told the system that you were doing this, here is a knowledge package for you.' Without you asking for it.

When we started this there was a Task Team Leader who said to me 'If you send me an e-mail I won't read it'. I asked 'What would I need to do to make you want to read it?' He said 'Only if the subject line had my project ID – that would make me feel like I might want to open it.' So that's exactly what we did.

> 'What would I need to do to make you want to read it?'

People came back and asked, 'How did you put all this knowledge together?' I said 'You told the system that you were about to do this project.' They said 'This is great!'

Teaching machines how to learn

Vivek tapped into the expertise of subject-matter experts in the Bank in order to refine the algorithm further, working with the Global Solutions Leads for specific topics.

We tested it first with the 'Water Global Practice'. They gave us the project description, we ran the algorithm, got some results for them, they came back and said 'It's missing this project and this project'. We refined it and did four or five iterations, until one of the subject-matter experts said to us 'You know what, your algorithm actually brought back some projects that we'd completely forgotten that we'd done!' That's when we said 'Now we've got it right!'

> 'Your algorithm brought back projects that we'd forgotten we'd done!'

The positive feedback from staff inspired Vivek and his team to seek further feedback and refine the algorithm further, and as a result of this, he began to notice a shift in the behaviour of staff. The quality of the knowledge packages was creating a change in the culture around information provision and tagging.

I discussed with people how it could be better. 'If you gave me a better project description,' I said, 'I could give you a more detailed response. You can e-mail it to me or better still, just update the system.' This was the first time that the system started to give them back something. They realised that it was important that if they feed it more accurate information, the system would help them more!

> 'This was the first time that system had started to give them back something!'

Current and future plans

Vivek is now seeking to further integrate machine learning into the other aspects of the World Bank activities, such as financial reporting. Machine learning is also being used to support other aspects of the KM Action Plan, including communities of practice – as sources and recipients of content.

Going back to the Knowledge Package, we created a large database of over 150 paid and free external information sources, which the algorithm used, and we have now added communities of practice (CoP) to this database, together with external experts – so people are also directed to the CoP. Now the KM folks within the Global Practices are identifying more resources that can be added in.

Automating feeds into communities of practice.

We are also contemplating feeding content into the CoPs – into the pages of certain Practices, for example the 'Fragility Community', to see how we can start feeding dynamic content from the knowledge packages into their platform, where people will come to seek knowledge in general (not just in relation to projects). We can give them an intelligent project feed of publications inside and outside the Bank.

Because our projects are the centre of everything that happens at the Bank, we want to throw those recently approved projects into the CoPs, so that the conversations start around that, so that people start tagging people, and are more aware of what the interventions are and the task team get more interesting results.

Confidence in, and confidence from, machine learning

Adding back a human dimension through communities of practice.

Vivek was keen to point out the value of an additional level of human validation, and also to explain the ways in which his algorithms are providing assurance to senior staff who approve projects.

We're getting the Global Solutions Leads to stamp 'gold standard' projects; examples of excellence within a sub-sector.

If these come up in the top 100 results, someone can then filter on whether they are recommended gold standard projects. We're flagging these as recommendations from humans. 'I'm doing a project, and now the Global Solutions Group has recommended this project as relevant.' That gives people more confidence – it's not just the algorithm. The idea is that the gold standard projects will come up in the top ten documents on the knowledge package.

Filtering with 'gold standard' projects.

We recently started hearing from practice managers and country directors who are responsible for approving projects. They said it would be great if they could use machine learning to know if we'd found similar work to a proposed project. They want to know so that they can ask the right questions of the task team before they approve anything.

The machine learning work was extended into other experimental areas, including automated handover checklists for Task Team Leaders changing roles. Margot completes the story:

> Projects will run seven to eight years and so they find maybe five team leaders over the course of a project; when one leaves another comes in. In an ideal world that person has everything at his fingertips: the budget is up to date, everything is there – all the relevant dots, all the people that he needs to be engaging with. Unfortunately, we don't live in an ideal world; this rarely happens. You walk into a project often not knowing what the heck is going on. From an efficiency and effectiveness perspective it's not ideal.
>
> So again, using machine learning, we're giving these leaders a package that pulls together everything that they need in order to hit the ground running. All of the background, budget information, tombstone information, people on the client side that they need to be engaging with. That's an automated process through machine learning.
>
> The one thing that we asked task team leaders to do in person (as all of the rest of the handover has been taken off their plate) is to write a page for the person who is coming in.
>
> This has been very well received. The guidance for that one-pager includes the following:

- What's going to bite them on the first day that they walk in the door?
- What's a systemic problem that this particular project has?
- Make it very straight and to the point.
- Talk to them like you're talking to your roommate!

'You walk into a project often not knowing what the heck is going on.'

Semi-automated project handover.

Reflections

Margot concludes with a reflection on the dual-stream strategy:

> We have a pipeline of other experiments now that we want to do. We know the foundational stuff is going to take time and we have to be seen to be delivering as we work through some of the stuff, which is really plumbing and basics!
>
> Experiments are really of our way of winning the hearts and minds of operations – it's letting them know that we're listening, we're dealing with some of the problems that they experienced – we're taking action.

'Experiments are really our way of winning the hearts and minds of operations.'

Having started her role by consciously 'resisting the call to just start doing something', Margot and her team have found the success of the various strategic initiatives and tactical experiments are generating development impact where it matters the most.

Mapping the story to the 'KM Chef's Canvas'

The World Bank has a deep heritage in Knowledge Management, and a well-resourced programme, which makes it difficult to single out just three highlights. We have selected:

Strategic context

KM has been integral to the work of the World Bank since the late 90s. The role of the current KM team is strongly aligned with strategic operations: 'Our job is to make the job of operations easier.' The team conducted significant engagement activities to understand these operational needs, conducting hundreds of interviews and many focus groups to surface the needs of the organisation, which were reflected in the knowledge action plan.

Processes

The Bank has well established and documented processes for creating, managing and maintaining information assets. Clear processes and tools exist to support the creation and effective running of communities of practice, and for the handover of roles between staff.

Technology and infrastructure

The Bank's activities with machine learning and artificial intelligence to create 'knowledge packages' is distinctive and has been very well received internally. There is evidence that the successful application of helpful, proactive technology is changing the way staff relate to information and the value they attribute to tagging and managing it as an asset.

11

Knowledge Management in General Electric: leading-edge communities

NARRATED BY DAN RANTA, KNOWLEDGE SHARING LEADER

Dan Ranta sits in the large open-plan office in the 1500-strong General Electric (GE) Research Campus in New York State, surrounded by his team and a number of large-screen monitors which are used for virtual interactions with internal and external customers. On his desk on the day we interviewed him was the book *Adaptive Space* (2018), written by General Motors' innovation lead, Michael Arena – a book about 'positive disruption', which could perhaps describe the role that Dan and his team play in GE.

> General Motors is also going through transformation like we are here at GE, so I'm really enjoying it. I like the transparency of the space here. I don't have an office to myself; rather we all sit together. It's actually an open environment where we invite clients in, so that they can see how we're working as we provide them with an array of KM services, but we also use video all the time.

Dan's previous corporate KM role had been with a global oil and gas company – a sizeable organisation of 35,000 staff, but a mere 10% of GE's workforce of more than 300,000; a challenge which he was strongly attracted to.

> This was a special job. I felt it from the beginning with key executive engineering leaders demanding that 'We've got to do collaboration better. We know it's not as good as it could be.' The businesses were largely siloed. There were nine businesses, nine vertical segments at the time, with untapped potential to collaborate down and across. I became really interested in the job – I thought this might be the biggest challenge of my professional career. I was right!

'I thought this would be the biggest challenge of my career.'

First steps as KM leader in a new organisation

Dan's earliest observation was that there was an over-emphasis on technology, and a lack of consistency and common approaches across the business. His first step was to identify and contact the many people identified with KM-related roles so that he could find what he described as the 'bright spots' in the different segments to help him with his agenda of consistency and standardisation. He was surprised to find over 75 people.

Finding the 'bright spots' in different segments across the company.

> The first thing I did was to invite everyone with a KM-related role to a day-long strategic visioning session. I just had to put myself out there – and I knew equally that they wanted to check me out as the new hire. I facilitated a nine-hour session during which all businesses were represented. I used that to get to know people – and to secretly find who might be our Knowledge Management focal points for every business, because I knew that I'd have a relatively small team of direct reports. I carefully tried to pick out who was closest to the top and started to generate a governance body – a knowledge-sharing leadership team across our company. This session was really special – it took us from strategy to action; we got a lot of ideas and we got a vision around knowledge sharing and most importantly our first KM roadmap.

Listening to Dan describe this first workshop, we were struck by his urgency and drive to make a first impression as a leader who was tremendously responsive and action-oriented.

'I felt the need to kill people with kindness and competency!'

> I felt the need to 'kill people with kindness and competency'! That was my strategy. You want to be accommodating, be flexible and be open to other ideas – because we've had so many good ideas from so many people across our company as to how to improve KM. Then you are in a strong position to demonstrate your own competency. After the workshop, I worked almost all night long and I had the first version of the strategic roadmap. I sent out a link to it through all the participants, the very next day. I wanted to show them that we're not just talking about something. I wanted to get it out there, let them opine on it and give me feedback. It was 'carpe diem' time for us. We needed to seize the day.

Recommendations and findings from the first workshop

Having worked through the night to process and analyse the views of the workshop participants, and recognise where there were existing 'bright spots' to acknowledge, Dan communicated the summary of recommendations listed here:

• Change the mindset and the branding from KM to Knowledge Sharing (and from technology to behaviour).

- Establish an initial project to build some early wins (five GE communities) and integrate this with an enterprise-wide KS Strategy.
- Work to create Collaboration Services for our GE-wide KS Strategy by working to find executive level sponsors from the business and from supporting groups such as Businesses, IT, Corporate Communications and HR/Learning.
- Create a KS leadership team – business focal points.
- Engage early with IT as a partner for KS development – ensure the project has strong IT support.
- Explore the creation of an enterprise-wide wiki – lay the governance foundation for GE Wiki.
- Work with internal resources to create some subtle KS and GE community branding to separate the new KS approach and work from existing and past KS-related efforts.
- Ensure that the security model for knowledge communities is clear and broadly communicated – there should be no ambiguity in this important area at GE.
- Create a comprehensive set of KS governance materials – build this directly into the GE Wiki.
- Build a KS team charter and structure that clearly shows how a central team can manage all KS-related activities for GE in the future.

Dan made a particular point of changing his job title from Knowledge Management Leader to Knowledge Sharing (KS) Leader to emphasise the behavioural focus that he was taking. One of his first actions was to launch a number of communities of practice, including a 'KnowledGE Sharing Community' which Dan describes as a way for him to crowdsource his entire programme. Working with this community, and his KM focal points in the business (which he refers to as his 'core team of brokers') he developed a set of objectives and goals for Knowledge Management where more than 65% of the items were short-term, to be accomplished in 90 days or less.

> We looked at all the 'W's: why, what, when, who was accountable to contribute, how you're going to do it and how you're going to measure it. Once we created our strategic focus areas, we were in a position to collectively create the 'why' and fill in the other Ws.

Changing the job title to emphasise a behavioural focus.

Building the KS Team at GE

The first strategic focus area was to build a central team, a small central team which would support the Knowledge Management focal points that existed in each of the business areas and bring about the necessary consistency in infrastructure and to start to build the first few communities of practice (see Figure 11.1). Dan was clear about the role of technology as an enabler and supporter of behaviour change.

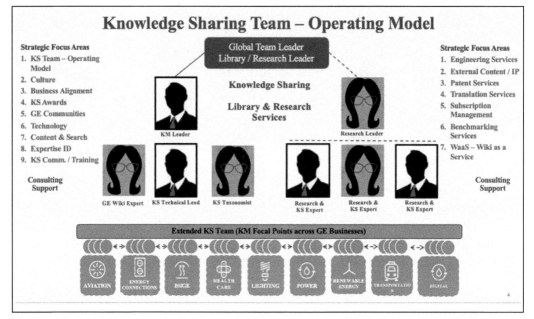

Figure 11.1 *Operating model of the Knowledge Sharing Team*

'Technology is the manifestation of the behavioural aspects of making knowledge-sharing work.'

It's not about the technology, but the technology is the manifestation of the behavioural aspects of making knowledge-sharing work. Once I was able to get a proof of concept in place, we were able to get the funding needed to fill other positions, like a wiki expert, taxonomist and a metrics and IT operations guy.

Sharing KM governance materials openly

Dan is a strong advocate of working transparently and internally crowdsourcing ideas for improvement from his knowledge-sharing community.

We have some really nice governance materials and have put them into our KM wiki portal space, where we have over 175 articles on how we do knowledge sharing. This is how we have worked to create our standards, get buy-in and share our approach openly, transparently with anybody and everybody across the company.

We mandate that all leaders and co-ordinators of our communities are members of our knowledge-sharing community. I guess I suck them in, without them even knowing it! It's the community space we use to blog and share all our governance materials for everyone to see and use . . . and help us improve. They see the questions and the answers, learn about the improvements to the community IT infrastructure and they ask, 'Why don't we have this, why don't we have that?' That's what we love, because 75% of our best ideas have come from the business – across all generations.

'75% of our best ideas have come from the business.'

An agile approach to community enablement

The high level of engagement with the knowledge-sharing community enables Dan and his team to rapidly iterate changes to functionality of technology, and the processes around their communities of practice, which have grown at a tremendous pace to include more than 130,000 members across about 170 live communities.

We listened to them and when it makes sense for the 'greater good' we put it into play across our process-based communities. Will we ever finish? Sometimes I wonder about this – when we get to something that's so perfect, that we don't have any other technical work to do. I don't think we're there yet, but maybe in about a year or two? We're really doing some fine improvements now – but we'll always be able to discover more. The faster you go, the faster you can go. That's a philosophy that I've always followed. We're very, very agile. Everything we do is based on agile development. We have regular scrum activity, just to be all on the same page. All this with a remarkably small team, given our customer base.

'The faster you go, the faster you can go.'

Dan described the services provided by his team as an 'ecosystem' for communities, with a growing range of customisable technical functions becoming added into the environment, including:

- automated wiki article creation
- RSS feeds, the delivery of targeted articles from 5,000 external technical journals and periodicals
- an ideation platform
- a 'discover connections' page for expertise location
- a way to connect mentors and mentees
- targeted problem solving based on tags that are a reflection of competencies in alignment with career development.

This is all underpinned by a common taxonomy, which he refers to as the organisation's 'circulatory system' and which even extends to the unstructured content in the library.

Communities, wikis, expertise and external sources, all channelled through the 'circulatory system' – taxonomy.

We're able to more precisely and surgically deliver things like RSS feeds through to the right people. We serve up knowledge that's from internal and external sources on a silver platter for the users within a community. If you don't operate like this, you are wasting people's valuable time.

Further innovation in community functionality

Our killer app is definitely our asynchronous discussion area – ask-and-discuss – which we've customised quite a bit. The questions come in as 'open' and they get tagged per a community taxonomy. This generates a match with experts or people in our 'expert pipeline' who are out there so that we can immediately involve them. That then generates an immediate alert based on a matching that happens with those tags. If you have expertise in particular areas of a community, a community discussion gets tagged with that. You get to know, 'Hey Chris, someone's got a question, you have expertise, do you mind helping them out? Just click here and answer.' We're building our whole programme based on professional pride and human generosity – people helping other people.

'We're building our whole programme based on professional pride and human generosity.'

We're focused on tacit knowledge exchange because of the fact that the 80 or 90% of all the knowledge that exists in any particular GE community is tacit in nature. We want to be able to tap into that experience-based knowledge and connect people.

More recently, Dan has integrated dynamic social network analysis into the community ecosystem, making visible the density and frequency of interaction between members of the community and enabling the go-to people, mavens and connectors to be identified at any time.

Figure 11.2 is taken from a view of GE's Knowledge Sharing Community, indicating Dan's centrality in communication to that group.

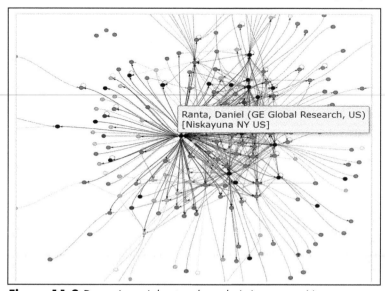

Figure 11.2 *Dynamic social network analysis in communities*

I'm two clicks away from being able to look at the collaborative patterns on our community sites through social network analysis – a 'sociogram' that's right there to be able to show members that have, and haven't been, really active. We encourage the sponsors and leaders of the community to use these sociograms to change-out the core team. We do regular health check activity and make sure that we're constantly nurturing, but anyone can easily go in and they can easily see who's been actually active. You can run but you can't hide! If you're a broker, you're a broker, and we'll want to make you a core team member and get in there and thank you for your positive engagement. All of the people that are active, we want to identify, elevate and thank them and continue to keep them motivated and transfer the positive behavioural aspects that they're exhibiting to colleagues. Others will then say, 'Oh, I can do that too!'. That's a key piece of, you know, building a collaborative culture.

'You can run but you can't hide!'

Distilling knowledge from forums into wiki entries

Not everything in GE's community ecosystem is automated. Dan was excited about a new service which involves Dan's team members in Bangalore and New York with the problem-solving discussion activity within the community 'Ask and Discuss' forums.

This is really, really super-cool – something I've always wanted to do – we provide what's known as 'wiki-as-a-service', where you just hit one button and the collective discussion – maybe five or six people who opined around the world on a particular topic in a forum – goes right to our team in Bangalore. They write the wiki article based on the discussion and you have effectively then turned that 'water cooler conversation' into something that's more powerful and put it in a fluid, dynamic environment where others can add to the knowledge over time. My team in Bangalore gives you a leg-up on creating this explicit knowledge and allows our knowledge workers to continue to develop it as we move forward. We love that the wiki flows right out of the actual discussions. It still requires some human intervention for sure, but we try to make the process as automated as possible.

Wiki-as-a-service, with the help of a team in Bangalore.

Roles and goals

GE has a consistent model across communities of varying sizes. The 'ecosystem' provides a common way of displaying the leadership roles on the home page of that community. Dan described the following roles, and his desire to see clear KPIs for every community:

We have a sponsor or co-sponsors, leader, or co-leaders, a co-ordinator who does the day-to-day work, particularly if it's a bigger community. The key role is core team members. Typically, somewhere between 10 and 30 of these in each community. They are your brokers, and they are key people with organisational power and influence. This is important in a command and control culture, since they give you coverage and

'What your boss finds interesting, you need to find fascinating!'

alignment. What your boss finds interesting, you need to find fascinating! We count on our core teams to bring other people in and to be active, leading by example.

Communities ranging in size from 120 to 6500 members.

The smallest community we have is probably around 120 people and the largest one is our ANSYS (engineering simulation software) community, 6500 people from across the entire company – I wasn't prepared to have parallel ANSYS communities in different parts – it was important to have one homogenous community. The same is true for reliability, electronics, inspection and other cross-company topics. Less is more with world-class collaboration.

Each community must have at least one business KPI.

I am challenging our communities to have at least one KPI that rolls up to the highest-level business objectives that exist within a business segment or are part of the enterprise-wide strategy. Some of our communities have the scorecards, other don't and I just keep pushing them to provide a single KPI as a minimum. 'What's your raison d'être? You got to be able to give me one thing. Come on. I know you can do it!'

Motivation for participation

Membership in GE's communities is not mandatory – it's a personal choice. However, Dan was quick to point out the personal case for joining and participating, using some Hollywood humour to make his point:

You probably remember the movie *Meet the Fockers*?

'You don't want to be loopless!'

At one point Robert De Niro tells Ben Stiller: 'You don't want to be out of the loop. You don't want to be loopless!'

The point is, when you have a lot of activity happening in a company like GE, do you really want to be that person on the periphery who is just e-mailing his or her ten friends?

'You win in this space by showing value.'

We drive people to our communities because it's good for them in a career-enhancing sense! You win in this space by showing value and being relevant. You end up putting something together that's so much better than if you'd gone it alone – it makes so much business sense. That's been our philosophy in terms of winning engagement within the company. Other things – let's call them 'losers' – then fall by the wayside!

Communities solving customer problems, an example from GE Renewable Energy

GE's communities are at their most powerful when applying their collective knowledge to customer problems. One customer challenge related to an issue with the post-weld heating temperature on tempered steel, which required immediate resolution. The project manager initially estimated three weeks of analysis to propose a solution – which would have delayed the project deliverables and added extra cost to the customer.

Instead, the project manager opted to engage the welding community across GE businesses to help him find a solution quickly. Within 24 hours, the discussion drew responses from 12 different welding experts resulting in the proposal of a quick fix to this customer problem. In this example, the welding community saved time and cost worth of 120 man-hours and above all it maintained a consistent level of customer satisfaction.

The 26 knowledge-sharing communities within the Renewables business collectively solved 324 customer problems over a 12-month period. The benefits and savings associated with the 'know-ledGE' sharing approach is estimated based on the cost avoidance in productivity. This cost avoidance is conservatively calculated at $503,000 in 2018.

Reflecting on challenges

Dan described his biggest challenge as 'transformational winds', and likened the variety and pace of change initiatives, and the challenge of maintaining excellent customer service, as being similar to riding a bicycle in different directions, yet always encountering headwinds:

> I'll never be in another place that's as big and is going through so many changes. The challenge is to remain able to deliver and to stay the course and build and improve our programme. I'm so proud of our team and our extended 'core team', and our focal points in the businesses that support community-based KM in the trenches. We have just literally hundreds and thousands of people in our community model, including sponsors, leaders, co-ordinators and core team members. It's their ability to stick with it, see the value and to continue to challenge us which makes us better.
>
> When you're doing a job like this, an orientation towards excellent customer service is so important. I have my 'rule of 99': you can do 99 things well and you know, you're like, 'Oh man, this is good, we are good. Let me get another cup of coffee and the next thing I do is going to be even better!' And then one thing goes awry which undoes all of the benefits in the eyes of the customer. What I share with my team and continue to remind myself of is: that's just the nature of the work. We're in a support role. We have got to be happy and energetic with boundless energy, supporting our businesses that are out there and need our help. When we get compliments for the team performance it just makes me feel so good. That what it's all about.

'You can do 99 things well . . .'

Reflecting on the skills necessary to perform the role

Listening is number one, listening to your customers with that boundless energy I talked about. You can't get down on yourself. No time for 'woe is me'. You keep listening and keep making it better, with great attention to detail. You have the mentality that even if you know you might be smart, the best ideas generally come from other people and it's your role to combine them – that's just a key piece of the change management process also.

Secondly, you have got to have a little swagger – you've got to be willing to go to leaders and tell them, 'Look, this is what I need you to do a little more effectively and here's how to do it.' I say, 'We do need you to get better and here's some examples: here's the three bullets'. I stick at two to three bullets; I don't want to overwhelm with ten things. They usually agree!

Listening, and maintaining a little swagger!

Finally, Dan reflected on a difficult decision which he made to change his reporting relationship in order to extend his network, despite the positive nature of the relationship and working for the 'coolest guy' in the world.

I initially had a boss who was very supportive. He was really super-cool – coolest guy I've ever worked for – but I said, 'I got to work somewhere else, I need to get more networked into the rest of our businesses.' So, I took a chance and I made a recommendation to change my boss and the HR leader supported me. I did it and I got networked across all of our businesses more effectively and then developed relationships there. That was very, very beneficial for our programme. I probably wouldn't even be here now if it wasn't for that. It's true you can make your own path, but sometimes you also need help.

Changing your boss in order to grow your network.

It's a combination of following your instincts and the luck of being in the right place at the right time with the right person. There's been a lot of that. I think you make your own luck to a great extent. So, things are serendipitous, but then your 'sticktuitiveness' gets you to where you're making your own luck too. The harder you work, the luckier you get!

'Sticktuitiveness'. The harder you work, the luckier you get.

Mapping the story to the 'KM Chef's Canvas'

The three areas we chose to highlight from GE's many strengths are as follows:

Technology and infrastructure

The development of GE's community spaces focused on tacit knowledge exchange and including dynamic social network analysis, and the integration of the different functional requirements and ideas arising direct from the stakeholders makes GE stand out in this area.

Interaction and internalisation

GE's KM strategy and story are built upon the success of their communities of practice, executed at a scale well beyond most other organisations. This may be the biggest, fastest implementation in the history of KM, anywhere.

Codification and curation

The underlying taxonomy which GE describes as its 'circulatory system', together with the streaming and channelling of external sources into community spaces, and the curation 'wiki-as-a-service' capability are clear strengths in this area.

12
Beyond KM: Collaborating, Learning and Adapting (CLA) in USAID

NARRATED BY PIERS BOCOCK (CHIEF OF PARTY, LEARN CONTRACT)
AND STACEY YOUNG (SENIOR LEARNING ADVISOR, USAID)

Stacey and Piers represent both sides of a successful contract to improve collaboration, learning and adaptive programme management across projects and programmes funded and supported by USAID. Stacey works for USAID in the Bureau for Policy, Planning and Learning (PPL), which set in place the LEARN contract for which Piers was Chief of Party. The contract supports strategic learning and Knowledge Management across USAID's development programmes and collaboration with PPL to develop and promulgate a framework, a maturity-assessment tool and set of knowledge and learning methods: 'Collaborating, Learning and Adapting' (CLA), www.usaidlearninglab.org.

Stacey begins the story:

> It started with the change in administration when President Obama took office. With each change in administration, there is typically some sort of reorganisation – then there's a fresh mandate. And at that time, a number of the programme cycle processes at USAID had fallen away. We weren't doing five-year country strategies or project design anymore; everything was really at the individual activity level. We weren't doing evaluation, and a lot of the disciplines of development had fallen by the wayside. One of the things that the administration had in mind was to restore those functions – and as part of that also to return the policy function to USAID.

'A lot of the disciplines of development had fallen by the wayside.'

During 2009-10 Stacey was part of an opportunity to do some pioneering knowledge and learning work on a pilot programme at the Uganda mission, applying the principles of learning and adapting to the development of a new country strategy. It was there that the phrase 'Collaborating, Learning and Adapting' (CLA) was first used to describe this intentional and adaptive approach.

The pilot in Uganda gave us an opportunity to really look at what had gone wrong in the past; to really look across the programme cycle and say where things had failed in the past.

There was a kind of 'Groundhog Day' phenomenon, where people do the same thing over and over again. It seemed fresh every time because we hadn't learned from the past – or a certain approach or a body of evidence had been superseded, yet was still in circulation and in practice. One issue was the way we approached programme plans; they were too detailed and too prescriptive. As soon as the ink was dry, reality would begin to diverge from what was in the plan, without any provision or processes for adapting when that happened. We realised that for the plan to actually be useful in guiding the work of the mission over five years, it needed to be much more adaptable.

'There was a kind of Groundhog Day phenomenon.'

Stacey built on the insights from the Uganda pilot, working with colleagues and building a team to embed knowledge and learning into the programme cycle, which helped make the case for investing in a five-year contract to support the work more widely across USAID's field programmes.

Piers was part of Dexis Consulting Group, which was awarded the contract, and he worked as Chief of Party, leading the work for the first four years of the programme.

What I liked about the concept was that it addressed the 'why' of Knowledge Management – to have an impact on development results. It also has a bit of a 'how' – through intentional, systematic and resourced collaborating, learning and adapting. In the request for proposal there were actually almost no specific deliverables at all! Just five big objectives – big concepts. So, in itself, the contract was applying one of the adaptable mechanisms – they didn't fall into the trap of government contracts which lay all out the targets and objectives in the RFP (request for proposal), even when it's a five-year programme. This was real progress for a USAID project in my mind.

A contract with no deliverables which walked-the-talk of adaptive management.

The idea of working with people like Stacey, with a complete blank slate and being able to build my own team with its own culture, on a programme with an iterative approach, focused on collaborating, learning and adapting was really appealing – so I said 'Yes'!

The imperative for the contract for USAID was all about improving development impact through an intentional Knowledge Management and organisational learning approach. The perception was that the development sector had been operating for decades, full of well-meaning, dedicated, smart people who want to make the world a better place – and yet it was still prone to repeating mistakes.

Piers expressed his frustration: 'Why have we not made more improvement? We know deep down that we are not learning to the best of our ability.'

Since this was a project about collaborating, learning and adapting, I was determined to build a team that walked the talk. That was the fundamental principle from the get-go. We know in Knowledge Management that any good learning organisation is based on people who are enablers for others to learn.

'Any good learning organisation is based on people who are enablers for others to learn.'

With a core team of believers, we then set about trying to create a flexible framework that would take the concept and make it practical for people in missions, to show what they should be doing.

Building the CLA framework

Working in collaboration with Stacey's USAID CLA team, Piers and his team undertook numerous interviews, understanding the history and the 'why it came to be' for CLA with various missions in the field, starting with Uganda. Piers picks up the story:

> Uganda was where the concept was first verbalised and they committed to try it there – they were the petri dish. We wanted to know what else was going on. There had never been a 'thou shalt' moment for CLA, but we knew that the Bureau for Policy, Planning and Learning was in the process of getting feedback on updating its programme cycle guidance. The previous version had some suggestions, this new version gave an opportunity to be more directive – 'you must do something to show how you are intentionally integrating systematic learning processes'.
>
> After the interviews, we helped Stacey's CLA team to develop a framework to bring together all the pieces and tested it. We looked at existing guidance, we looked at what had worked, and what hadn't worked in development, externally and internally. We found examples of other missions behaving in a way that we would say is effective learning.

Learning from internal and external examples to build an inclusive framework.

The CLA framework (Figure 12.1 on the next page) addressed the programme lifecycle (Collaborating, Learning and Adapting), and the enabling conditions (culture, processes and resources); breaking down six key areas to help programme teams to think about each aspect individually and then more holistically, asking a number of questions through a self-assessment process, undertaken by programme teams. Piers continues:

> It's basically an organisational development framework which is relevant to the international development sector. It looks at collaborating, learning and adapting, and at the enabling conditions – culture, processes and resources to do that. Two hemispheres: 'What are the things you do?' and 'How you do it?'
>
> At the same time, we tried very hard to avoid the trap of saying 'Here is the template for how you do this' and instead created a self-assessment process that supported a flexible and customisable approach. Using the

'What are the things you do, and how do you do it?'

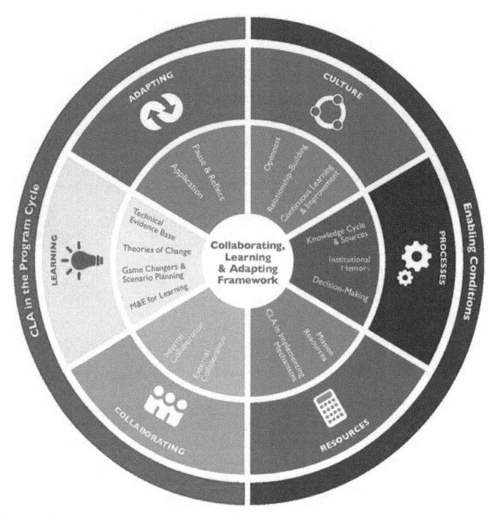

Figure 12.1 *The Collaborating, Learning and Adapting framework*

framework, our role was to facilitate the group, they would identify what was and wasn't working, and we would then give them examples of other places where it was.

The framework is a lens through which to look, so that they can get concrete about actions they can take: 'What does this look like for us?' The end product is some form of CLA action plan which provides 'What are some practical, small steps?'.

Setting realistic improve-ment targets and concrete actions.

We're not falling for the comprehensive plan that everyone signs off on but where nothing ever gets done. This is about making incremental improvements in our processes. The framework's self-assessment and action planning process helps people identify where they most need to improve, helps them come to practical suggestions, based on experience borne form other parts of the agency.

Exploring the components of the CLA framework

The six segments of the framework break down into a further 16 components:

1 Internal collaboration: regularly and strategically engaging with teams within the organisation, beyond information sharing, to co-create/co-manage.

2 External collaboration: identifying and strategically engaging with key external stakeholders, beyond information sharing, to co-create and leverage synergies.

Collaborating

3 Technical evidence base: staying aware of and contributing to the shared knowledge about a particular technical field and using it to inform programming.

4 Theories of change: articulating and testing our understanding of why and how we expect activities to lead to desired goals.

Learning

5 Game changers and scenario planning: identifying, planning options for, and monitoring the most significant variables outside our control that will impact our ability to achieve intended results.

6 M&E (monitoring and evaluation) for learning: designing M&E efforts based on what we most need to know and using them to inform decision making about current and future programming.

7 Pause and reflect: leveraging learning and reflection to make and act on decisions about any programming modifications that may be needed.

8 Application/adaptive management: creating timely opportunities to pause in our work to reflect and have honest conversations about how things are working.

Adapting

9 Openness: having a culture where people are willing to share ideas/opinions, listen to alternative perspectives and try new and innovative approaches.

10 Relationships and networks: having strong relationships based on trust and good communications that are leveraged across the system, to share knowledge about and influence the system.

Culture

11 Continuous learning and improvement: valuing learning and iterative approaches enough to make time and space for them in order to continuously improve.

12 Knowledge cycle and sources: working through the knowledge cycle – generation, capture, synthesis sharing, application – with data and contextual information from a variety of sources.

13 Institutional memory: using processes and systems to capture, store and facilitate easy access to organisational information and staff's tacit knowledge.

Processes

14 Decision making: articulating clear processes and levels of autonomy and engagement for how and by whom decisions are made.

Resources

15 Mission resources: incorporating CLA into staff's scope and workload, with sufficient support from the programme office, champions, and a support contract.

16 CLA in implementing mechanisms: setting expectations and providing support for CLA with partners by including it in activity and mechanism designs, scopes, and budgets.

Using the CLA maturity assessment with programme and project teams

In order to be successful and impactful, it was felt that the process of self-assessment should be dialogic, democratic and enjoyable and lead directly into action planning, as Piers describes:

'The process was set up to bring people together to have a conversation.'

We knew we could send out surveys ahead of time, but the wise and experienced organisational development and organisational learning people in the team recognised that the real learning comes out of the group conversation. The process was set up to bring people together to have a conversation – but even that is prone to going off track. So, we came up with the idea of playing cards – concrete examples of what maturity would look like for that particular topic. Originally it was called the CLA matrix, because it was a maturity matrix. But that felt too 'boxy' and not fun – and we insist that this needs to be fun. (The graphic is now round, to illustrate how each component associates with all of the others.)

'A simple maturity matrix was too "boxy", and not fun.'

Once people have decided where the hot buttons are, where the areas of conversation are, we use the cards – big colourful cards – to show what maturity looks like. Then individuals use smaller cards to show where they would place the organisation, like a card game – they reveal their hand. Sometimes they agree, but often they don't – and that's where the valuable conversations come in. Out of that, we get the challenges. It's a democratic process with people from all levels of the team talking about it.

'We focus on where they want to go.'

We don't use the whole framework at once – we focus on where they want to go. We'll provide an overview of CLA, then we'll meet with individual teams and ask – 'choose just two components from each side of the "wheel" – let's talk about those'. That's where we focus and they come up with actions. We let them guide the process. Across multiple teams in a mission you will end up covering everything.

Identifying evidence and measuring successes

As the team approach the end of the initial five-year LEARN contract they expect to have reached around 80 missions. One of Piers' measures of success was the number of missions with CLA plans: the degree to which strategies were really using the learning from other evaluations. 'How many evaluation reviews are actually leveraged rather than sitting on the shelves?' In order to surface the evidence and the examples of CLA in action, a 'Case Competition for CLA' was established, which now runs annually, and has become a significant celebration event on the USAID calendar, as Stacey describes:

> We've also been running the competition for a number of years. The cases have been immensely valuable in helping to understand really on a very practical level, with a narrative that demonstrates impact – how the CLA approaches were used and what the value has been.
>
> Lo and behold, we now have over 200 examples of CLA from around the world that you can filter by location, sector and CLA component – all based on voluntary submission from missions and partners. Partners wanted to be recognised, missions wanted to demonstrate that they were using CLA. The winners get a certificate, they get highlighted at our annual 'Moving the Needle' conference and we get stories!

Creating a case competition to discover stories of impact.

The CLA cases can be searched online, graphically and through a variety of filters – see usaidlearninglab.org/cla-cases.

Empowering a CLA community of practice

With the common language arising from the CLA framework, the potential for missions to share resources and questions presented itself. A community of practice (CoP) seemed like an effective way to facilitate knowledge sharing and spread CLA practices. The CLA team and LEARN convened and actively facilitated a CLA community of practice among USAID staff. With a lot of work and some time, the community has taken shape and taken off, as Piers explains:

> Like most of the things with CLA, there was something that already existed – it just needed 'juicing' – needed to be made practical. There was already a collection of individuals who had self-identified to be part of a CLA community on an internal USAID platform, but it was characterised as a group of 'lurkers' with one or two people who were very generous. Someone would say 'How do I do an after-action review' and someone from a mission would say 'Hey, here's a template'.
>
> We thought a CoP was a really good idea, but we needed to truly make it a community, not a mailing list. So, we asked those people 'What would you really like to talk about?', and that drove the agenda, which drove the engagement.

Moving a community of practice beyond being a group of 'lurkers'!

Reflections on the CLA programme

Looking back of the five-year contract, Piers described the challenge of taking a deliberately open and adaptable contract, and generating an engaging, actionable product.

> The greatest challenge was trying to translate the concept into practical actions that people would want to take.

A change to the programme cycle guidance also created an imperative for projects to use CLA 'standard processes', which Piers had initially seen as a potential issue.

> There was a worry that if you make CLA mandatory, then people will do it because it's a check-the-box thing – but what it actually did was to raise attention to the importance of demonstrating intention and systematic and resourced learning approaches in your context – putting it on the radar and then supporting it in very concrete ways.
>
> We have found in our data hundreds of examples of CLA in action. 21% are requirements from the programme cycle guidance, but 79% are voluntary applications of CLA components. This is great to see – we were afraid that people would only do things because they were required.

'We were afraid that people would only do things because they were required.'

Stacey was particularly proud of the energy and excitement which the programme had generated through its combination of the self-assessment framework, community of practice, local champions and Case Competition celebrations.

> I see people light up, and it's really something to see – because it's a very bureaucratic place and people feel really burdened a lot by how many hoops they have to jump through and all the impediments between what they're doing day to day and the potential that they can see for our development programmes. When they encounter this work, they get really excited and the burden has been lifted and they go on to do really cool things that actually advance development.
>
> And then the other side of that is the evidence-based work that we've done, which I think fills a real gap in the Knowledge Management and organisational learning space because there is evidence gathered through a variety of methods, and the evidence demonstrates impact at the level of organisational effectiveness and at the level of development results. And so that evidence validates the energy and excitement that I see on my colleagues' faces. The evidence base we've developed is a resource that lots of organisations can and do use when they're trying to make the business case in their own organisation, trying to persuade their leadership to get into and devote resources to learning.

'I see people light up, and it's really something to see.'

Mapping the story to the 'KM Chef's Canvas'

The three areas we chose to highlight are:

Evaluation

The Collaborating, Learning and Adapting framework itself, and the self-assessment process, demonstrate a mature level of evaluation. Material impacts are identified, celebrated through a 'CASE Competition', captured and shared in an evidence base of successful CLA cases which is publicly searchable.

Governance

'Collaborating, Learning and Adapting' (CLA) is clearly embedded in the programme lifecycle and is 'on the radar' for both the programme teams and central teams. Application of the techniques is measured, and it is clear that USAID staff see it as strategic and valuable, such that they voluntarily participate well beyond the mandatory aspects of the programme.

Processes

The CLA process and resources has evolved a well defined framework, a well documented process and product (set of cards) with clear facilitation guidance which includes an opportunity for stakeholder feedback.

13
Knowledge Management in Schlumberger: 'Eureka!'

NARRATED BY SUSAN ROSENBAUM (DIRECTOR OF KM AND CAREER DISCIPLINES) AND ALAN BOULTER (KM AND PROCESS WORKFLOW)

Schlumberger is a name well known to Knowledge Management practitioners as one of the early explorers and pioneers in the field, regularly celebrated with KM awards and sharing at conferences. Perhaps that enthusiastic pioneering spirit reflects the exploratory nature of the oil business? More likely, though, their success reflects the personalities and characters of the 'Eureka Team', which is led by Susan Rosenbaum. Despite the length of this KM programme, Susan remains as irrepressible and dynamic as if Eureka were a start-up.

Alan Boulter, who has worked with Susan for many years, sits in the UK Schlumberger office next to Gatwick Airport. His measured, archetypally British personality is the perfect foil for Susan's enthusiasm and Texas drawl.

You'd see a number of awards on my desk – the company recognises seniority very strongly; it's a key thing. When you reach a particular milestone, for example 15 or 20 years, there are some pretty big celebrations and rewards. These are celebrated around the world – when you pick up a magazine or look at something digital they will always have seniority awards. If you go to the office in Sugar Land (Texas) the walls are absolutely full of awards and patents.

'We value seniority and we celebrate achievements.'

My current responsibility is 'Knowledge Management and Process Workflow' – I look at KM in a more connected way to see how things flow in the organisation and ensure that people know where to turn to at which specific time. It's a big organisation and it can be confusing, so trying to map out a path for people is important.

'I look at KM in a more connected way.'

The initiative for Eureka – which is the backbone of the KM programme – was started off by the then CEO Euan Baird, and initially focused on the technical, research and engineering domains. Baird felt that we would be a much stronger organisation if we all worked together and shared our knowledge. Many parts of our business, such as offshore operations, are expensive – millions of dollars a day. Any lost time that we could help to prevent for a client was really important. That's how the business case was built.

'Millions of dollars a day.'

KM in Schlumberger – InTouch and Eureka

Schlumberger describes Knowledge Management as a collection of initiatives, processes and tools that are designed to accelerate the flow of expertise around a highly technical workforce.

One of the first elements of the programme was 'InTouch', which is the primary way for Schlumberger to align dedicated resources inside the organisation in support of field operations – which Alan describes as fundamental to the business: 'our bread and butter'.

Providing 24x7 access to technical expertise.

InTouch is more than a helpdesk with full-time experts. It's a programme; a joined-up initiative to support our people in the field. They might look through the InTouch database and search to find vetted, reviewed documentation, and if they can't find it then they are referred to a range of experts at different levels. First-level experts are available 24x7, while the next level not quite as frequently, as they are more senior experts. People can submit information to be included in the InTouch database and add updates to existing documents as well; all of these are then vetted by the technical experts. It's a pool of experts who are available to answer short-, medium- or long-term questions, which also get fed into InTouch (the database). That is an expensive resource (many hundreds of full-time experts) which has needed a lot of dedication from the organisation to make that work. But the value is clear.

Another major part of the overall KM approach is the large, diverse number of professional communities of practice (CoPs) and special interest groups (SIGs) which are supported and managed by a small central team.

'Sharing the millions of years of experience we have in the organisation.'

Eureka relates to the way we work together internally – on a longer timescale, to share the millions of person-years of experience we have in the organisation to find solutions and help people learn; to grow themselves and to grow their careers. A large part of Eureka is inward-looking – support for each other. It is driven by groups of people who share an interest in a topic, not necessarily in the same part of the business, but with the same background, such as computing, electronics or drilling. They can reach out to each other; it provides a diverse network to tap into.

You can ask anything. This is a great culture in which to ask questions; 'there are no dumb questions' – that phrase keeps popping up whenever you talk to people! People are always asking, always learning, always sharing. People are much more likely to get into trouble if they don't ask the question, than if they ask for help.

'Eureka provides the professional networks for your entire career.'

Eureka provides the professional networks for your entire career. By being involved and engaged in your own groups – virtually or face to face – you get to know people who you may bump into years later, who are a source of reference or advice. It builds up your professional network.

Schlumberger has always been an early adopter of technology. The web domain slb.com was only the 50th to be registered. From the mid-90s onwards, a number of bulletin boards (BBs) and discussion forums were being actively used by the technical staff, but it was hearing a presentation from one of Schlumberger's key customers which was the genesis of the Eureka programme.

Susan picks up the story of how Eureka was born in the late 90s, possibly as a result of corporate one-upmanship!

> In 1997 our CEO, Euan Baird, went to an event and started hearing about Knowledge Management. He returned from the meeting and said, 'We need to do Knowledge Management! We need to start sharing knowledge across the company.' That's why it started.
>
> We needed to do it because we've always worked worldwide, the business was growing, and we were questioning what we could put in place to support the business need and help people in operations and in R&D to share their knowledge around the world.

'The CEO came back and said: "we need to do Knowledge Management!"'

Inspired by others and based on our business needs.

The growth of Eureka

Susan charted the course that Eureka had begun at its inception, extending it from its original active and emergent set of communities and discussions into an organisational structure with a recognised governance and constitution, without losing its pioneering spirit.

> The objective at the beginning was to connect people and share knowledge. We had elected leaders from the start. We had face-to-face events planned and there would be new communities and events every year. They would get together virtually and physically, meet each other, and talk about what they were doing. The bulletin boards kept going, the meetings happened, but there wasn't really much of a plan beyond that. I was a management sponsor for the IT software community, and to me, even as a sponsor, I couldn't see much happening – it wasn't clear.
>
> When did the structure of Eureka become more formal? When I got the job!
>
> I can't remember if I complained or what – but I was given the job!

'I can't remember if I complained or what – but I was given the job!'

Alan continues the story of how Susan and the team carefully added in the layers of governance, guidelines, objectives, roles and processes.

> Over the last ten years we have built up expectations on communities that they will deliver something concrete – produce something that they can give back to the business. In the early days, we had communities being created that overlapped with other communities – but over the past ten years there has been more governance, which has helped a lot.
>
> Eureka has a documented constitution, which we have updated over time. It's available for anyone to look at and it defines our core values,

Communities are expected to produce something concrete that they can give back to the business.'

how we operate, how communities are formed, and how leaders function. In the early days, we called it our constitution; now we refer to it as a set of guidelines.

We have standards that we maintain, but I think it's OK to have some looseness, for example, people asking the same questions in discussion forums.

Roles, processes, guidelines and training.

We have roles and responsibilities for Eureka roles, leaders, sponsors and subsidiary supportive roles. We have training for people – how to use the tools and how the processes work. For more information, see the Appendices, pp. 252–3).

Community leadership: expectations, development and support

Community leadership democratic elections.

Community leadership is a voluntary role; however, leaders must be democratically elected every year by members of their community. The team secures commitment from the manager of each community leader that they will be able to make the time to lead, but it is widely recognised that community leaders gain from the experience, both personally and professionally. Susan and Alan oversee the community and SIG 'portfolio' and apply the right balance of challenge and support to sustain and encourage over 400 leaders.

Balancing challenge and support.

We ask for all communities and SIGs to put together annual objectives and to get agreement for these with their sponsors – and we hold them to account. If they say they will be holding a webinar every month, and they don't, then we will ask them, 'What's happening? How can we help you?'

'We don't work as police or controllers.'

That requires quite a lot of background, back office work, to track all this, but we don't work as police or controllers – it's not like that. We're more concerned about the health of the communities, and if there's a problem, we want to help them.

It's become almost instinctive for us. If you asked Susan and me independently to list the ten most successful and least successful communities, you'd get very similar lists. We can see the traffic, we know what's going on, we know how visible the leaders are.

'You only track what you can track – that won't represent the full activity of a community.'

We also have metrics that we have used more in the last 5–10 years. The difficulty is that you can only track what you can track – and that doesn't represent the full activity of a community. You can measure bulletin board conversations, webinars and website postings, but we were concerned that we were evaluating just on the basis of what we could see – the tip of the iceberg. However, we found over the years that the tip of the iceberg tended to be a good indicator for what was beneath the rest of the iceberg too.

When we go back and say 'Hey guys, what's happened?', they say, 'We've been really busy – we struggle to get the newsletter out every month,' and we ask, 'How can we help you?' Sometimes it's just down to a bit of training, or a conversation to encourage them.

Training for community leaders

Early in her role leading Eureka, Susan took action to develop a dedicated training programme.

I realised it wasn't clear what a leader should be doing. They ran for election, they got elected, and then they just kind of made it up to get by. I reached out to an external consultant who helped us put together a face-to-face training programme. The Eureka team would fly around the world to deliver it – a full day on how to be a Eureka leader – it was fun! When there was pressure on travel expenses due to the drop in the price of oil, we turned the key points into a virtual programme, which is still how we deliver the training today, and it's still very effective.

At the start of each year we hold a series of training programmes (see Appendices, pp. 252–3): how to be an effective leader, how to use the various tools, then later, how to run a successful webinar, how to write a newsletter. We track the training quality, feedback and attendance, and update the content each year.

In 2018, we had 400 Eureka leaders, and on each training call, we'd get up to 100 people participating. We have run a survey for all members, and we solicit feedback frequently from members, to understand what they want from Eureka. A leader will often do an annual survey asking, 'What topics should we focus on this year?' or 'What do you want to do this year – more webinars, newsletters . . . ?' If the leaders do it well, they will talk to their sponsors to get a steer on the most strategic themes to serve business interests – not just what comes up from the members.

> 'I realised it wasn't clear what a leader should be doing.'

Connecting community leadership with professional development

It is not unusual for large distributed organisations to introduce communities of practice or similar networked structures. However, the way in which Schlumberger has integrated community leadership and participation into professional development and talent management is very distinctive. Alan explains the role of Schlumberger Eureka Technical Careers (SETC).

> Training programmes for community leaders.

SETC provides the opportunity for technical professionals to gain recognition from their peers and to advance in a career ladder parallel to the management career ladder in terms of compensation and rewards. The technical population can advance in their careers, gaining increased visibility without managing people. It's important for the organisation not to have their technical professionals distracted by nontechnical stuff.

One of the important 'pillars' of SETC is 'mentoring and community leadership'. We want to encourage our technical professionals to mentor others as they go up through their technical careers, to pull through those who are coming behind them – that's a really important element.

To progress, technical professionals don't actually need to have been

> Connecting KM with the technical career ladder.

> 'Pulling through those coming up behind them.'

a community leader, but they must make a clear, significant contribution to knowledge sharing and Knowledge Management. They need to contribute towards the values of Eureka – sharing, motivation and innovation.

Celebration and awards for reaching 'Principal' and 'Advisor'.

When employees reach the Principal and Advisor level (two of the higher levels), this is publicised on the Schlumberger intranet, and there are local celebrations. Leaders of communities will publish congratulations for community members who achieve any levels – these acknowledgements are often creative, with graphics and photos. We celebrate these milestones a lot. People receive glass crystal awards that you see on their desks – tangible and visible ways are important.

Another pillar of SETC is 'professional visibility'. It's not enough to be a technical leader in your own field inside the company; you also need to be proactively connecting with and influencing others outside the organisation. Some people will have high levels of external visibility, through professional associations, for example. It is important for people to be known externally and we're well represented in external publications. It's important for our people to be externally visible but being visible inside the organisation is key too.

'It makes sure that we share knowledge and don't just have a world leader who doesn't share internally.'

It's not enough just to be the best expert – that's the bottom line. You need to be visible, getting out there, leading and proactively sharing your knowledge. All these factors tie into you receiving an SETC recognition, which impacts pay and career progression.

I think that ensures that we use the knowledge and don't just have experts who are recognised externally but who don't share internally.

Career network profiles

To support the Eureka Programme, and to make expertise and experts even more visible, Schlumberger has created its own 'yellow pages', called career network profiles (CNPs). Alan explains:

Twenty years ago, people couldn't look up other people within the organisation to learn about their expertise. We created the career network profiles to give people an internal biography. This is more than an expertise directory, though, and includes an assignment history; the CNPs also now have links to externally authored publications, which are important for our technical population.

'Everyone has one, but it's up to the individual to decide how to populate it fully.'

People project themselves to the organisation through it, as opposed to having endorsements from others like LinkedIn. There are no private CNPs – they're all available. Everyone has one, but it's up to the individual to decide how to populate it fully.

If you go to meet someone new, people will always go to the CNP first. We get 10–12 million hits per year on CNPs.

Reflecting on the biggest challenges, opportunities and proudest moments

With Eureka celebrating its 20th anniversary, Alan and Susan have much to be proud of, but are still hungry for greater active involvement of community and SIG members.

> We've had such an open model – experts, novices and everyone in between, open for anyone to join – sometimes that can give a bit of a false reading to a leader or sponsor when they look at their community population and think 'Wow, I've got 2000 people! I'm going to change the world and get feedback from everybody.' Then they host a webinar and only 80 people join, and they wonder what they've done wrong!
>
> But if you look to the internet, you'll see groups with thousands of members, but only a few contributors. Leaders run a survey for 2000 people and only get 80 replies – 'It would only take 4 minutes – do you really not have the time?'. That's still a challenge.
>
> In terms of expectations, though, they are doing more than they ever did. We have had over 800 technical webinars this year; hundreds and thousands of hours of people learning and sharing. It's phenomenal! The value is getting greater, but the model – the number of people we actively engage – is always a challenge on which we work.

'Hundreds and thousands of hours of people learning and sharing. It's phenomenal!'

Susan noted that, as leadership engagement has increased, Eureka communities have become a natural way to work and support other corporate programmes, and that other transformation programmes in the organisation are looking to integrate communities.

> One thing that has definitely changed is the way the senior management team understand Eureka. When we started, they never really thought about it or got engaged with it. Now the perception has changed: 'Yes, of course we have Eureka and people are involved!'
>
> We find that when we have initiatives in the organisation, we hear immediately from senior management who want to create a Eureka community for their initiative – this is how they connect. We now have communities focused on topics such as continuous improvement and global stewardship, showing Eureka's expansion beyond 'just' the technical population   it's really good!

Susan also reflected on where the Eureka programme 'was lucky' in the beginning, through circumstances which couldn't necessarily be replicated. Having a passionate sponsor with long-term faith in the programme was key for her.

A programme which is embedded in other transformations.

> When we started Eureka, the Chief Scientist at the time was a huge supporter – he loved the grass-roots nature of it. Other senior managers, had it fallen under their responsibility, when it didn't seem to be doing much, or it wasn't clear where the value was . . . they might have stopped it. However, he believed in and supported Eureka until it started doing something – we were lucky to have him as the sponsor. For something like this, you need to give it at least 3–4 years. That's tough to defend, but he was the guy who did that for us.

'For something like this you need 3–4 years, which is tough to defend.'

More often than we know, information shared through the Eureka channels results in tangible business improvements. One example came recently from a member who noted that he always watches for postings or webinars in Eureka that describe alternative methods to optimise well delivery. One such set of information expanded his vision to go beyond the norm in their drilling operations and evaluate a change to what had been a long-accepted drilling practice. The change he tested enabled his team to deliver wells for their client four days early. This enhanced practice is now the new 'best practice' used by all, thus showcasing real value initiated by knowledge sharing through Eureka.

Proven business value

Looking to the future, Alan could see new opportunities in the area of innovation.

A desire to extend from knowledge sharing to innovation.

Innovation: we can't say that we have 'conquered' this yet in Eureka. Somehow, we feel that we're not yet making full use of all our experts to feed the innovation funnel. Don't get me wrong, innovation is happening all the time – I just feel that this is something that we could do even better; there are more opportunities.

Finally, as Alan and Susan looked back together over dozens of 'Eureka moments', testimonials from communities to celebrate the 20th anniversary of Eureka, they allow themselves a moment of pride.

People have these Eureka moments all the time.

'They are blown away that it's a grass-roots thing.'

They say, 'I can't believe how many people are helping me.' When we read through these quotes, you can't but help have your face light up and you think 'Wow – we must be doing a really good job here.'

Despite what was said earlier, the number of people actively involved makes us proud. We can see the impact inside the company. Also, the number of other external companies who ask us for presentations about what we do because they've heard about it . . . and they're like 'Whoa!' . . . that makes us proud. Often when speaking with our clients or suppliers, they are blown away that it is a democratic, grass-roots thing. We're a very small team supporting hundreds of leaders. Not many other organisations have the same model.

What better way to finish the Schlumberger story than with five of the best of those Eureka moments?

Eureka moments.

'The Eureka community never sleeps.'

'I am just an intern but was really surprised that so many people interact with me.'

'The experience of being a Eureka leader couldn't have been more exciting.'

'Eureka is not simply a platform to share, it's embracing diversity among disciplines and ideas.'

'Knowledge is fascinating. Shared knowledge is powerful. Eureka makes both possible!'

Mapping the story to the 'KM Chef's Canvas'

The three areas we chose to highlight from Schlumberger's many strengths are:

Leadership

Leaders across Schlumberger are clearly aware of Eureka and seek to integrate it into their own agendas. The history of sponsorship from the top of the organisation, and the long-term commitment to resourcing the team at a senior level, both underscore this.

Roles

Schlumberger has clearly codified a number of KM-related roles and responsibilities and connected these with professional development and progression.

Processes

The Eureka programme has evolved, improved and documented all underlying processes and principles, and can demonstrate how the various elements of the programme connect with each other. Alan's responsibilities for process workflow also indicate that this is a priority area.

14

PROCERGS Brazil: using knowledge and innovation to make government more efficient

NARRATED BY LUCIANA MENEZES, KM LEAD, AND JOSÉ JAEGER, INNOVATION LEAD, PROCERGS, PORTO ALEGRE, BRAZIL

Gestão do Conhecimento

Compartilhar é multiplicar

'To share is to multiply'

That's the adopted mantra of PROCERGS' Knowledge Management activities, which emphasises the importance placed on knowledge sharing. Luciana's Knowledge Management unit is based adjacent to PROCERGS' Innovation Lab and is part of KMI (Knowledge Management & Innovation). As witness to numerous collaboration and facilitation efforts they have pictures and artefacts from projects, workshops, events and from other practices.

There is also a collection of KM reference material: from books on organisational models to Knowledge Management textbooks available for study and consultation by the unit and staff; some examples of knowledge-sharing techniques (such as the fishbowl conversation technique), learning reference models adopted by the company (such

Create an environment that stimulates the culture of innovation and knowledge sharing.

as model 70:20:10), creation methodologies (such as Design Thinking), and other materials displayed on a mural, plus a bookshelf that shows awards won over the last 15 years. Figure 14.1 illustrates the examples mentioned.

Figure 14.1 *CIC Mural*

The challenge

Headquartered in Porte Alegre, with over 1,000 employees spread across the Brazilian state of Rio Grande do Sul, PROCERGS provides information, technology and communication (ICT) solutions and infrastructure for the state to keep it running.

Besides having more than 700 application systems supporting the current actions of the state government, PROCERGS also has an agenda that includes modernisation and rationalisation. It adopts an entrepreneurial approach to the development and production of its ICT solutions and services and recently generated over $300m in sales.

Since its establishment 45 years ago, PROCERGS has been facing the challenge of identifying and introducing new technology and processes that improve efficiency and service to the public (in a region with more than 11 million inhabitants in the south of Brazil that borders Argentina and Uruguay), whilst keeping government running effectively.

PROCERGS' analysts and software developers are well versed in the needs – current and future – of their clients in government. KM plays a pivotal role creating an environment in which they can thrive and share and introduce new ideas.

Luciana traces the evolution of her unit:

> Approximately 15 years ago, a study was started on the subject of Knowledge Management in a technical area, the DTI – Technology Division, through an employee who was then responsible for bringing

the subject and its practice into the company, introducing, as the first practice of more structured KM, the 'Knowledge Wednesday'. Created initially as a technical event to bring employees together to exchange knowledge on technical matters, having improved over the years, incorporating new approaches (behavioural, innovation and others), it has become a well recognised practice internally and externally.

Recognising the importance of generating new solutions and introducing improved technology, in 2010 the Innovation and Knowledge Centre (CIC) was created in PROCERGS' planning area. It acts in a systemic and integrated way with the other areas of the company and contributes to the creation of an environment conducive to innovation. CIC comprises two units: one focusing on KM, headed by a Knowledge Manager; the other on innovation headed by an Innovation Manager. Both work closely together.

Then in 2015, in order to give greater support to the company's innovation actions, the Strategic Innovation Programme (PEI) was instituted. Its main objective is to 'apply innovation to government processes using information and communication technologies to transform public service and citizen service'.

Today, PEI aims to complement the positive image of PROCERGS as an agent of innovation and reference in digital government. Knowledge Management is an essential part of this programme.

Using Innovation and Knowledge to improve public services

Building on the symbiotic relationship between innovation and KM

PROCERGS' KM team has the responsibility to research, disseminate and encourage the use of techniques, tools and methodologies that support the creation, sharing, use, protection, identification, development and organisation of strategic knowledge. It also seeks to create an environment conducive to Knowledge Management and innovation. These directly link to guidelines contained in the strategic plan and with the Innovation Hub of CIC.

Company managers across the business take responsibility for managing knowledge and intangible assets in their area. CIC team members support those activities through a variety of KM and innovation practices, methodological approaches, tools and techniques.

Knowledge management and Innovation are the same. KM connects people to tools that have developed new solutions and products.

A relationship delivering results

Innovation Management works with KM and the results are impressive. Many artefacts of knowledge and innovation were generated through practices, including tools for expanding creativity and exploring best practices. José Jaeger describes three of them:

- **Ideas Portal**: a social tool geared to the generation and sharing of ideas and demands across the company – see Figure 14.2.
- **Innovation Working Group**: concept of a multidisciplinary work group that develops activities focused on experiments and prototypes, acting as an Innovation Lab.
- **Challenge or Hackathon on Innovation**: a competition to promote ideas for technological solutions for the state government, of collaborative and participatory nature, linked to the strategic programme of innovation of PROCERGS. Having gained this experience, we also provide mentoring and support in the innovation challenges of other state public administration bodies.

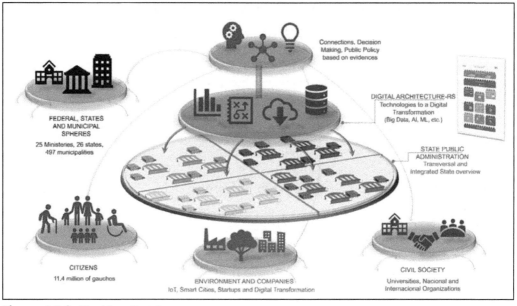

Figure 14.2 *The Ideas Portal*

Leadership, culture, formalising the role and process

From day one, PROCERGS' management team supported CIC, even when state governments have changed and pressure has been applied to budgets. For their part CIC has maintained close dialogue with senior management. The capture and sharing of knowledge and innovation is a key component of the company's cultural values and resulted in a number of national and international awards.

As one of the established business processes and part of the organisation's strategic guidelines, KM has a formal document, the 'normative documentation', that sets out the objectives, roles, interactions with other business areas and fits with the organisation's strategic innovation programme. It is regularly assessed, and staff members are asked as part of their regular evaluation what they have contributed to KM and innovation. KM sits in CIC, as seen in Figure 14.3. It works in close alignment with Innovation Management.

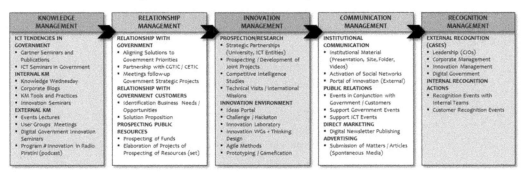

Figure 14.3 *CIC Organisational Framework and PEI Structure*

KM activities in PROCERGS

As part of their remit to investigate new technologies and trends, the four-person team in CIC participate in seminars and research with prominent ICT consulting groups.

Their internal activities focus on communication, collaboration and facilitation. Luciana details how these work:

- **Knowledge Wednesday**: a virtual and face-to-face event in the HQ auditorium each Wednesday for employees to know and share about what is happening in the company and the market, what projects are being or have already been done, what are the technologies and methodologies in research, development and use. This practice began with sharing among employees 15 years ago and has evolved to include external expertise by including guests and new themes and making it available virtually for all staff.
- **Corporate blogs**: repositories of information and knowledge, tool for the development of communities of practice and a discussion forum, among others.
- **KM tools and practices**: Practices 1.0, 2.0 and 3.0.
- **Practices 1.0** are already fully internalised and happen throughout the company without the need for intervention by the KM team: intranet, institutional site, methodology, processes, information security, circulation of periodicals, document repository, normative documentation, training face-to-face or read, physical and virtual library.
- **Practices 2.0** is the current focus of KM actions: Knowledge Wednesday, blogs, the Ideas Portal, corporate social networking, practice communities, discussion forums, agile methods, thinking design, storytelling coaching, fishbowl and animated videos.
- In addition, there is a set of 3.0 practices under way, characterised by the generation of knowledge artefacts and lessons learned in

discussion groups and work groups that work on new approaches, methods and tools of innovation: the creation of toolboxes, the instrumentalisation and multiplication of knowledge to the employees, to apply these approaches, methods and tools and to reconfigure their stocks of skills, demonstrates the new context present in the KM area.

Increasingly, KM and innovation look outwards, beyond the boundary of the organisation. Luciana illustrates how:

- **PROCERGS Users Group:** a network of collaboration with ICT co-ordinators and managers of the end areas of state agencies, with open participation for any public servant of the State of Rio Grande do Sul.
- **Seminars on innovation in digital government:** sharing of innovative cases in digital government.
- **Innovation workshops:** support in the dissemination and application of innovative approaches, tools and methods to governmental bodies in a network of ICT managers.
- **Support to innovation challenges** of governmental body **or** entity: mentoring and support in the achievement of innovation challenges of state public administration bodies.

People have said the sessions KM run helped professionally and personally.

Using storytelling to communicate public policy

One of the most innovative initiatives PROCERGS has participated in recently is the 'Intelligence Network to Citizen' which, through the use of big data and data science projects, aims to connect data, people and objectives to support decision making by the public administration and the citizen.

The purpose of the work is to 'connect people, objectives and data of public organisations, partnerships and the regional society (more than 11.4 million inhabitants) to help everyone to make better decisions, to learn and to innovate, through the use of the new and disruptive technologies, act preventatively and proactively in the guarantee of rights, in the delivery of goods and services and to generate enhanced public value to citizens'. Among actions and reflections made or in progress, the network seeks to understand how government services and products are used during the whole life of the citizen.

Storytelling was one of the KM techniques used and supported by PROCERGS and the State Secretariat of Planning, Governance and Management. The first project was looking for an understanding of problems (such as school dropouts) and the generation of hypotheses, as inputs to be used on data analytics tools, by the data science's team.

Luciana explains further:

> We brought experts from various sectors to discuss the problem of dropout among students in the state education network, the focus of the pilot project.
>
> Using a brainstorming technique called Carousel, we analysed possible events in the student's lifecycle. Carousel brainstorming is a co-operative learning activity focused around movement, conversation and reflection that can be used both to discover and discuss background knowledge prior to studying a new topic, as well as for review of content already learned.
>
> Each expert put up one Post-it note with a factor or event during these stages (prenatal, childhood, adolescence, adulthood, late adulthood and post-life). Included were: chronic absence; dropping out of school; illness; loss of parents; sexual abuse; drugs; and many things they thought might, or used to happen, in real life. Later, the set of events or factors were read and stories told around them.
>
> Common themes were grouped to create a set of hypotheses: parents in prison; living in a dangerous neighbourhood; and poor school transportation.
>
> Data analysis tools were then used to investigate the hypotheses raised against data produced by the Secretariats of Education, Health and Security. These results were shared with sectoral experts, for validation. Finally, a set of statistical models were created to help predict the probability of the student dropping out during the year.
>
> In the next stage of the project, with new inputs of data and connections, the storytelling was applied again in the construction of a persona, based on a real-life case. The aim was to find results that could bring new possible responses and solutions for actions and public policies.

Reflections

On overcoming barriers

Luciana reflects on the progress that's been made and new barriers that emerge:

> Initially, the main barrier was the internalisation by the employees of the importance of explicit and shared knowledge. Today, due to the evolution of KM indicators and continuous process improvement, these barriers have been overcome.
>
> Emphasis on the importance of innovation, especially the digital transformation process, has caused concern about the current work model and knowledge and skills of the people and areas involved. This is a moment of great importance for Knowledge Management, where new practices and ways of working need to be chosen, experienced and learned. This leads to new barriers to the process of evolution as old mental models slowly change.

On surviving a change of government and sponsorship

PROCERGS has to cope with leadership change (state elections) every four years. There is an organisational transition plan in place, for example, to deal with the handover in 2019. KM and innovation are important components of the process of change and see it as an opportunity not a threat since they are called on to generate new ideas and are open to new ideas themselves from the incoming administration.

On the importance of building networks across the organisation

Luciana describes her journey:

> When I began to play the role of Knowledge Manager, Knowledge Management and Innovation (KMI) was already in place with a number of established practices. I also had the challenge of continuing work already started and recognised in the company by the previous Knowledge Manager. This challenged me: as well as maintaining and evolving current practices, searching for new fronts, exploring new practices, I had to find ways to take KM in PROCERGS, using 3.0 practices that had recently emerged.
>
> In addition to the essential sponsorship of the executive level, building a network of partnerships and collaborating across the business and with people was fundamental for the implementation and consolidation of KMI practices. After all, it's the people who make Knowledge Management happen. And practice is the best way to bring it to life.
>
> The organisational environment is conducive as is the support that is permanently obtained from the managerial levels. Moreover, the characteristic of our business, technology, which changes very rapidly, means that we are constantly updating ourselves, our products, methodologies, processes, tools and new ways of thinking and managing.

Above all, Luciana suggests a knowledge manager looking to formalise KM in their organisation should:

> Start small, think big and develop in a planned and persistent way.

On measurement

> Because we are a company that seeks to learn, we adopt indicators that measure and signal the results of KMI practices and their effects and how much lessons learned are being identified and worked on in the company.
>
> Every area completes a monthly evaluation report and the performance of Knowledge Management and Innovation is one of the questions to be addressed.
>
> Another measurement is the market recognition of the work we do,

since the company is often invited to share its KMI case with various public or private entities and universities.

On the skills needed for the role

Luciana has a comprehensive list that many in the KM arena will find valuable:

Systemic vision, multidisciplinary approach, openness to the new, obtaining learning, establishing empathy and relationships with people and possessing knowledge about the company, its business, people, main processes and organisational culture.

Attributes knowledge managers should have.

On the future

Lessons learned have been increasingly incorporated into the company culture. The improvement of the Knowledge and Innovation Management process takes place through learning practices, through evaluations and reflections on lessons learned and outcome indicators from the practical perspectives applied by both KMI staff and the executive level of the company. We need to build on this. The greatest risk is that the KMI loses its strategic position, and gets its resources reallocated through government change, which occurs every four years; previously a major risk factor, although as time passes and KMI's process consolidates and improves, this risk is diminished.

Mapping the story to the 'KM Chef's Canvas'

PROCERGS, alone among the global organisations we spent time with, is focused on providing more efficient government and services for the citizen. The housing of KM and Innovation together illustrates the drive to develop new ideas and solutions. KM provides the facilitation and collaboration tools and techniques to surface innovative solutions and products.

Strategic context

The Knowledge Management and Innovation team's goals are totally aligned with those of the organisation. The output of their work informs policy and is mapped to strategic guidelines.

Improvement

PROCERGS CIC division (which includes KMI) provides an environment that stimulates the development of new ideas which improve or replace existing processes and services. KM has a formal document setting out objectives, roles and interactions with other business areas. KM reviews its toolkit and processes on a regular basis and staff are required each month to assess the performance of other divisions, including CIC.

Interaction and internalisation

There are many examples of the KM team engaging with its stakeholders: Fourth of Knowledge; Knowledge Wednesdays; Innovation Hackathons; and seminars. We were impressed by their approach to a major project (big data and data science) which seeks to understand how government services and products are used during the life of the citizen. The use in expert group sessions of storytelling and personae to map the lifecycle of a student surfaced issues that might otherwise have remained hidden.

15

The Olympic Games: Knowledge Management and learning pathways

NARRATED BY CHRIS PAYNE, HEAD OF OLYMPIC GAMES
KNOWLEDGE MANAGEMENT

Chris Payne, a former British Army officer, now Head of Olympic Games Knowledge Management at the International Olympic Committee (IOC), reflects on his experience building knowledge and learning capability.

> My military experience has helped a lot over the years. I learned early to live with ambiguity, focus on people, make decisions on at times incomplete data to maintain operational momentum, and, perhaps most importantly, get the politics off the table as much as possible, right at the start of any project. My time at the military college at Sandhurst has been a bedrock. I especially like John Adair's action-centred leadership model. It's simple but highly adaptable and can help remove a lot of often unnecessary complexity. I have always found that reflecting hard on challenges in the context of the model is a great way to take ground, certainly in any highly people-centric venture like the Olympic Games.

The challenge

The Olympic Games is a wonderful celebration of human achievement shared with a huge global audience through a series of spectacular events over a 16-day period every couple of years. Behind the scenes, it requires management of a lot of complexity, given the huge number of stakeholders involved. And it also presents huge challenges of scale, given that each edition starts from nothing and grows to be one of the biggest peace-time mobilisations of people and equipment. To put it in a different way, every two years the IOC initiates a new project – a start-up in a new country, a new culture and with a new team, with an immovable deadline, that requires significant growth to be effective, and then disbands.

It's a daunting challenge, but it's never a surprise. The IOC works closely with an Organising Committee for the Olympic Games (OCOG) for each edition. It takes seven years to deliver, building progressively and following a carefully worked out schedule. Many of the KM activities are built on milestones specified in the schedule, others are required *ad hoc* to meet challenges as they emerge. Whilst each edition of the Games is distinctive, there are, of course, repeatable approaches, reusable experiences and documented lessons – what an opportunity, therefore, for Knowledge Management to prove its value supporting one of the world's most watched events.

The evolution of Olympic Games Knowledge Management (OGKM)

The origins of OGKM extend back to the Sydney 2000 Games:

> In the early 2000s it became clear that knowledge transfer processes and associated learning services should be managed more directly by the IOC to support the growing challenges of organising the Games. This came at the end of a period of significant evolution for the Games, which in turn drove an increase in operational complexity and challenge. It was a natural evolution to focus more on managing knowledge and learning in response to this. At the same time in Sydney we had an organising committee that had planned and delivered the 2000 Summer Games very professionally – with defined project management, clear deliverables, developed planning cycles, and so on. They produced a lot of quite structured information and ideas about how to work, that IOC wanted to capture and nurture. Sydney were equally keen to share – 'We don't want all this stuff we've done to go to waste'. So the first organised KM programme was built on the work done by the Sydney team. They can take a lot of credit!

As the Olympic Games continued to evolve, with each edition throwing up specific knowledge challenges, so the KM programme had to evolve. Chris continues the story.

> Go forward a few years, the growth of the product, the evolving operational requirements, new cultures – basically a lot of ongoing change – and the focus shifted to finding ways for KM to support smarter, more efficient working. Not just sharing information but supporting the search for more innovative ways to do things that will save time, effort and money. In 2013, when I started, I had to identify ways to empower people to learn faster (and to understand it is generally OK to fail fast, too, so long as you learn), to deal with change and move away from a copy cat approach. We've had to maintain the information and lessons from previous Games – what you might call classic transfer of knowledge

'The first focus was equally on knowledge and learning.'

– but also shift the emphasis even more towards learning instead of just information sharing.

Against the backdrop of change, embodied in the IOC's new Olympic Agenda 2020 programme, we've had to retire blocks of knowledge which are no longer relevant and seek out new knowledge to be aligned and responsive to the needs of a new type of Games, one that is leaner and more cost-effective. We have refreshed our vision regularly, and restructured twice within the five years, to ensure the right focus on supporting the change. Most recently, we have integrated planning processes for the human resource evolution of the OCOGs, focusing much more on capabilities. I think that our growing role in learning and development is now as important as, if not more than, KM, and it'll be interesting to see where these evolutions take us next. One characteristic will remain – we will always seek to create a range of services that each OCOG can adapt and use in a way that best supports their own situation. Everything we do must be based on real practical needs.

> 'We've had to retire blocks of knowledge which are no longer relevant.'

The OGKM services, structure and activities

OGKM is structured into five areas: Coaching, Training, People, Knowledge and Analysis. It employs a small team of eight full-time staff and several external advisors and it has a long-term partnership with the World Academy of Sport, an external education provider, which supports the programme in many ways. Key activities supported by this hybrid but close-knit team include:

The Olympic Games debrief

This is a substantial week-long thematic debrief which typically happens around two months after the closing ceremony of the Paralympic Games. This debrief will involve several hundred staff participating in a full lessons-learned exercise, identifying recommendations and content for future OCOGs and recommendations for process improvement for the IOC. Interestingly, the debrief is always held in the city that will next be hosting the Games – hence the Rio 2016 Games were debriefed in Tokyo (which will host the 2020 Summer Games), and the 2018 Pyeongchang Winter Games were debriefed in Beijing (hosts of the Winter 2022 Games). The rationale for this is that the future host city is the primary 'customer' for the learning and insights and should hear them first-hand in a setting that allows plenty of time for networking between different organising committees.

> Coaching, training, people, knowledge and analysis.

> The future host city is the primary customer for the learning and insights.

The debrief is attended by representatives from future Summer *and* Winter Games, as much of the learning is programmatic, rather than event-specific, and cultural context is also important. Chris Pollard, who headed up Information and Knowledge Management for the London 2012 Games, acknowledged that in some functional areas, the knowledge transfer from the previous Winter Games (Vancouver 2010) was more readily applicable than from the previous Summer Games (Beijing 2008). Recommendations which are relevant to all future Games become enshrined in the Operational Requirements, part of the Games reference materials, which are regularly reviewed to remove, refresh and add content.

Knowledge transfer is dependent upon context.

Games reference materials

OGKM co-ordinates the development and provision of key reference materials to assist and support the OCOGs, Candidate Cities and cities considering bidding for an edition of the Games. These materials comprise the Olympic Games Framework, Host City Contract – Operational Requirements and the Olympic Games Guides. The Games Guides represent a significant body of explicit knowledge relating to every aspect of the Games. They are a regularly updated thematic collection of recommendations and good practices distilled from the experiences, lessons and debriefs of previous Games.

A regularly updated thematic collection of recommendations and good practices.

There are currently more than 40 guides totalling more than 7000 pages of information, supported by videos and case studies. Documentation is primarily in English, but the OGKM team are actively exploring translation options (including machine translation).

Topics include: Accommodation; Arrivals and Departures; Brand Identity and Look of the Games; Ceremonies; City Operations; Communications; Culture; Digital Media; Engagement; Event Services; Finance; Food and Beverage; Information and Knowledge Management; Language Services; Legal; Logistics; Media; Medical Services; Olympic Spectator Experience; Olympic Villages; Operational Readiness and Test Events; People Management; Olympic Torch Relay; Technology; Ticketing; Transport and Venues and Infrastructure.

Host cities carry a contractual obligation to provide content to OGKM on an ongoing basis to ensure that the 'flame of knowledge and learning' is passed forward.

Olympic Games Knowledge (OGK)

OGK is an evolving platform which hosts all the information collected through the IOC's various knowledge transfer approaches, giving the OCOGs access to thousands of reference documents and videos that they can refer to when seeking to plan their own Games. The OGKM team have also been experimenting with Google Street View-style virtual walkthroughs of different sporting venues and the athletes' village, through which the various reference documents appear, in context, as the virtual explorer navigates their way around. The Games happen in the venues, so accessing data and information via a spatial venue interface is very valuable, and shortcuts several steps to acquiring the right information.

Knowledge reports

Waiting until the conclusion of the Games before a full debriefing could lead to the loss of insights. Knowledge reports are produced from mini-debriefs and the curation of relevant documents, immediately after any significant activities to capture learning for future OCOGs. The process for knowledge reports is also used to capture data and statistics from the OCOG as it evolves. Increasingly, content is captured in many forms, some using video interviews.

The Games Experience Programme (GEP)

OGKM co-ordinates a series of behind-the-scenes visits for future OCOGs to learn first-hand through group visits to the host city at different stages of planning, testing and delivering the games. A fixed location – a campus – is identified as the home for all the observation and experience during the Games and a series of different activities are run, including visits, round tables, lectures, networking events, and so on. These are vital learning opportunities, mostly with a social flavour, which the visiting OCOGs prepare for in detail. Pavel Alferov, who co-ordinated the Sochi (2014) visit to the Vancouver 2010 Games, described a process where the Russian visitors assembled a list of over 5000 questions for their Canadian hosts during their observation and experience visits. Lord Coe, whilst Chairman of London 2012, has been quoted as saying that he used the event to 'look and learn and soak up every last piece of knowledge to help us with our planning – and the golden rule of staging an Olympic Games is that you can never plan too much'.

Patricia Vasconcellos, an observer from Rio at the London 2012 Games, articulates the difference in observation-based learning and desk-based learning. 'In terms of the transfer of knowledge programme, 'being here' is fantastic – you go from the papers to real life.'

> Learning from a behind-the-scenes visit.

> 'Look and learn, and soak up every last piece of knowledge to help us with our planning.'

Secondment, shadowing and mentoring programmes

In addition to the volumes of explicit knowledge and reference materials, the opportunity to participate in learning debriefs and the Games Experience Programme, longer-term opportunities exist for deeper experiential learning. These range from short-term shadowing work to longer-term secondment. Chris, who worked on the London 2012 team, describes his secondment experience to Vancouver in 2010:

'The very best way to learn is to assume responsibility and take on a role, rather than visit and observe.'

I think the very best way to learn is to assume responsibility and take on a role, rather than visit and observe. You have to take your 'mother-ship job' hat off and go into a lower level in an organising committee and learn by doing. You must be dedicated to the job, the budget, you fall in line with their KPIs – it's hugely valuable learning. You come back with a rich set of experiences that you can call on. For example, I was shocked by how little snow ended up on the ground at Cypress Mountain given the amount that was there just a couple of months before. The process that the Vancouver Organising Committee went through to deal with this threw up a huge amount of learning. Perhaps the biggest single lesson was the importance of a willing, 'can-do' attitude. No one aspect is more important than any other; everything is interconnected in delivering such a complex event and everyone must be willing to help everyone else, at all levels.

'Little islands of knowledge'

We found that the people who had experienced a secondment quickly became little islands of knowledge that could be constantly used as references for testing things – they were incredibly valuable.

Workshops

Interactive workshops are organised throughout the lifecycle of the organising committee and are tailor-made to suit the OCOG's needs. Overseen by the corresponding function within the IOC, these workshops (as many as 100 different types) are run by the IOC functional areas accompanied by external experts, who have often worked closely with previous OCOGs. Examples include cross-cultural awareness, operational readiness and games management.

Chris emphasises the place that external advisors have in supporting the various workshops during the OCOG journey.

The IOC is actually a pretty small organisation when you consider the scale and complexity of the Games. We work with a lot of advisors and they add significant value in all sorts of ways, plus they give us a lot of flexibility to deploy resources to support the OCOGs. I would say the workshops, each one tied to a milestone, is the backbone of our work with the OCOGs; it provides the cadence or rhythm of meetings. And we need people to help us deliver these. But this also means we must place significant emphasis on training, so that this distributed workforce is up to date with current thinking and can support the many changes to the way we do things that are now necessary. We're also moving to a more robust way of evaluating this workforce, so that we are sure the services provide solid value to the OCOGs. In summary, the decision to build capability or buy expertise is a common challenge. We choose to buy a lot of expertise, but this creates other requirements in terms of the KM programme.

Executive education, coaching and communities

Chris sees this as a key component throughout the lifecycle of the Games.

> One of the fundamentals for us is the importance of executive-level coaching – getting senior folks to actually touch and feel the Games and the challenges. OGKM has a big role to play in this. If you talk to enough people from past OCOGs, you begin to see a narrative which is the same. When you start out, the learning curve is very steep, and without any intention, you'll be prone to make mistakes. If you can really support them in the early years, then it helps a lot. We're doing a lot of workshops which are needs-driven, based on their analysis of what they want to focus on; we then fill in with executive education.
>
> We're also doing situational mentoring, providing mentoring to executives based on the situations that the mentor will have encountered before.
>
> We are working on the concept of an annual leadership summit to get them together to network – introducing more of a cross-OCOG exchange. In the early years, it's all about building a really strong executive partnership with the senior folks.

When you start out, the learning curve is very steep.

Additional services from OGKM include specialist information research services and analysis, supporting the collection of artefacts and publications from each Games, working closely with the Olympic Games Study Centre and the Olympic Museum, plus providing access to a community of trusted external advisors (consultants with Olympic Games delivery experience) for specialist technical issues which the IOC is not resourced to address: cybersecurity, for example. Chris emphasises the importance of a couple of the analysis projects:

> OGKM, perhaps not typically for KM, runs a programme to capture data at the Games to measure service levels. We are pushing to widen the scope of this project, to ensure we have top-quality measurements in support of Games optimisation. Our focus is on providing datasets, and analyses of them, that are accessible, informative and actionable by the relevant decision makers.
>
> Our structured interview programme captures the knowledge and experience of OCOG executives at five points on their journey. We have

thousands of interviews for each Games edition, captured using video. Working with the University of Lausanne, we also apply analysis techniques to the interview transcripts. This research helps us understand trends in Games delivery, from the perspective of the people doing the work. And of course, we provide the interviews online as a very useful way to share and learn through simple storytelling. It's a bit of a homebrew operation but highly effective.

Creating learning pathways

The OGKM team work with OCOG staff to ensure that all the knowledge and learning services are consolidated into 'learning pathways'. Each pathway is tailored to help the OCOG deal with a specific set of challenges in a specific context.

> It's all about mitigation and reducing risk, helping them to understand what they can and can't do, and helping them access services which are available and relevant to them, based on a specific activity at a specific time. If done well, the pathways provide a roadmap for just-in-time, just-right learning.

Chris has structured his team to support this:

> Right at the start, the OCOG needs to have a clearly laid-out learning vision and carefully articulate the 'knowledge journey' each one of them will travel. Everyone who comes in must know the opportunities open to them. It follows that the OCOG is in most respects a learning organisation, and so from there we need to ensure that OGKM services are representative of the learning journey of the people who ultimately need to deliver the events.

The team continues to be refocused to meet a growing need to deliver the Games in ever more efficient ways.

> The current thinking is that the OCOG should take longer than it has in the past to carefully define what it wants to do – three years initially with a relatively small team dealing with the challenge of how they are going to implement some of the recommended changes, make wiser procurement choices, clarify responsibilities across core stakeholders and ultimately reduce the costs. During that phase, we have increased the opportunities for coaching, mentoring and executive education.
>
> One of the classic mistakes is to equate 'doing stuff' with 'having a lot of resources'. By holding people back and making them really think about what they need to do, as opposed to what past Games have told them they should do, we can avoid waste and promote efficiency.

Much of Chris's passion to continuously refine the way OGKM responds to OCOG needs arises from his own experience in the London 2012 Organising Committee, prior to joining the IOC.

I don't think I could do my job effectively now without having had the experience of London 2012. I did nine years with that project. We won the bid in 2005, and I then focused on the technology part of the Games, doing a number of different roles in that space. Technology underpins a huge amount – it's a wonderful area to work in and really understand the DNA of Games delivery. Many things change and a lot of what was relevant in London may not be relevant elsewhere. But one core fundamental is always the same, and it's the perfect space in which a KM programme can really flourish – properly equipped, motivated and empowered people with the headspace and support to deliver events on the ground. It's not enough to have loads of documents and e-mails and be expected to read them all; it's not enough to just recruit people and it's a mistake to assume that one way is the right way. Everyone must understand what they're there to achieve, be confident in their abilities, know what flexibility is permissible, and then be ready to act. I've tried to evolve OGKM with this always in mind – the thin red line that I've been following from the beginning.

'I don't think I could do my job effectively now without having had the experience of London 2012.'

Future plans

Chris reflects upon where he sees this 'thin red line' leading to in the future:

I think it's all taking us to something that I wouldn't necessarily describe as KM. I don't come from a KM background as such, and I've always struggled with the term. I think what we are trying to put in place is better described as a Games learning model built on strong communities. So I think there will be evolutions in what we call ourselves, and that's pretty important, it sets our identity. If I go to the 'KM World' conference, it's all about SharePoint and taxonomies – that's very important, but not really where we're at!

The key thing for us is getting that passion for learning and sharing right into the people who deliver the Games.

We need to get much better at understanding where cognitive technologies can support us. There are so many opportunities in this space, and I feel we're a little behind the curve. There are two areas we are actively exploring: machine translation coupled with automatic video and audio transcription, and virtual-reality simulation based on a multi-event delivery environment for training purposes. These things can be hugely effective and save us a lot of time and effort, I am sure about that.

As for the knowledge component, well it never sleeps, it's a constant, flowing through everything we do. It's becoming more social all the time, less easy to control. I'm not sure sophisticated KM systems work well in our space, certainly not when you consider operational time constraints, language barriers and maintenance overheads. Better to move the emphasis to point-in-time and just-in-time learning and ensure that the knowledge resources can be found easily – or specifically commissioned via efficient research capability using reliable data – to support that learning. And make sure the social elements are encouraged via communities and a high degree of interaction between all the right actors involved in any event delivery activity.

Last, but important, we are actively expanding our integration with the Paralympics. This will be a fundamental for us in the future. Some of our core activities are already worked jointly, and this will be expanded. The OCOG must deliver both events, and so obviously the learning should be fully integrated and consistent. There will be a big push in this space for the learning opportunities around the Tokyo 2020 Games, and a lot of doors will be opened I am sure.

The biggest contributions to the success of the OGKM programme

Chris was quick to recognise the importance of executive sponsorship and the attitude towards learning. Christophe Dubi, the IOC's Executive Director of the Olympic Games, was involved with the programme right back at its inception in 2000.

> I have a strong executive sponsor. He understands the programme and the value it brings. And has been a direct part of the evolution over the years – that counts for so much. I also get a lot of learning from him through regular dialogue and testing ideas. And I think this is perhaps the essence of any success we've had – the attitude to learning must be right. There is no silver bullet; you must be so open to finding different ways that will work, constantly exploring options, pushing boundaries, not be afraid of failure. Any area where we encounter a closed attitude to learning and where failure is punished, is a dead end!

Mapping the story to the 'KM Chef's Canvas'

The IOC's applications of Knowledge Management to the successful delivery of the Games is an excellent example of an integrated, holistic approach. As a result of this, identifying just three areas to highlight is difficult.

Strategic context

OGKM has an unerring focus on the learning requirements of individuals in an organising committee. Every 'knowledge asset' is aligned with its needs at a specific moment in the timeline for Games delivery.

Interaction and internalisation

In the development and provision of learning pathways, tailored for organising committee staff, much attention is paid to learning in person, from observation experience and through executive coaching.

Codification and curation

The lifecycle management of the Games reference materials, and in particular the Olympic Games Guides for each functional area, are excellent examples of knowledge being distilled and refined through experience and expertise. This is further enhanced by the desire to use innovative technology for navigating the knowledge landscape.

16
Médecins Sans Frontières: knowledge without borders?

NARRATED BY ROBIN VINCENT-SMITH, MSF OPERATIONAL CENTRE BRUSSELS (OCB)

Robin Vincent-Smith is an irrepressibly energetic and yet deeply humble character, hence it's rare for him to sit still – and even rarer for him to talk about himself.

> I'm literally all over the place, but you can find me. I've always got one of these smartphones with e-mail and WhatsApp. I'm always findable, but I don't have an assigned desk.

He flits between hot desks, booths and library spaces in the Brussels office of Médecins Sans Frontières (MSF), looking out on the open-plan, activity-based headquarters, full of artefacts and posters which reflect the humanitarian work which they support and engage in. Poignantly, as you enter the building, your attention is caught by a memorial list of MSF colleagues who lost their lives in Kunduz Trauma Centre, Afghanistan.

The human consequences of MSF's work are clearly reflected in the way Knowledge Management and related disciplines of project and change management are applied and refined.

> I was recruited to this position five years ago by the General Director because there was a problem with headquarters-level project management. We'd had some bad experiences; projects had gone wrong with people, money and time lost. My initial mandate was to set up what Gartner calls an activist project management office – an internal consultancy gathering all the best practice and advising project sponsors and project managers. Quite quickly we noticed that, whereas project management starts from the moment you start hiring a project manager and writing a charter, and it ends when you have delivered, change management starts from the moment you start talking about this and it ends years after you've delivered whatever it is going to deliver. Change management was the second focus.
> The third element that came along was knowledge.

'We recognised that we were haemorrhaging knowledge at horrific rates.'

'I've chucked away my job title!'

We realised that we were doing things again and again and reinventing the wheel. And we recognised that we were haemorrhaging institutional knowledge at horrific rates – so we added that in my job title as well! Next, we acknowledged that changes needed to be made to our management culture and structure, and so organisational design came into the picture too. Today, these are the principal areas in which I support MSF: project and programme management, change management, Knowledge Management and organisational design.

The final evolution is to say that I've just chucked away my job title. My e-mail signature now reads:

'My name is Robin. I'm here to help. My agenda is up to date. Book me!'

From a knowledge project to a knowledge service.

Launching the Knowledge Management project

MSF launched its 'Knowledge Management project' with a baseline review of capability, using a model tailored to the development sector.

We benchmarked ourselves using an assessment tool for development organisations, mainly to identify the priority areas to work on in terms of Knowledge Management within MSF OCB. We identified a series of these, and attacked them one by one, as part of the project.

Now the project lifecycle has come to an end, we're essentially in the service lifecycle; Knowledge Management is a service that I provide, but I don't do it alone. We created the knowledge and information team, which includes a representative from each department.

Robin reports centrally to the General Directorate and provides his services with the help of a distributed team, comprising 'knowledge and information representatives' from every department. He breaks down his knowledge services into a number of discrete areas.

Facilitating magic and meaningful meetings

Robin noted that meetings consume a huge amount of people's time at MSF, and that they are fundamentally moments for knowledge exchange and creation, which can be enriched through facilitation and training.

The service that I get called the most often to provide is meeting facilitation or workshop facilitation. Because we've come to recognise the value of a neutral facilitator, and as I work for the General Directorate I often have less stake in what's going on – I'm neutral.

I get asked to facilitate more meetings than I have time for, so I launched 'a magic meeting masterclass' to empower people to facilitate meetings within their own and other units. I'm trying to increase the capacity of that service across the house – so there is now a bunch of 'Fantastic Facilitator' volunteers who offer this service to the house.

The magic meeting masterclass details a range of facilitation, team learning and knowledge elicitation techniques.

Meetings as moments of knowledge exchange and creation.

> The mantra for the masterclass is really important. It says 'Don't organise meetings. Don't go to meetings. (Unless they derive clear value!)'. We look at the objectives – are we there to discuss, debate, co-create, improve, decide or inform?
>
> In preparation, we look at the physical room set-up and consider the roles of the meeting owner, facilitator and active participant. Then we look at timings, how are we going to take decisions – consent, consultation, consensus, democracy, autocracy.
>
> Then in the meeting itself the role of the facilitator is to get people to speak, laugh and move in the first few minutes so that they feel at ease. I make the agenda visible as a Kanban board (a visual workflow tool from Lean Manufacturing) to help people observe where they are in the process and add to/re-prioritise when necessary.
>
> Then as we go deeper, we refer to all kinds of different methodologies – After Action Review, World Café, 1-2-4-all, design thinking exercises, brainstorms – depending on what the meeting is trying to achieve.
>
> Finally, converging: we plot decisions on a feasibility/impact matrix. Then we debrief and check out – and have a drink afterwards!
>
> I spend quite some time coaching others – because I think this is a basic business skill – to run magic and meaningful meetings through structured freedom. Meetings are about transferring knowledge: people's opinions, people's ideas and people's expertise. If you frame this correctly, then knowledge transfer happens happily; but if you don't, it doesn't.

'If you frame this correctly, then knowledge transfer happens happily; but if you don't, it doesn't.'

Maintaining the intranet and leveraging Office 365

Robin and his team take responsibility for the intranet and other digital information displays around the MSF HQ.

> We have an intranet within MSF Operational Centre Brussels and a home page which sits on top of that intranet; these are my babies and I ensure that they are maintained, alive and relevant as much as possible. We also hired a full-time internal communications manager, which I think is a very key role in terms of the knowledge service that we provide.
>
> If I need to share some knowledge and insights widely, how do I transmit my message in a homogenous way in view of all the other messages are being transmitted? We have newsletters and dynamic displays – screens in the individual meeting rooms – which offer additional channels for sharing.
>
> I'm not an expert on Office 365, but people will come to me and say, 'Look, I need to interact with the other members of my team. I need to

exchange knowledge with other members of my team. How do I best do this within our environment?' This is an area in which we partner with IT. I never thought I'd hear myself promoting Microsoft but it's such a great leveller because everybody gets access to exactly the same tools. Anyone can e-mail everyone, everybody's got access to OneDrive, the equivalent of Dropbox, etc.

'The most effective people in the organisation . . . are those that are embracing the Office 365 architecture.'

It's just a great level playing field. It facilitates, for example, inter-departmental or international working groups.

I've noticed that the most effective people in the organisation – the ones who really get things done – are those who are really embracing the Office 365 architecture and are leveraging it to its maximum. It's really helped to de-silo the organisation.

Back-pocket mission-critical knowledge

Robin reflected on the impact of ever-shortening attention spans, and the need to package knowledge in quick-read guides, designed to be 'read on the plane before the movies start'.

People very rarely take the time to read 200 pages. They want some kind of executive summary or succinct version – and during emergencies we have to deploy people very, very quickly, and so don't really have time to walk them through a long training. You just have to chuck them on the plane!

Exploiting a 25-minute window to refresh knowledge.

We noticed that (and this is now irritatingly not the case in many new planes) there was always a period of 25 minutes between the time you actually physically sat down on the plane and the time the movies came on. We thought we'd try and exploit that 25-minute window. We produced these pocket books – thin, A5 booklets which you can fold up and stuff in the back pocket of your jeans. You can read them in that 25-minute period between sitting down in the plane and starting the video.

They are executive summaries of a whole series of guides and practices and processes and tell you where to look further if you need to. They deliver the main messages we want to transmit. So this allowed us to do very swift, very efficient, very targeted and very prioritised knowledge transfer. It took off. As a result, we produced them for different scenarios: for example, a multiple-casualty scenario, a cholera scenario, a vaccin-ation campaign, the classic kinds of emergency scenarios where we have to deploy large teams quickly. That way everybody's singing from the same song-sheet.

'Everybody's singing from the same song-sheet.'

Gamification, virtual reality, video-newsletters and immersive training

The multiple-casualty scenario has evolved from 25-minute back-pocket reads to 25-minute gamified learning experiences.

You arrive in the field as a doctor, and you may have to manage multiple-casualty situations. This is something which many medics won't necessarily have done – unless a bomb went off next to their office!

We produced a 3D, virtual-reality, multiple-casualty experience through which we can really immerse people in the situation and what it's actually like to go through a bombing (see Figure 16.1). Whilst we found this useful for training purposes, we also found it useful for communication and fundraising purposes. It was just very powerful to be able to bring MSF donors and partners into our reality without having to transport them physically to the field.

'It was just very powerful to be able to bring donors for MSF and partners into our reality in two minutes with virtual reality.'

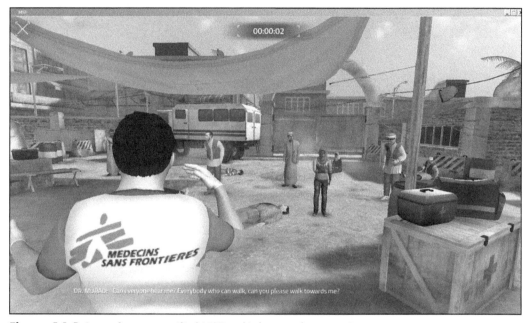

Figure 16.1 *Scene from a gamified MSF multiple-casualty scenario*

We gamified parts of the cholera guide, too, with an interactive map of a cholera treatment centre. Infection control is crucial. The map is focused around washing hands, water points and patient flow.

I think it's about recognising the reality of why, how, when and where people enjoy absorbing knowledge, and providing multiple formats. We keep the books – some people like them – but we also provide the digital alternatives and so people have both, and we look at video or gamification as an alternative if we think the return on investment justifies the spend.

'It's about recognising the reality in which people absorb knowledge.'

The same is true for our newsletters. For example, a newsletter will be printed, but increasingly the owner of the newsletter will just speak into a smartphone for two minutes – just reading the text out and posting it as a video. And that way we cater for different needs.

With face-to-face training, we have volunteers playing the role of badly injured people and people completely traumatised running around. We

Booklets, games, virtual
reality and actors . . .

set off fireworks and smoke, we make it as real as possible. And then, and in order to address a wider audience that can't necessarily be present at face-to-face training, we created a video game which anybody can play anywhere. In the game you can actually explain the choices that are made and the reasons why you have to do certain activities; you could lose points for doing a bad triage, and so on. Even non-medics can play it; anybody can play it. It walks you through this concept of triage and the reality of MSF teams across the world as they receive in their medical facility a truck full of injured people. Every time we try something new, we learn a lot from the experience. I'm constantly rethinking the way that we absorb knowledge and constantly trying to adapt as well as possible.

'I'm constantly rethinking
the way that we absorb
knowledge, and
constantly trying to
adapt.'

We haven't got to 'The Matrix' yet, though!

Knowledge-enabling the MSF quality principles – self-assessment framework and a river diagram

MSF has embraced workshop approaches to develop a self-assessment framework which describes 'what good looks like' in measurable detail for the core quality principles which they espouse. This common language enables peer connections and knowledge exchanges to be more purposeful, and for good practices to flow from those who have them to those who need them.

For a long time, we struggled with the notion of 'quality' within MSF. Our activities may simply involve jumping on a donkey and disappearing into the bush with basic drugs and coming back six months later . . . or building a university-level hospital offering orthopaedic surgery . . . and everything in between!

It's very, very hard to decide what we understand by 'quality' as an organisation, so the operations department built a framework, which became really useful for allowing people to self-assess against ten different principles (Figure 16.2 opposite).

A common language for
connecting to share
good practice.

For example: How are we doing in relation to the quality principle of 'interaction with the local population'? Am I really in dialogue with the local population about their needs? There are great lessons to be learned about how each individual quality target has been reached or not reached.

We train all our new field co-ordinators and project medical referents (key positions in the field in charge of strategy and daily management of operations) at a two-week face-to-face training course in Brussels. We outline the quality framework and then invite them, from their personal experience, to choose one area where they feel they've reached a high level of quality and one where there is still work to do. They then share with their peers, who ask questions for clarification and offer advice on how to work on the area to improve – a kind of peer assist. All of this happens live during the training. I talk for about five minutes in the morning and then they go away; they prepare and then they present to each other. It's a very easy day for me as a facilitator!

10 Quality Criteria for MSF Projects

Ask the right questions — Reflect with your team — Find the right tools — Learn from each other.

Here you will find **10 quality criteria** to assess your project.

They are meant to help you deliver a good project to your beneficiaries.
They are adaptable to any context. They are addressed to all team members. You can comment on each of them and share your good practices with your peers.

Relevance

Effectiveness

Do no Harm

Integration

Population centered

Coherent

Staff support

Resources

Learning

Agility

Figure 16.2 *10 quality criteria for MSF projects (msfqualities.wordpress.com)*

'Peer learning is much
more powerful than a
plenary session.'

And it is always fruitful because peer learning is much more powerful than a plenary session.

This process of self-assessment using a common framework provides the basis for a peer network which is sustained beyond the training programme.

> You can look at your projects through the self-assessment lens and that's very useful – but also you've got access to a peer network, a community of practice of other field co-ordinators, some of whom you've just met at the training.
>
> We've launched the community of practice for the hundred or so field co-ordinators across MSF OCB. This has introduced the notion that it is healthy and normal to ask your peers for support – and the quality framework offers a frame to do it from because you can call up your friend in another project and say, 'look, I'm having problems with this quality level: I'm not "integrated with my environment" enough . . .'. It just gives them a frame around which they can have a constructive discussion about how to improve the quality of their project. It's a frame for knowledge transfer.
>
> Finally, they build a river diagram together on brown paper on the wall, so they can see where they are relative to their peers, and whom they can learn from. We're not at the stage yet where we've got live real-time river diagrams for all 100 projects on a beautiful dashboard. But that's absolutely the goal.

'It's a frame for
knowledge transfer.'

Welcome packs – introducing KM to newcomers at MSF

Robin saw the opportunity to curate a welcome pack for new starts in MSF as a way to on-board them, and have these new internal customers experience the value of the knowledge services provided by the team.

> In a way, we brainwash people right from day one with KM, because we wrote the welcome pack! It's a simple two-pager. There's a bar of chocolate in there, which is the most important thing – chocolate is good for the brain. The pack also contains the organisational chart and the strategic summary that describes the direction of travel of the organisation – and it's got a map of the building. It's immediately useful.
>
> So right from day one, a newcomer is exposed to the services of Knowledge Management. In the welcome pack, we list the kinds of knowledge and information tools that a newcomer can make use of, one of which is 'Diggr' – our enterprise search engine – a kind of 'Google for MSF' that we invested in using Adelean and Elastic search technology a few years ago. If I'm a new staff member and I want to go looking for information, this is where I look for it. All of this is presented in the welcome pack.

Future plans – from 'on-boarding' to 'off-boarding' and 'baton-passing'

Robin continues to look for opportunities to blend knowledge sharing, connection and elicitation (capture) with the lifecycle of MSF people, with a particular emphasis on supporting and engaging those who are leaving the organisation.

'So you're leaving MSF?' Up until now, interestingly, what was happening in our Brussels office was that staff were asked to give back IT equipment and sort out their admin with human resources and that was pretty much it.

It's also important to think about people's well-being; how do they feel about leaving the organisation? People are emotionally committed and to leave is often hard. A lot of international staff struggle when they go back out into their home society. We wanted to focus on well-being and supporting people through the 'off-boarding' process, and we have developed an alumni network to support this. We want to promote alumni as a kind of peer support network. 'So you left MSF too – how has the real world been for you?'

'A lot of international MSF staff struggle when they go back out into their "home" society.'

The other important element is knowledge transfer. When you leave, you could take all your knowledge and experience with you, but obviously we'd rather staff left some of it behind – otherwise we'd be haemorrhaging institutional knowledge. So we're trying to create a kind of 'goodbye pack', which may also contain chocolate or a bottle of whisky – I have to figure this out – we're not there yet.

This pack would cover those elements, the practical stuff, like giving your IT equipment back, contacting HR, but also very importantly, knowledge transfer into some kind of handover document, some kind of 'end-of-mission document'.

This is already done for staff in the field, where the deal is often: 'You don't get your plane ticket home until you've given your end-of-mission report to your line manager'. This is a hard line – that was how I did it when I worked in the field. It worked because that way you really made sure the knowledge was downloaded before people left, because you know that once they're on the plane home, they're out – both mentally and physically.

'You don't get your plane ticket home until you've given your end-of-mission report to your line manager.'

You can't play the same trick at the Brussels office, because people aren't catching planes and of course it's illegal to withhold people's salaries!

However, what we can do is we can facilitate the writing of a handover report by providing a really simple, engaging template, and by offering 'baton-passing' if needed. In baton-passing, a neutral third person, a facilitator, will interview the outgoing person to help them curate their key insights, interview the incoming person to help them organise their key questions, and then facilitate the meeting of the two to ensure that the 'baton' is passed from one to the other.

Facilitated baton-passing.

Reflecting on challenges and strengths

Robin took an introspective angle when reflecting the biggest challenge which he had faced during his five years shaping and leading Knowledge Management.

> The biggest challenge for knowledge sharing in MSF has been ego. And it starts with one's own ego! Perhaps it was a good thing that I didn't start from a position of an expert when I started. I knew pretty much nothing about the topics of project, change and Knowledge Management and I had to learn and to manage my own ego.
>
> When I'm in a facilitation role, I cannot express an opinion – it's the number one rule. You have to remain impartial, neutral: otherwise you've blown your role as a facilitator. I also have to manage the egos of everybody else – because we're all attached to our authority and our hierarchy and people dominate meeting 'air time'. That means ensuring that everybody's voice is heard, one after another in a circular mode for example, and ensuring that decisions arise from consent. Once you've removed ego from the equation, all of this becomes so much easier.
>
> The greatest expression of gratitude that I receive in my 'knowledge' role always comes from people I have helped to organise, clarify and express their ideas, to fully understand their own 'knowledge assets', then render them transferable.
>
> I can literally observe the relief and satisfaction on their faces. I help people to communicate – I am an interpreter. I've been described as 'clairaudient': 'I can hear clearly'. When I'm facilitating, I'm essentially a translator – an interpreter. You observe two people not understanding each other for whatever reason and you just help them to speak to each other. It's funny, I studied languages at university, but now I don't necessarily translate between English and French, I translate between English and English or between French and French, but it's the same concept. It's just getting people to understand each other through facilitation.

'Once you've removed ego from the equation, all of this becomes easier.'

'I've been described as "clairaudient", which in French means "I can hear clearly".'

Mapping the story to the 'KM Chef's Canvas'
Culture

KM is deeply linked with MSF's quality principles, which in turn build upon the organisation's values and principles. Robin is frequently adapting his range of services in order to address cultural challenges – for example, through the improvement of meeting facilitation. KM is intertwined with 'on-boarding' and 'off-boarding' of staff with the creative approach to engagement even extending to the use of chocolate!

Interaction and internalisation

Robin, who heads up KM, describes himself as 'always findable'. There is a significant focus on the quality and effectiveness of collaboration and facilitation in meetings. Learning and training resources are very human-centred, immersing staff in an authentic and emotionally engaging process, through gamification and virtual reality. Organisational design is an area which forms part of the responsibility of the KM team.

Improvement

The KM services are constantly under review, and MSF is quick to experiment with new processes and technologies. The integration of KM into the quality principles of MSF and the use of self-assessment and river diagrams enable a shared approach to improvement, using positive deviance to identify and learn from strengths.

17

Transport for London (TfL), UK: learning to be world-class

NARRATED BY LIZ HOBBS, KM LEAD, TfL, UK

Liz is a practical, no-nonsense project manager, equally at home in a hard hat down a tunnel with fellow site workers or facilitating a senior management lessons-learned session in a swanky office. Liz is a bit of a 'magpie', adept at collecting snippets, tips and knowledge from others.

> . . . anything I could drag from anybody related to Knowledge Management, because with my background being project management on stations, I'm thinking what the heck do I, as a project manager, know about Knowledge Management, other than we don't do it?

Her office environment reflects this: a newspaper article where a consultancy had conducted lessons-learned sessions for London Underground; project management books; Knowledge Management books, including Chris Collison and Geoff Parcell's *Learning to Fly* (2004). Of course, there is also her computer, which 90% of the time is showing the TfL KM Portal.

The challenge

No other city is as recognised by its transport system as London: its red buses, black cabs and Underground 'Tube' trains, trams, overground and river services are known the world over.

As the integrated transport authority, responsible for meeting the Mayor of London's strategy and commitments on transport in London, TfL runs the day-to-day operation of the capital's public transport network and manages London's main roads. Since more than 31 million journeys are made daily across London, this is no small task.

TfL's programme of transport capital investment is one of the world's largest. It is building the 60-mile west-to-east Elizabeth line (Crossrail), modernising Tube services and stations, transforming the road network and making it safer, especially for more vulnerable road users such as pedestrians and cyclists.

As a public, not-for-profit, organisation, TfL reinvests every pound of income (nearly £11bn in 2017/18) into its transport network. It is committed to reducing costs and reinvesting all income to run and improve services.

The Project Management Office in London Underground (a TfL operating company) previously talked about setting up a lessons-learned database, but there had been no co-ordinated approach until senior management launched Project Horizon in 2010. This was a fundamental review of TfL that aimed to create one organisation, merging the support functions which had been carried out in a variety of places across TfL. In doing so it sought to deliver significant savings, drive improved processes and provide clearer accountability. Liz takes up the story:

> Project Horizon, in looking at the organisation, realised that we weren't actually exploiting experience or learning from previous projects. So they put together a job description for a knowledge manager, assistant knowledge manager and some temporary posts to go out and gain the information they thought we were lacking.

'When I saw the job description and one of the biggest points was to go and build a lesson learned database I buried my head in my hands and thought, but it's not just about that'

'I don't want a database, I want a repository, I want a portal, I want a knowledge hub.'

12 months to develop a strategy together.

Developing a KM strategy to tackle project learnings

It was late 2012; Liz was situated in a group called 'Continuous Improvement' as Head of Knowledge Management, tasked with developing a lessons-learned database.

> I moved into the team that provided TfL's initial project management framework. Lessons-learned was always linked to the end of a project at that time.
>
> We talked about having three pillars for Knowledge Management: the very tacit, difficult-to-codify, areas of knowledge-sharing events, special-interest groups or communities of practice, and the explicit, linking to how we actually identify what things we need to change in the project management world through the lessons-learned repository. I did everything I could to try and not refer to it as a database, because people see databases as static.

Rather than rush in to develop a strategy and action plan Liz took time to consolidate her thoughts as to what Knowledge Management might mean for TfL.

> It's 'How am I going to get cynical project managers to buy into the need for sharing their knowledge?'. For me, it was never about a database; in fact, that came a year to 15 months after.

From the branch line to the main line

The KM initiative started within London Underground's Project Management Office (PMO), reporting to the London Underground Executive Board. TfL recognised that it needed to demonstrate to the whole organisation that KM was of value. Liz takes up the story:

> Part of what I had to do was to refresh and integrate eight sets of project management frameworks across the organisation. We linked Knowledge Management into the new, integrated, framework or pathway; the pathway was mandated by endorsement of the Transport Commissioner.

A horizontal discipline across a set of siloed organisations.

As the organisation was seeking to transform, Liz set about assessing cultural attributes and barriers that needed addressing for Knowledge Management to work.

Build KM into existing work processes.

> On first joining London Underground, one of the first things I did in trying to assess the culture across the whole organisation was put together a cross-TfL working group.
>   I'd worked on an 'interface manual' (everything a project needed to know and do when it got on site – Oxford Circus, for example, has 100 interfaces). And in doing the research I'd got to know many people and who to contact. Together with my boss, Arnab, who had a wide network, we were able to assemble a set of people who could help in each of the TfL companies.
>   I called it a working group: not a special-interest group and not a community of practice, because we had specific work that we needed to get done. And part of the role of the working group was to harvest lessons-learned reports from across the organisation, before doing a baseline report of where we were.

Importance of being able to draw on existing networks to create a cross-organisational working group.

Early 'show-and-tell' events

TfL launched its knowledge-sharing drive with a series of peer-to-peer project community events held every six weeks, at which an individual project team would describe where they were in a project, share their lessons to that point and give recommendations for other projects. Liz and her team would then organise presentations relating to any new or amended processes that project teams needed to know. Attendance was high, ranging from 60 to 125, depending on the project topic. Liz remembers this session as being memorable:

> I'd previously facilitated a lessons-learned workshop for the Integrated Stations Programme (ISP) that surfaced a couple of issues around collaborative working and shift productivity reporting which they sought to address. At the six-weekly project community event, ISP described how they'd introduced changes into their working practices. A programme

manager from a huge project that was kicking off came up and spoke to the team and said, 'Can I come and have a look at this in practice so that we can roll it out?'

This occurred 12 months after the initial kick-off and gave Liz and her team a success story they were able to share.

Productivity increased from around 40–50% to 84% as a result of embedding the outputs of a lesson learned exercise.

Introducing special-interest groups (SIGs) or communities

Concurrently with the launch of the show-and-tell events, TfL also set up six SIGs based on the different elements of the business. These included Construction; Health and Safety; Planning; and Risk. (See the Appendices, pp. 254–5 for an extract from the Terms of Reference for Knowledge Sharing SIG.) Each group initially provided feedback on the integrated project management framework then looked at where they might improve processes and share in the show-and-tell events. As Liz notes:

From six SIGs to 27. One of the most effective is people change with a Yammer user community of 650 people interested in how change impacts projects.

> I started organically growing the champion's network that exists across TfL. It was quite multi-faceted and more organic than I think I expected it to be.

Capturing learnings from major projects

Many of TfL's projects can take a decade to complete and so it is important to capture lessons on the way. Liz believes that mechanics drive behaviours. She adopted the 'learning before, during and after' model. Liz explains how her team of three went about it:

Lessons should be captured as they happen, otherwise they are prone to memory bias and also many of the team will have left.

Embed lessons into the processes of the business.

Create value as you develop a portal.

> There were a couple of things I did on 'mechanics drive behaviours'. The first was that I de-coupled the lessons-learned report from the system where learnings were previously captured; the second was that I built it into the Stage-Gate® reviews. (Stage-Gate is a method for assessing and managing new projects and products.) So, the gate managers would start asking, 'Have you been onto the lessons-learned portal?', which obviously was a bit further down the line. 'Have you looked to see if there are any lessons from your next stage of the project and have you got any lessons that you can put on the portal from what you've learned?'
>   So, whilst we were building the first iteration of the portal, we thought: 'How do we build value? How do we get project managers to see value? We need to go out and facilitate lessons-learned workshops.'
>   'We need to show them – actually we need to ask the questions that make them think'. One of the questions that I asked the working group was 'What do we think a good lesson learned is?' I did toy with the idea many times of changing the terminology to 'lessons identified', because

until you tell me you've done something with it, it's not a lesson learned. We never got to that and it never got changed, but for me that was the challenge: 'Show me what you've learned and how you've done it.' So we would facilitate lessons-learned workshops in the first 18 months for the team and the champions. I think we facilitated about 150 lessons-learned workshops in total.

A lesson identified is not a lesson learned unless it is acted upon.

The lessons-learned portal was released in May 2014. Liz and team had been in position for 12 months at that stage, and used the facilitation of lessons-learned workshops to start building up the portal content.

In 15 months, the use of the portal grew by 294%, in terms of lessons acquired.

How TfL prepare for and run the workshops

The team conducts a pre-meeting to surface the objectives for the lessons-learned workshop, a mandatory event that is part of TfL's quality assurance. More often than not, guidance is required on how to construct the e-mail invitation to those involved in the project, which includes internal as well as external planners, contractors and project management personnel. The inclusion of external contractors was initially questioned, but this changed once TfL people understood that 'If you don't understand how contractors see us and the impact TfL can have on the contractors' business, how can both parties learn?'

Each workshop opens with a fun element and is conducted on a 'no blame' basis. It looks at three things; 'What went well?', 'What could have gone better?' and 'What did you do or would you do differently going forward?' Liz describes one particularly memorable workshop:

I was doing it for a really cynical project manager, and I can say that, as we are friends! We were facilitating; it was the end of the project, so we looked at the whole project lifecycle. I'd got two discipline engineers in the room (discipline engineers cover things such as fire and mechanical and electrical power). We were going through the lessons and I was writing stuff up and asking questions. One of the project team said, 'But of course this delayed the project'.

So I said 'No, explain; tell me more, tell me more, I want the whole story.' They said 'Well, the discipline engineers say they own this particular asset, and the premises engineers say they own it.' I said 'Okay', and they said 'They've got two different standards.' So one would sign it off and the other one wouldn't. The two discipline engineers were sitting next to each other. So I said, 'Project team – talk amongst yourselves!'

I took off my facilitator's hat and played the role of project manager. I went up to them and said 'You only have one asset owner, guys; at the very least can you reference each other's standards. But it would be ever so much better if you actually got in a room, talked to each other, decided

Make sure the workshops are fun!

The need for a combined
standard.

When the cheapest ends
up costing more.

'. . . go and put two half
days in my diary, I now
see what lessons learned
is all about and I'll be
taking this lot to my next
project with me.' [Project
Manager after the
lessons-learned process].

Dancing in the rain.

who owned the asset and develop a combined standard, don't you
think?'

Then it was time to take my project manager hat off and put my
facilitator hat back on. We got some really good lessons from that and
about procurement, where they'd been sort of told to go down the
cheapest route. It had ended up costing 100%-plus more than going for
the most technically competent approach. And that's the sort of evidence
that we would start to be able to feed back.

But on the Friday afternoon, we sat with the project manager and his
assistant project manager, because project managers always give 'it' to
the assistant project manager to upload to the portal, because that's the
boring bit.

We sat there for a good couple of hours and the project manager
asked, 'Can we do one more?' – because we were helping them write
the lessons. I said 'They're your lessons, they're not mine. It's your
experience but wouldn't it sound better if you did this or if you added this
bit of context?' So, we're teaching them, coaching them on how to write
lessons. And about four o'clock I said 'Do you know it's getting awfully
late and it's wet out there. Don't you want to go home?' And he's still
asking: 'Can we do one more?' and I said 'Really? Yeah, okay.'

I left the meeting and went outside in the pouring rain and I was
dancing up and down, such was my delight to have someone who was
cynical and now gets it.

Curating the lessons learned

While the lessons-learned process had proved its value, Liz saw huge
potential in consolidating the lessons arising from the various
knowledge activities: portal; knowledge-sharing events; and special-
interest groups. TfL wanted to make the lessons learned a key part of
process improvement. In order to achieve this, they created 'wiki pages',
where lessons around a common theme are gathered then tested with
the SIGs and finally included in a set of 'knowledge articles' to educate
people. The consolidated learnings are fed into the process.

Reflections
On taking on a mandated role that managers did not initially embrace

I struggled for many years, because though Project Horizon had effectively
given me a mandate by creating this KM role, and told me to go and put
together a strategy and a lessons-learned database, senior managers,
for some reason, never thought that they had to buy into it themselves or
actually talk about the key messages of why we should be learning! I
think that was my biggest lesson.

On reaching out to the KM community for advice and verification

One of Liz's early exchanges with the global KM community was during a conference call where she and her boss Arnab presented three slides on their KM approach. Liz recalls asking if anyone who was on the virtual call had any advice:

> We presented the knowledge-sharing events, the special-interest groups and then the lessons-learned portal. And we got what I thought was a really good response: 'You don't really need to do anything else because if you can crack those three areas you're pretty well on your way.' I said, 'But tell us what else we need to do', and they said 'Just go and do it'. I think we had quite a lot of external endorsement at the very beginning as well, which gave me a lot of hope.

On choosing the right business partners

Liz believes that to make an impact, KM needs to be seen to have advocates throughout the business. Here's why they went for the projects as partners:

> We did start with projects because that's where we thought we'd get the quick wins: 'Let's see if we can support projects by learning, getting them lessons from the different parts of the project lifecycle.' Within that 15 months, I'd pretty much got lessons from every part of the lifecycle.

Go where the business needs help.

On measurement, governance and monitoring

> We used the lessons-learned project as our flagship, but the approach turned out to be so popular that we had to revise the strategy some 15 months ago because we couldn't process the number of lessons going onto the portal! It comes to a point where you then need to start doing things with the rich source of data that you've got.
>
> We measured progress by use and the quality of the lessons being input. That quality really improved over time and became a key measure; for example, it became important to draw out what actually happened and to put context in, rather than submit high-level one-liners such as 'London Underground has a great engineering team.'
>
> Now they will document 'What actually happened and what impact did it have on the project? What do we think caused it?'

Adapt the strategy to meet the results from early interventions.

On KM as a transformational tool

Liz reflects on how the application of the lessons-learned KM technique has transformed the way TfL undertakes projects:

I had an example where there was a project team that hadn't really got the power process on their radar. They didn't understand the timescales required and it ended up costing an extra £1.5 million on design. But then the process owners went out and did a big knowledge-sharing event, a lunchtime learning event to educate people who were linked with projects for the power process.

Success is also visible on what we call LOCROS West (London Overground Crossrail West). The sponsor and the project manager from LOCROS East looked at all the issues they'd had and amended that in the contract for the West. What they learned from the issues clarified a lot of scope elements. I think things have changed in terms of the culture and willingness to learn.

On maintaining and improving special-interest groups

TfL has engaged its stakeholder groups throughout the evolution of its KM activity, the 27 special-interest groups being a case in point. After the initial burst of enthusiasm Liz discovered that their working practices were becoming quite individualised. So she and her team convened networking events involving the SIG heads to establish a common way of working that all could subscribe to. The lessons-learned approach worked, and within three months they had agreed terms of reference for future SIGs that acknowledged the importance of continuous process improvement.

Effective stakeholder engagement is essential.

In 2015, there was a big change to the construction design management (CDM) regulators' SIGs. The Health and Safety SIG used their time together to develop what the projects needed to know, what training the projects needed and what communication they needed to make sure that all projects knew of this legislation change.

And that, for me, is exactly what they're there for, because you're hitting the whole group, you're actually defining what it is that people need to know. You're disseminating it in a form that is easily accessible.

On getting senior management buy-in

This is a perennial challenge for most KM programmes and TfL is no different. Liz notes how often she had to re-sell to one board or another as their attention moved elsewhere or new people came in. She describes how, after building KM activities into organisational key performance indicators (KPIs) over the last four years those 're-sell' discussions have become less frequent.

There are a couple of programmes that build lessons learned into KPIs; learning is now a senior management responsibility, it's on the agenda at team meetings. People are not picked on but they are asked 'What have you learned this quarter, is there a particular lesson?' So there are now groups of champions within programmes that not only facilitate lessons learned, they're responsible for inputting key lessons, they're responsible for sharing them across the programme.

Liz describes how she got buy-in from one board:

Rather than present for 2½ hours, I got three lots of people from my champions around the business to come and share how they'd used Knowledge Management and lessons learned. I also got someone from Crossrail. One of the directors turned to Karen (from Crossrail) at the end and said 'But you're fine, you had board level support from Andrew Wolstenholme.' And I said 'But gentlemen, that's exactly what I'm asking you for, your support, to be responsible for cascading key messages across the business and giving your staff the time and the space to contribute to this and feel they can do it without fear.'

Bringing others in to sell what you do.

Figure 17.1 shows what the board signed off on:

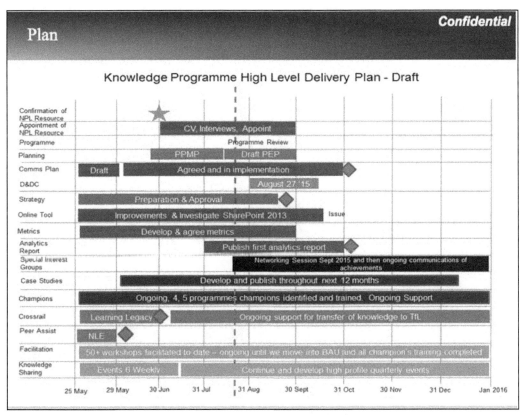

Figure 17.1 *Knowledge Programme High-level Delivery Plan at TfL*

On the skills and behaviours needed for the role

I think you can learn them. In terms of skills you need: communication, empathy, persuasive skills, storytelling. I always start my lessons-learned workshops with stories.

On the change in the last four years

Having a structured approach (the Stage-Gate® process) for project development already in place that people are mandated to complete was important. Building lessons learned into that process was like pushing an open door. Even though Liz has moved on from her previous role, the combination of a strategy, formal processes and KPIs for people means the lessons-learned programme has become ingrained behaviour.

I have to say that I'm fortunate to be in a position where I can walk around a number of our offices and constantly hear 'Is that a lesson we've actually learned? Have we actually learned that? Are we doing lessons learned?' And it's a far more open culture than it was four years ago.

Mapping the story to the 'KM Chef's Canvas'

TfL's KM programme was driven by a reorganisation in one of its major operating companies, London Underground. Housed in the Project Management Office, it focused initially on identifying and feeding back lessons on major projects. It aimed to embed 'learning before, during and after' into the way it works and that has proved successful. It also aimed to get people collaborating and sharing expertise across the various businesses that comprise TfL. That too has worked. We particularly liked:

Interaction and internalisation

TfL now has 27 special-interest groups (SIGs) and a common code of practice that each adhere to. The KM team facilitate countless learning and 'show-and-tell' events where people from inside and outside the organisation share project experiences.

Improvement

As reporting lines changed and KM was located in Continuous Improvement, so the emphasis moved to process improvement: embedding lessons in TfL's Stage-Gate® new product/project development process to ensure that knowledge supports investment decision. They have been able to measure progress by the quality of the lessons input to their lessons-learned portal.

Support

Facilitation is a key part of the ongoing support TfL's KM team provides to the business. They have a defined process for running workshops that all follow.

18
Syngenta: leaping into networks and cultural KM

NARRATED BY NICOLA THOMSON, CAPABILITY AND KNOWLEDGE
MANAGEMENT HEAD, PRODUCTION AND SUPPLY, SYNGENTA

Waiting for Nic in the reception area of Syngenta's UK headquarters in Manchester, you can't help but notice a large sculpture which they refer to as the 'backbone'. It's a visual reminder of their purpose and values – and it's everywhere, as Nic explains as she guides me through the open-plan office to her desk.

> We've got a lot of whiteboards with huddle zones, small working areas where we have orange glass boards that we can discuss and work around and then capture notes and ideas on them as they emerge. If we want to, we can instantly get together and have a discussion or problem-solving session. In my area we have 'scrums', where once a week we gather around a board with Post-it notes and talk about what's on the agenda for the week: who is in or out of the office? What do we need to do? Am I on track or not? It also gives you that great sense of achievement, because you're physically removing from the wall a Post-it note of something you have achieved, rolling it into a ball and putting it into a bin. A nice feeling!
>
> So here we are at my desk, I've got a number of gadgets here – wireless headphones and iPad for Zoom and Webex video calls – oh, and I've got a model of the Syngenta backbone in front of me.
>
> It describes where we're going to – our ambition and strategy – and where we have come from – our brand and story. Right in the middle, that's where our purpose and our values sit. The Syngenta purpose is really fundamental to us – it's about what we do and why: bringing plant potential to life.
>
> Our purpose and our values are at the core of everything we do at Syngenta – they have really been deeply woven into the Syngenta culture.

Syngenta is a Swiss-based global company which produces agrochemicals and seeds and conducts genomic research, improving global food security by enabling millions of farmers to make better use of available resources. According to its website:

Through world-class science and innovative crop solutions, our 28,000 people in over 90 countries are working to transform how crops are grown. We are committed to rescuing land from degradation, enhancing biodiversity and revitalising rural communities.

LEAP: Learning from Experience and Accelerating Performance

Around Nic's desk are a number of posters which illustrate the work of the LEAP programme, which Nic has led since its inception in 2009.

'Being able to increase the capability in people was as important as increasing our capacity in our assets.'

It all started as a project, designed to address some challenges in the organisation at the time. The leadership team recognised that there were a number of challenges facing us which needed some focused attention. The demands on the supply chain were enormous at that time and continued to grow year on year (and as they continue to do). Linked to this was the recognition that being able to increase the capability in people was as important as increasing our capacity in our assets – our manufacturing sites. You need to do the two things together really. It was also decided that we needed to have a greater focus on up-skilling or increasing the capability in the supply chain – hence the work to partner with an internationally recognised business school in France.

We also were looking at some of our number predictions for the future, and could see that over the next (at that time) 5–10 years there would be a lot of people who would have been with the company for a long time, therefore with a lot of experience, who could be walking out of the door. They could be retiring – but it made us think about not only those that were retiring, but people at any stage of their career, whether moving from production and supply to commercial, or moving from Syngenta to another company. What we couldn't afford to do was to let all of that knowledge and experience just disappear without trying to sow it back into the organisation somehow and pass the corporate knowledge and insights onto future generations.

Sowing knowledge back into the organisation.

'We couldn't get to the knowledge we needed, to make the decision.'

In addition to this we recognised that we were reinventing the wheel left, right and centre. It wasn't that we didn't have knowledge, we had mountains of it – we couldn't get to the knowledge we needed at the moment we needed it to extract the key learnings to make the best decisions.

Sponsorship for the LEAP programme

Nic was quick to connect the early success of the programme with the strong advocacy and role-modelling which they gained from Mark Peacock, an Executive Committee member.

Characteristics of an effective KM sponsor

We were sponsored by the Global Supply Leadership Team, but we were extremely fortunate that the Head of Production and Supply at the time was on the Syngenta Executive Committee.

He was a passionate advocate for what we're trying to do. He really believed in developing people, connecting and collaboration. He was a great sponsor at a very high level and took every opportunity he could to either give us words in e-mails and announcements, to give us a video interview, to be there when we were making presentations, so wherever he could make his presence felt, whenever he could talk to people about what we were doing, he would do it. A lot of our success in those early days I think were due in no small part to what he did in advocating and talking passionately about what we were doing.

'He believed in developing people. He believed in connecting and collaboration.'

Building LEAP networks into the heart of the programme

Like so many Knowledge Management programmes, the LEAP programme had the development of communities of practice (known as networks of excellence in Syngenta) at its core.

We knew that what we needed to do was to create networks – communities – so that we could put people who had problems in connection with people who had solutions and, in doing that, share that good or best practice, share the learnings and capture those insights. The first bit of the initiative was to set out eight new 'networks of excellence'. They had a clear purpose. They were unofficial – so we never made people join them. We spent a lot of time talking creatively about how we communicate, how we engage, how we publicise, to try and create the pull from within the organisation.

'We never made people join them.'

They all needed certain things to draw people in and a lot of the early days were spent actually trying to identify what it was that the community really needed, that could be used to hook the people.

Finding the hook for each network.

We created virtual homes for them, with resource libraries, photo libraries and discussion boards. We also had a 'who's who and who can help' directory for their network, as there was no facility to do that across the whole of the company at the time.

Nic and the LEAP team paid particular attention to training the network leaders. The training introduced potential network 'core teams' to the roles within networks and ensured that the members had a plan to take them through the first 100 days of the network after its launch. One innovative part of the training was a board game, 'Network Snakes and Leaders', which used the familiar snakes and ladders board to explore different scenarios which could befall a network during its early stages.

Training network leaders with a board game.

We had a role profile for network lead, the sponsor, topic leads and the core team. We then extended it when we introduced ambassadors and regional leads into the programme. Wherever we had key roles we had job descriptions which echoed the Syngenta job descriptions format.

In the two-day training, we used a lot of evocative speeches – a lot of mobilising and inspiring. We chose a few people around the organisation who we knew had a belief in what we were doing to talk about why they think we should be doing this. From a change management perspective (we used John Kotter's model at that time) it was all about creating the vision for people. We brought in individuals who could paint that picture of the 'better' place to be, and this would start building momentum and the energy to get us up and running and to really start 'turning the flywheel'.

Turning the flywheel.

Supporting network development with charters and frameworks

Elements of a network charter.

The LEAP team provided a template for networks to use to build a charter, leading them through such questions as:

- What's the purpose of the network?
- What are the key topics that need to be worked on?
- Who will take on the main roles?
- Do they have a plan to get going?
- What behaviours will they adopt?
- What do they want to do in those first 100 days, and what resources and support do they need?

Nic recalled the importance of the charter construction being collaborative.

'We'd lost them from the get-go!'

One of the networks we really struggled with had problems because the network lead created the charter himself in the meeting – the rest of the core team were looking around thinking 'So what am I doing here? This is not my network!' And that was it. We'd lost them from the get-go.

Measuring network development and maturity

Initially, the LEAP team focused on measuring what was measurable (predominantly lagging indicators), before moving on to using leading indicators from a maturity self-assessment.

Our first measure was quite basic in terms of numbers: how many people joined the network, how many of those people were contributing in terms of posting articles or asking questions or answering questions versus how many were visitors or surfers. We then moved onto think about discussion boards, how many discussions were kicked off and what were the response rates? How many will reply in a certain amount of time, how many were closed down and summarised in certain amount of time. We then introduced our wiki (MediaWiki) into the suite of knowledge assets and include wiki contributions in our measures. So how many wiki pages were created? What were the refresh rates? How many times were they looked at?

Once the network was up and running, we then started looking at a network maturity model. We initially ran that quarterly and went back to running it annually. We were using that as a common measure across all of the networks, and encouraged network leads to discuss their strengths, offers and needs with each other.

In addition to the maturity measurement and cross-network good practice sharing, the LEAP team set in place a recognition scheme for knowledge-sharing behaviours in the networks. Nic describes these as one of the biggest successes – one which is enduring.

Lagging and leading indicators for network capability.

The TREE awards – recognising the right behaviours

The TREE awards were inspired by a recognition programme in ConocoPhillips, namely the 4G awards: Give, Grab, Gather and Guts (courage to share failures). With the agricultural nature of Syngenta's business, the most natural translation of these awards was: Transfer, Reuse, Embed and (Share a difficult) Experience. Hence the TREE awards were born.

We wanted to encourage this continual sharing of knowledge, so we decided against an annual celebration. Once a quarter we'd have a look and people would submit their success stories aligned to their networks. The network core team would then decide which were bronze or silver.

We set up a senior governance group for the programme and this group would decide which of the silver TREEs should be elevated to gold recognition, using the following criteria: the power of the story, the degree to which it exemplified the category, and most importantly, the business impacts.

Criteria for TREE-winning stories.

We had glass trophies made for both silver and gold awards and had a tree laser-etched into the middle of the glass trophy. We were running the TREE awards probably two or three times a year initially, and have now reduced it to an annual scheme. It could be that in a given year we don't receive so many submissions of the right quality for 'experience' and therefore don't issue a gold 'experience' award. We didn't want to compromise on the quality of the submissions by forcing them. We felt if we actually lowered the 'pass mark', we were doing ourselves or our reputation a disservice. People loved having the awards on their desks – they became a focal point for discussions. We also worked with an external journalist to write the TREEs (silver and gold) as stories which would then be published on the intranet to widen the recognition to a bigger audience. People's names were mentioned and recognised, which was great for them (and a form of reward in its own way). It also publicised the programme; those who might not have heard about LEAP were now reading about TREEs and within minutes would be reading about LEAP.

LEAP radio

One of the members of the LEAP team had worked on local radio stations in the past and proposed the idea of a dedicated LEAP podcast.

> We had LEAP radio – essentially a podcast in which we were interviewing people who were experts in the company. Leaders, either direct leaders or people who are leading in their field – we spoke about what they were doing, what their insights were, what their experience told them about what they were doing and where we're going, and we captured them as a series of radio programmes or podcasts.

Connecting organisation learning and individual learning

With the 'L' in LEAP standing for Learning, Nic described what she called the 'learning suite' of activities within the programme.

Learning from leaders, leavers, experience and projects.

> I call it the learning suite; learning from leaders, learning from leavers, learning from experience and learning from projects. Those were the four primary things that we needed to make sure that we're learning from.
>
> LEAP radio was a way of learning from leaders. When we knew people were leaving the organisation, we would provide exit interviews with them to capture some knowledge and experience to populate the LEAP wiki.
>
> Learning from experience took the form of a workshop where an experienced person still with the company worked alongside some people who were new in that field. The process used was that the leader gave the new starters some scenarios and explained how and why they made decisions they did – it was a little like telling a story.
>
> The final piece was on the project learnings. We started work on how we manage our project portfolio and as part of that, how we ensure that whenever we have projects in Syngenta we're capturing the learning in a better way.

The LEAP programme (see Figure 18.1 opposite) was established to develop capability in the Production and Supply function of Syngenta. In order to complement the informal knowledge sharing and improvements arising from the networks, combining leading-edge external thinking, a formal relationship with INSEAD Business School was established, providing a Masters-level leadership development programme with an alumni network which integrated learning and insights back into the broader LEAP programme.

> We did a lot of work alongside INSEAD Business School to create an academy where we could start the 'up-skilling' of our emerging future leaders in Production and Supply. We put them into the academy to develop the capabilities and experience when it came to supply chain practices.

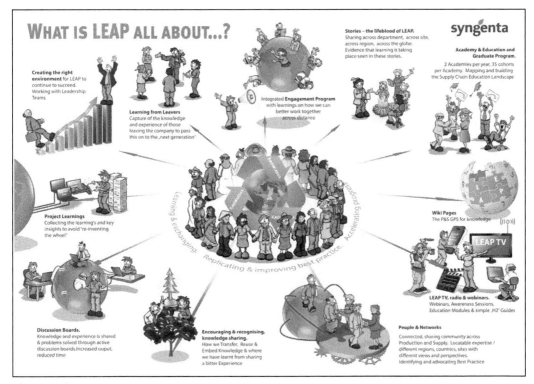

Figure 18.1 *Publicity poster explaining LEAP and its components*

Reflecting on challenges

As Nic looked back over the past nine years, and forward to the future, she reflected particularly on the challenge of renewal and retaining attention.

I think the biggest challenge has been to make sure that people don't think of what we're doing as last year's initiative. Our challenge is to keep the focus and attention on Knowledge Management. We've tried talking about LEAP version one, two, three – dealing with it a bit like a software release each year, to maintain attention.

We recently moved into Office365, which has actually given us a completely new-look environment. We're playing with the features which are new and will lead people back to us – that's been a stroke of luck for LEAP.

We just restructured the networks – so rather than looking at them in terms of the functions within production and supply, we have raised them up to a higher level, adopting the supply chain SCOR model approach: Develop, Make, Ship, etc. This has resulted in fewer networks, which are bigger in size than previously. We've tried to renew the look and feel of what we're doing – but ultimately it's still essentially about 'How do you network?', 'How do you collaborate?', 'How do you share?' And 'How do we capture, store and retain knowledge?'

'Our challenge is to keep the focus and attention on Knowledge Management.'

Mapping the story to the 'KM Chef's Canvas'

The three areas we chose to highlight from Syngenta's many strengths in people-oriented Knowledge Management are:

Culture

Syngenta pay particular attention to knowledge-sharing behaviours and have a very well established recognition scheme (the TREE awards) in place to acknowledge where the right behaviours have been demonstrated. The LEAP programme has been positioned as a cultural transformation programme, making use of established models of change management.

Roles

Roles for network leaders are well defined and supported with training programmes and maturity assessments. Sponsor, topic lead and core team roles are also fully documented.

Interaction and internalisation

The LEAP programme is rooted in the creation and support of collaborative networks, with direct encouragement to share knowledge through the TREE award recognition scheme. Expertise has been celebrated and shared through a series of webinars, under the brand of 'LEAP radio'.

19

Linklaters: knowledge, value-add and innovation

NARRATED BY RACHEL MANSER, GLOBAL HEAD OF KNOWLEDGE MANAGEMENT, AND IAN RODWELL, HEAD OF CLIENT KNOWLEDGE AND LEARNING, LINKLATERS

Number One, Silk Street, London. Sitting in the reception area of Linklaters' London headquarters, it's easy to reflect that the address describes the culture that lies within. Quiet quality and unhurried professionalism; receptionists whose quality of service would grace a top hotel. Rachel and Ian met me and took me from the sanctuary of the client entrance into the hustle and bustle of Silks Café, where knowledge and ideas are shared by employees and partners over coffee (and exceedingly good cakes). It was from here that first Rachel, and then Ian, shared the stories of their respective 15 and 26 years at Linklaters, and their work in the area of Knowledge Management.

> I'm a qualified lawyer who started out as a professional support lawyer (PSL) – that is to say, someone whose job was to ensure that a particular practice area (my world was competition law – or as the Americans call it, 'antitrust') was always at the cutting edge of the law. The investment that the firm makes in professional support lawyers ensures that we are safeguarding quality and driving efficiency through our practice areas. It would make no sense to have every single person following every piece of legislation – nobody would have the time.
>
> My role has included a collection of responsibilities – it included keeping our precedent documents up to date and acting as an in-house counsel for all of our lawyers and also our clients at times. Ultimately though, it's all down to quality, efficiency, mitigating risk.
>
> During my first ten years in the firm, I was always curious about how we could make our systems and processes better. I was particularly interested in the technology side and how to enable access to knowledge. I took the leap and moved sideways into the Knowledge Management team, first for the UK region and then eventually the firm globally.

'Ultimately though, it's all down to quality, efficioncy, mitigating risk.'

Rachel was quick to acknowledge that in taking her sideways move, she was stepping into an existing legacy of Knowledge Management activity, although it was not always labelled as such.

Knowledge Management started off in a very traditional 'let's get our documents in order' way. Over the past five years there has been a sea-change, particularly in terms of using technology to make us much more effective in enabling us to leverage our collective global knowledge for our clients.

That said, Knowledge Management is still a phrase we don't use very often.

'We have always tried to put things into layman's terms.'

We have always tried to put things into layman's terms, so it's simply about quality, efficiency and mitigating risk.

For Ian, the journey from information, to knowledge, to learning started when he joined the firm's real estate practice.

Knowledge is at the heart of business for a law firm – clients are buying knowledge. It usually leaves the organisation in the form of documents – it's the lifeblood of the organisation.

The simplest form of KM is to just ask someone! When law firms began to get over a particular size, it became not so easy – so KM became about putting people in touch with the right person or document – to stop reinventing the wheel.

It's far more effective and efficient not to start with a blank sheet of paper, but to have an existing precedent, checklist or template which represents the firm's views, experience and insights on a particular issue. In many ways, these precedents are the firm's crown jewels.

'In many ways, these precedents are the firm's crown jewels.'

We also realised was that there was a lot of other particularly valuable material that was created during the course of working with clients that would be useful to others. It could be a note of research, a letter of advice; a particular set of drafting that may not be included in our precedents or it might be training materials. It was a case of identifying the knowledge content, then adding metadata to it, so that others could then retrieve it.

Ian went on to describe the importance of aggregating and curating vast numbers of documents which are generated on client matters.

Navigating 90 million documents to get to the heart of the organisation.

I think we have something like 90 million documents in our document management system. Much of that will be repetitive content which may not have unique enduring knowledge value; hence having a curated 'body of knowledge' is absolutely key.

Over time we have built playbooks for what should be done in particular circumstances – so our precedents are supplemented by checklists to cover particular contexts and situations. In some practices, these have spun out into in-house textbooks or manuals. And, in many ways, those form the knowledge heart of the organisation.

Shaping Knowledge Management in the Linklaters culture

Ian continued to describe the culture at Linklaters, the intensity of the work and the challenges of creating consistency in a partner-based firm.

Whether it's a law firm or whether it's an in-house legal team, the greeting in the lift is always a question: 'Busy?' – to which there's only one answer! If people are working on a critical deal, you'll sometimes hear 'I left the office at 3:00 in the morning and had to be back at 7.00'.

The key issue is time, because in an industry where you measure your minutes of chargeable time, it is a challenge to make time for doing something such as knowledge sharing which is non-chargeable. There are also other self-imposed barriers to knowledge sharing; people might pre-judge and think 'What I've produced may be too general or it could be too specific to be of use to anyone'. Alternatively, they might think 'If I put it into the public domain then I'm open to criticism.'

Lawyers are inherently competitive – and often competitive against themselves as individuals – they are so driven. One of the things we often talk about is the lawyers' mindset: perfectionist high achievers. You've got people who are deeply driven to succeed: ambitious, incredibly hard-working, fiercely intelligent, but at the same time they can be ultra-self-critical. 'The excellent is often enemy of the good' – you can become obsessed with perfection rather than creating something that is pragmatically good enough to succeed.

Finally, one of the challenges of a partnership-based firm, with over 400 partners, who all own the business, is that you tend to see a lot of local initiatives and local governance. What we have increasingly done over the years is to try and bring more consistency and co-ordination to what people do.

> 'The greeting in the lift is always "Busy?" – to which there's only one answer!'

> Internal dialogues which limit knowledge sharing.

> The lawyers' mindset: perfectionist high-achievers.

> Bringing consistency and co-ordination to local initiatives.

Rachel described the opportunities, challenges and tactics for her approach to growing the KM capability and capacity in the firm.

We're a knowledge business. We have a huge amount of knowledge that is generated on a day-to-day basis. The key is actually identifying it and then tapping into it and then crucially helping people reuse it.

The first project we did was to actually redo the intranet and search systems and that was really wanting people to be able to find information and to connect, to collaborate. It's the basics; back to that simplicity of lawyer language. 'We want you to find what you need; to tap into the global brain and to really deliver excellence to clients.'

Our role is not to fix what isn't broken. It's to help our senior champions – we call them 'knowledge and learning partners', and our professional support lawyers who are working in each practice area to capitalise on the inherent culture of wanting to help colleagues. We tap into that to encourage knowledge sharing. We also use these champions to get engagement and buy-in for global systems and problems, often by seeding ideas in their weekly team meetings.

We use those sessions to push out things that are going on globally, but we've got to be quite careful, because we don't want to come in

> 'We want you to find what you need to tap into global brain and look good in front of clients.'

> 'Our role is not to fix what isn't broken!'

Balancing global
consistency with local
needs.

and say: 'The centre says you must do this', since you know that in this culture that would fail immediately. It needs to be put in the context of each part of the business, because law is different depending on whether, for example, you're talking to a corporate lawyer in Germany or a finance lawyer in Lisbon or Tokyo.

As mentioned, Knowledge Management activities in law firms often lean towards documented 'explicit' knowledge, in the form of precedents and the underlying information architecture. Rachel felt that a balance between managing explicit and sharing implicit knowledge was most effective – collections and connections.

Balancing collections
and connections.

'Ensuring the culture that
we have is maintained
and gently pushed
along.'

It's far easier to deal with the former. It's very easy to put a technology programme in place – we have a multi-year programme to do that. In terms of connecting people – whilst you can do that with technology (for example, searching for people via metadata), a lot of our learning work is actually about bringing people together. It's about fostering the really good knowledge exchange that is happening in every practice area. It's the subconscious things – ensuring that the culture that we have is maintained and just gently pushed along.

For example, a key thing is making sure that the connections are built early – we deliberately get our junior lawyers together on a global basis. Wherever you are in the world, you all come together in the early days as you start to build those friendships and connections – we call this the New Lawyer Programme. It's a very informal programme, but to me the biggest benefit you get is you're laying those foundations of connection. The same happens on a practice-by-practice basis. This is something important which has naturally evolved; one of those things to gently push along.

Gaining the benefits of a standard approach

Rachel has described how she is pursuing a culture where knowledge flows as naturally as possible; recognising that is only healthy to control a certain amount of the activity.

'"Simple and useful" are
our design principles.'

There are a lot of things that we can do from a central perspective. All of the technologies that we use – we have spent a lot of time and effort making sure that those are useful and lawyer-friendly. 'Simple and useful' are our design principles. The whole point is about enabling access to our collective wisdom across the firm through a standard approach, but then enabling as much flexibility as possible; same tools, same basis but relevant to a particular practice area. We can also control standard information processes, the resources we procure, and have standard career paths around the world.

Roles underpinning Knowledge Management and learning: knowledge and learning partners and professional support lawyers

Ian described the role of 'knowledge and learning partners' within each of the practice areas who take responsibility for governing and championing knowledge activities.

Standardisation with flexibility.

> In a way, they're our key communication channel – because the most effective communication is always partner-to-partner. We encourage them to talk to other partners about what we're doing in the knowledge and learning world. They also have some responsibility for professional support lawyers, who are a key part of the knowledge structure within law firms.

Partners as champions for knowledge and learning.

Linklaters employs around 100 professional support lawyers (PSLs) around the world. Ian describes them as 'the kind of people who make things happen'.

> Typically, what they will be doing is drafting and updating the precedents; producing current awareness; charting regulatory and legal change; and feeding that back to ensure our lawyers are kept up to speed with what's happening. They will usually be responsible for designing and delivering local legal training. Every time we have a new intake of lawyers or a group of qualifying lawyers, substantial training programmes are needed.
> Most groups have weekly meetings and these usually include a knowledge slot where the PSL will provide updates. For example, they might talk about a particular legal development: to remind you that 'this case has just been reported on' or 'a reminder that we're expecting this to come into force this week', etc. PSLs are like the Special Forces crack units of the knowledge and learning world.

'PSLs are like the Special Forces crack units of the knowledge and learning world!'

Networks and gangs

Groups and networks form an important part of the professional development of lawyers in Linklaters. These rely on face-to-face and virtual connections around complex legal matters, with all lawyers equipped with laptops or tablets for video conferencing.

> As a lawyer, when you start, you immediately become part of a 'gang', because you're in a cohort of around 40 people. These become an incredibly intense set of relationships which people often stick with throughout their lives in the firm. You also have your practice areas 'gang' with whom you become very close, given the intense nature of the work.
> The weekly meetings are a forum for knowledge exchange. There is also a formal training programme and the groups go away together once a year, where we see a lot of cementing of people-to-people relationships. When you look to the future, where real estate costs may

'When you start, you immediately become part of a "gang".'

Protecting the culture whilst shifting towards virtual working.

mean that people work increasingly in a more agile way – we will need to think carefully about how we maintain this fantastic culture of trust which underpins knowledge sharing.

From Knowledge Management to innovation

Rachel sees a natural pathway from focusing on knowledge to identifying good examples of where innovation is coming into the firm, and where opportunities exist to amplify or connect ideas from lawyers and clients.

Amplifying and connecting ideas from lawyers and clients.

> There are huge amounts of pressure on cost from clients, changes to technology, new forms of competition and changing expectations. You pull all that together and you can see that this an industry which is ripe for innovation. The fact is that we are already far more innovative than we think. The KM challenge is joining it up. It's a natural segue from the world of knowledge – it's all about transferring what we know and make, and thinking about how to monetise it.

Automating precedent documents for client.

> For example, automation is a hot topic in innovation, whereas we have been automating documents for over a decade; we actually started by doing it for clients.
>
> Innovation is about helping the firm think differently. We spent a lot of time thinking about what the definition might be – but simple is best! It's about enabling people to challenge the present and shape the future; so much of it is actually about empowerment. It's about being a catalyst, and saying 'We as a firm need to think differently and we need to encourage ideas'. We think that a lot of these ideas will come from our people – particularly the ones on the front line. We also need to look outwards to other industries and we do that actively.

Innovation is about helping the firm to think differently.

> However, none of that is very useful unless you can translate it into practical action to address some of the major issues facing the firm. Lastly, all of that is for nothing if you don't shout about it. If a great idea happened in Moscow, we want to make sure that's being looked at in Düsseldorf, New York or Seoul!

Think.
Do.
Shout.

> It's about thinking, about doing, about shouting – hence Think, Do, Shout (Figure 19.1 opposite) became the three pillars of our innovation programme. I sometimes think, is this almost too simple for Linklaters? But it really resonates.

A sandbox for innovative ideas.

Linklaters organises programmes of work underneath each of these three pillars with support from the innovation lab – which incorporates a 'sandbox' for trying ideas.

> The innovation lab started off being more virtual. Then we realised people would like to have a place where they could come and collaborate and think differently. We have an area in the London office for this. It's a place which is different, where you can draw on the walls and where you are encouraged to think in a different way.

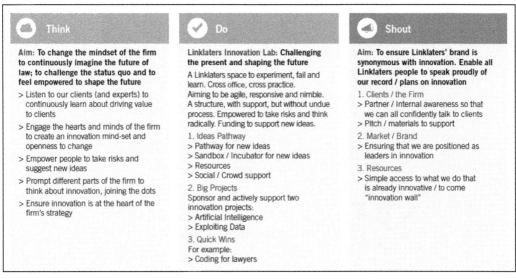

Figure 19.1 *Think, Do, Shout at Linklaters*

We have an 'ideas pathway', so that when people are thinking of ideas they can add them to our online ideas pathway – the whole firm can access it and can then 'like' and rank ideas up and down. Lots of these ideas that are coming through can be signposted to relevant people who can help them. Sometimes we just need to connect dots, but where there are genuinely new ideas, we prioritise and move them forward.

Democratic ranking and voting on ideas.

We then give the idea some funding or a bit of project management support from the team – whatever they need to help them. But we try not to say 'Give it to us and we'll do it.' You want people to feel empowered to process their ideas themselves and then you get a better chance that they will become embedded.

The importance of empowerment.

The 'coding for lawyers' idea

One example of an idea from the innovation process was 'coding for lawyers'. This idea has enhanced Linklaters' capability to embrace artificial intelligence by providing the training necessary to build bridges of understanding between lawyers and technology innovators. Rachel explains how it came about:

In one of our first meetings, we brought in some junior lawyers to meet with me and three other partners. In our first meeting we said 'Let's just listen, just listen to our juniors'. One of the first-year trainees asked 'Why don't you teach coding for lawyers?', and it was such a simple thing and because we have this innovation infrastructure in place, we felt 'Absolutely, why don't we just do it?'

Coding is actually not far removed from the legal thought process because it's all about logic and problem solving. We can all see that technology is going to have huge implications for the world of law. What we're not doing is trying to teach people to become coders and stop being lawyers; it's more about learning a language and understanding. We're giving them enough knowledge to be able to say 'OK, I can look at my problem in a new way and I can explain to you, a qualified coder, this is what I'm trying to do'. We're trying to create lawyers with a sprinkling of technology to bridge the gap with technologists who have a sprinkling of law. The more we can do to prepare a workforce for their own personal development and for the benefit of the firm, the better. In terms of recruitment, this sends a very strong to message to the market that we invest in people.

From internal to external: delivering Knowledge Management services to clients

As Linklaters' reputation for Knowledge Management has grown, Ian's role has evolved into one of a provider of services and consultancy to clients.

Knowledge services adding value to client proposals.

What we've seen increasingly over time is clients asking for guidance on their own knowledge systems. We've also had clients asking partners 'One of the things that we are trying to do is to get better at how we share knowledge – is there anybody that we can speak to in your team?'

What I do now is work mostly with external clients on a range of non-legal requests. These are mostly training-related but I also get drawn into conversations about how they can share knowledge more effectively or collaborate better – or I'm a conduit to colleagues with particular technical expertise. On occasion, we have given more strategic guidance and even seconded some of our people on short-term assignments.

Reflections on past and current challenges and memorable moments

Rachel contemplated the current challenges to the knowledge, learning and innovation agenda in Linklaters, with a particular emphasis on the 'problem' of satisfied customers:

We just had a global engagement survey where one measure was: 'I can find the knowledge and information that will help me do my job'. We had more than 94% positive responses.

There is a risk that people somehow feel it's no longer their responsibility.

However, I think a challenge is that because we have such good Knowledge Management globally, there is a risk that people somehow feel that it's no longer their responsibility to contribute. So it's about making sure that we keep going out with that message that this will only work if we keep investing in the culture of knowledge sharing as part of the responsibility to the broader firm (and our clients).

Looking back over her time leading knowledge and learning at Linklaters, Rachel reflected on the volume and complexity of activities to keep in alignment.

> Knowledge and learning (K&L) is a huge collection of so many different disciplines. It stretches all the way from formal information, data, research, learning in the classroom to very funky interactive worlds. Being able to pull all that together working as a global team of over 300 people directly involved in K&L, so that we have a common a sense of priorities, is a challenge. It is very much achieving a balance of a vision and sense of direction, with the freedom and empowerment to align to the context of the office or practice. That's been my approach, as someone who has been in the centre a long time.

Characteristically, Ian's final reflection was a benefits story which summarised the personal impact of Knowledge Management for one of his colleagues.

> Twelve years ago, we launched a new knowledge system, and shortly afterwards one of the lawyers that I knew came down to see us.
> 'This is just brilliant', she said. 'I was here at 2:00 in the morning and I needed to write a note on the difference between 'best endeavours' and 'reasonable endeavours'. I just put it into the system and answers came up straight away. I found all these other examples that people had written and I was able to go home!'

Mapping the story to the 'KM Chef's Canvas'
Culture

The KM programme is fully embedded in the team processes of Linklaters, and the team, as former lawyers, are fully empathetic to the specific culture and pressures facing their colleagues. They spoke openly about the 'lawyers' mindset' and the challenges of competitiveness and perfectionism. KM has now bridged naturally towards supporting Innovation in the firm.

Roles

The KM programme benefits greatly from the global presence of senior 'knowledge and learning partners' at strategic levels in the firm and the large team of professional support lawyers providing knowledge updates to legal teams. KM roles and responsibilities now have an external client-facing dimension, with KM capability recognised as value-added service.

Codification and curation

Critical legal knowledge is updated through professional support lawyers, and precedent documents are highly prized and described as the 'firm's crown jewels'. Access to information is supported through a document management system containing 90 million documents and a professionally resourced library.

20

Defence Science & Technology Laboratory (Dstl), UK: guarding against organisational amnesia

NARRATED BY DR DOMINIC DAVIES, TECHNICAL FELLOW, KNOWLEDGE MANAGEMENT SYSTEMS, DEFENCE SCIENCE & TECHNOLOGY LABORATORY (DSTL), UK

Dominic (Dom), a chemist by training, is a senior public-sector Knowledge and Information Management (KIM) veteran:

> I have been working in the field of Knowledge and Information Management (KIM) within Dstl for the last 17 years. I have had roles ranging from supporting research projects, through management, to now being responsible for improving the way we manage and exploit knowledge and information throughout our organisation.

Dstl believes that effective KIM requires infrastructure, both physical and electronic. This goes beyond IT and libraries, to include spaces for people to interact, such as coffee rooms or break-out areas.

Dom is based at one of the three core Dstl sites. He and his team of two work in an open-plan environment with fully flexible desking. Personal wallpapers on laptops and crates for keeping day-to-day equipment are the ways of personalising their workspace.

In the office Dom is based in there are at least three different styles of workstation, with many awards and mementos of visitors and foreign visits in glass cabinets around the office. There is a massive picture of Stonehenge that brightens up the environment and acts as a piece of acoustic art which reduces disturbing noise in the building.

The office space is quite light and airy with windows on three sides and a two-storey atrium in the middle.

The challenge

Dstl is an executive agency of the UK Ministry of Defence. They deliver science and technology (S&T) research and advice to the Ministry of Defence and other parts of government. Much of the research and advice they deliver is supported through contracted work with academia and industry.

As an S&T organisation, our main asset is knowledge and information. We need to have high levels of current awareness of the state of S&T in our research areas. We need to avoid repetition of work which has already been carried out, by us or any other organisation, and we must record what is learnt in our work to ensure it is available in the future. This is not just about what was done in the last couple of years; often we find ourselves having to refer to work which was carried out 30 or more years ago when it suddenly becomes relevant again.

There is no expiry date on Science & Technology (S&T) research.

As one of many examples, Dom cites a decision to purchase fighter aircraft for the Ministry of Defence's aircraft carriers that necessitated looking at information dating back 70 years and dealing with insurgents in Iraq and Afghanistan:

Centaur and Audacious class carriers from the end of WWII were the last CATOBAR carriers. CATOBAR, Catapult Assisted Take-Off Barrier Assisted Recovery, is a system used for the launch and recovery of aircraft from the deck of an aircraft carrier. Much information relating to CATOBAR would be this old. When we were deciding which F35 (Lightning II) variant to buy for our aircraft carrier we suddenly had a potential need to understand CATOBAR again.

The threat we had in Iraq was incredibly high-tech and it was very much what our systems had been built to counter. The threat we hit in Afghanistan was low-tech and the sort of work we've done looking at this sort of low-tech threats was very old. We had to ensure we were re-using this work rather than trying to regenerate it. This is what I mean by S&T not having a particular lifespan, because that work was not recent, probably about 30 years old, if not more in places.

A lot of very clever computer scientists are frustrated by the rate of delivery and the limitations of what can be achieved on corporate systems compared to their research environments. Dstl people are good at discussing their work in person and on IT platforms, but need to get better at capturing and storing the outcomes and content of these discussions or presentations, etc., as they contain so much knowledge which only exists in people's heads. Hence capturing tacit knowledge is a challenge. The decreasing budget for defence research post-Cold War means that Dstl faces a 'retirement cliff-edge' as many of its subject-matter experts approach retirement age.

'. . . you put two scientists in a room and tell them to start talking and more often than not they actually will start talking and start realising there are not necessarily synergies but there are links where you have knowledge relevant to what that person is trying to do, even if it's just informative rather than innovative.'

The positive aspects of Dstl's culture is that they have many scientists and engineers who love talking to one another about their work. In the last detailed benchmarking exercise, Dstl identified that the culture for knowledge sharing was good but slightly 'stove-piped' and not well supported by technology.

Striving to prevent organisational amnesia

Dstl started taking KM seriously about 18 years ago through the formation of the Knowledge Agent Team, who delivered direct KIM support to the research programme. Since that time a gradually increasing importance has been given to efficient and effective KIM across the lab and in strategies.

There is recognition that knowledge and information management is important to the organisation, with two strategic actions in Dstl's recent corporate strategy and a high-level, broad overarching policy for knowledge and information management. Processes are documented for those information and Knowledge Management activities which are suited to process. The strategy has two clear strategic objectives around knowledge sharing and improving KM engagement tools and processes. Dstl is defining specific activities which will go to contributing towards delivery of that strategy. Dom expands on how this came about:

> It's hard to identify a single issue or event which focused the need to improve KIM. A generally increasing groundswell of unhappiness with the current situation played more of a part. People find it difficult to retrieve information they know exists; they cannot access the expertise they need; and so on. I suppose the starting point came after the last comprehensive benchmarking which led to deployment of a 'social' business collaboration capability and a semantic wiki capability.
>
> These two capabilities raised the profile of KIM activity in Dstl and set the tone for actively bridging the gap between software delivery and its being used as a part of a KIM tool set. They raised the profile of KIM significantly and gave us the opportunity to have engagement in other areas.
>
> They also highlighted the challenge of information management (IM) in the organisation. Since IM is foundational for KM we decided to take the opportunity to improve the underpinning IM capability to support KM activity whilst continuing to improve the more human aspects of KM.
>
> In my area of responsibility, we do not deliver or own IT – that is Knowledge Information Services (KIS) and the Chief Information Officer's role. We exploit what KIS deliver, but work with them to influence the future strategy, taking in to account KM; increasingly it is more common that the platform is delivered and managed by our IT service provider but the day-to-day running and governance falls to us. Fortunately, the KIS team understand the importance of KM to the organisation.

The overall aim of Dstl's KIM programme is to prevent organisational amnesia, to avoid repeating work which they, or others, have already done and to ensure that all advice given is based on solid foundations. With a need to access information often decades old, Dstl needs to be confident about information authenticity to counter the risk that inaccurate or incomplete information be taken as authoritative.

Dom has a clear view on how to differentiate between knowledge and information:

> We have developed a simple and easy-to-use differentiation: information is or can be a physical or electronic thing, a report, a video file, etc., whereas knowledge is a personal thing and always resides in an individual; it brings together disparate information sources, often through an experienced and knowledgeable individual.

Dstl is striving to improve the use of current systems and tools whilst concentrating technology on automating some activity to reduce the burden on the individual. It has had a strong focus on ensuring Information Management delivers trusted information stores and quality search, and makes efficient use of their storage estate.

Developing a knowledge ecosystem

Knowledge Management is seen to be an ecosystem, rather than a process, because content doesn't move from one Knowledge Management tool to the next in a linear fashion. Instead, different kinds of data, information or knowledge will be best suited to different niches. Despite the technological prowess of staff in Dstl, the most critical component in the knowledge ecosystem Dstl is developing is *people.*

Dstl uses a range of different IT platforms and services to support the activities and techniques it deploys. The term 'ecosystem' was chosen to reflect the way knowledge tools co-exist and interact in a dynamic way. There are three aspects analogous to an ecosystem. Dom describes them:

The knowledge ecosystem: co-existent, co-dependent and co-evolutionary.

Co-existent: The flow of knowledge in Dstl, the sharing, storing and exploitation, forms a complex system of interacting elements. While they may sometimes appear to be competing for our attention, they have the shared purpose of getting the right knowledge to the people who need it, when they need it, so that we can all do our best work.

Co-dependent: The different strengths and limitations of the elements mean that no one element of the ecosystem dominates; we need all of them to make sure the flow of knowledge is uninterrupted. Some are good for identifying what knowledge gaps you may have, while others are better used as repositories for our collective knowledge. The elements depend upon each other for knowledge – knowledge generated in one system may flow into another for storage. Yet another element may draw upon that knowledge to support discussion or the generation of new ideas.

Co-evolutionary: Because the elements are co-dependent, they evolve together. If we change the way we use one element, either by adding functionality or finding something new we can do with it, we'll see a change in the way the other elements are used. Sometimes an element may be used in a way that was not originally anticipated as those interacting with this element find a novel application. This creates emergent behaviours in the ecosystem.

Curating and finding salient knowledge, information and expertise

For a science and technology organisation, access to the academic and industrial literature is critical. Dstl spends about £1.5 million on this each year. They use a federated search service to enable as much of this content as possible to be accessed from one search engine. There is a small physical library service, which holds the key S&T reference books that are not available electronically, together with training material and military history books.

The MOD Chief Scientific Advisor's reports collection is curated under the Athena service. It is a record of defence research and reference material dating back over 100 years and containing around 750,000 items. This collection has been invaluable in the past, as it has been the only remaining source of information which, though over 40 years old, was suddenly needed again to support urgent operational requirements.

Distillery and CatalyST are Dstl's enterprise social media platforms. Distillery is the internal platform and CatalyST is outward-facing for collaboration with academia and industry and other external partners. Engagement with Distillery is very high and the platform is used for an extensive range of purposes. One of the most successful use-cases has been the rapid identification of knowledge and expertise within the organisation. Dom explains more:

'If you try and delete Distillery, I'll chain myself to the data centre.' A scientist who is an active user of Distillery.

> In one case, an answer was needed to a question by 2 p.m. in the afternoon. The initial post at 7 a.m. had been answered with academic and defence literature reports relevant to the question by 9.30 a.m. By 11 a.m. a range of subject-matter experts in Dstl had been put in contact with the person who posted the question and by 12.00 the person was confident they had all the information they required and two hours to write up the answer. This could not have been achieved at this speed before we had this capability.

CatalyST has the same functionality as Distillery, but due to the need to control intellectual property and security on the platform, it is not as open to the organisation as Distillery. However, the functionality is delivering significant improvements to the ease with which Dstl collaborates with suppliers in academia and industry. As the platform is available via the internet, for authorised users, it is allowing secure

Creating an effective information architecture to enable assisted search.

People deploy a search engine thinking it's a piece of technology which once you've installed it, is there. You also need to have a look at optimising the information architecture so the search can work better; they look at best bets – they don't look at the failed search statistics

and efficient collaboration with partners who previously would be contacted via e-mail, telephone and post.

WIkiD (semantic media wiki) acts as the central searchable hub allowing Dstl to link information assets, people, activities and organisational constructs.

Figure 20.1 illustrates the importance Dstl places on creating the right structure to identify and manage its information. Dom describes it:

We have categorised our information into four types: technical information (our lifeblood); project information (the way we deliver most of our work); organisational information (how we run our business); and personal information (stuff which our people keep to manage their own development and because it is of interest to them).

We have created places for each type of information to be stored in. There are more detailed filing structures within each area, but as long as it is in the right place we can understand how long it must be kept for, or if we need to keep it beyond the normal retention schedule because it has enduring scientific and technical value. It also allows us to set up our search in such a way that you can choose just to search in the right area of the storage estate.

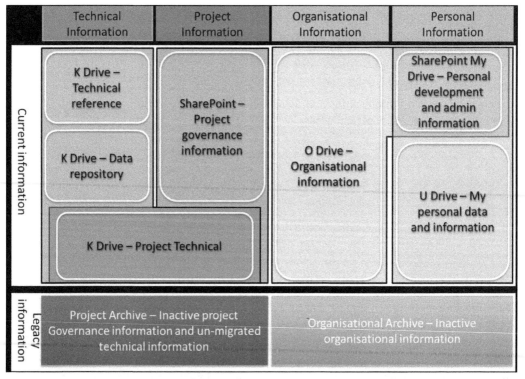

Figure 20.1 *Dstl's information management structure*

This structure means that as long as it is in the right place at the top level any mistakes in the lower levels will not result in information being lost to the search functionality.

Search improvement features prominently in Dstl's KIM programme. By optimising the information architecture so that it is categorised by purpose (see above), it enables a clean search scope and delivery of better search results for researchers.

Preventing future knowledge loss

A change in the financial climate for defence, post-Cold War, combined with a large number of long-serving staff aged 55 or over who will retire in the next decade or sooner, presents a significant challenge to Dstl. Dom cites one such example:

> There are a lot of good people in the personal protection area, trying to make sure we don't lose a huge amount of accumulated knowledge and expertise. They are trying to understand how decisions were made, to better understand why we have the sort of personal protective equipment we do.

'If you add up what 50 years' worth of defence research spending was, you're talking about a catalogue which represents many billions of pounds' worth of government expenditure.'

This effort is being driven by one of Dstl's Knowledge Advocates and is supported by the KIM team, who have adapted the process that has been developed by others and created a cadre of people trained to facilitate knowledge-capture interviews and help equip others to do so as well.

Dstl is working on stop-gap measures such as knowledge capture and 'talking head' sessions to prevent knowledge loss. But another part of its efforts is focused on removing single points of failure by making knowledge and information more accessible to all.

The Athena Collection is where authoritative technical material of enduring value should be held. Unreviewed information is more suited to the technical reference libraries and the data repository.

> At the core, information management, information technology solution level, it's about really getting to grips with how we organise our technical information and making sure that we have technical reference libraries.
>
> The researchers can actually build a technical reference collection which will ensure, in the terrible situation that we lose a number of staff at little or no notice, that they've at least left behind a reference collection.

Reflections
On the interface between KIM Services and IT

S&T is much more than the experiments of laboratory scientists; it encompasses equipment design and use, human factors and operational research, ranging from tactics right up to war gaming. Each of these areas generates a broad range of information and knowledge. The role of the KM team is to support innovation. Dom explains:

We have used Web 2.0 business collaboration technologies and wikis to support change. Make your tools easy to use and avoid over-reliance on one platform.

There's a lot of interest in understanding how our information and knowledge activities link together. When you look at the wiki capability, we are starting to link things which are not necessarily expected to be together. We register technical assets before we put them on the long-term S&T storage system and we link those technical libraries to projects and capabilities or to personal innovation projects.

A lot of this is being driven by people working on innovative ideas because it supports their ability to do the visualisations and analysis of the information we hold.

On technology and equipping people to use it

The technologies you deploy to support your KIM activities must be fit for purpose and as easy to use as possible; they need to add value and not be a hindrance to the user. We have moved away from bespoke and heavily customised IT solutions based predominantly on one or two key platforms and now we use a range of commercial off-the-shelf and open source tools which are as out-of-the-box as possible. Open standards and application programming interfaces allow these platforms to interact cleanly, in many cases.

Though one tool might be able to do it all, the user experience is often poor, which decreases user engagement, and there are risks to becoming utterly reliant on one platform, both in terms of what happens if it falls over and how easy it is to understand where each activity should take place.

There will always be people who need support.

People can understand what they should do but be unable to actually do it, hence training and guidance material is needed to develop individual competence. It is a big mistake to assume that, if it is obvious and easy to you, it will be the same to everyone else. No matter how simple you think your concepts are or your user interface is, there will always be people who need support. Training is not, however, limited to the use of IT; all the human-centric K&I tools and methods also need competent people to deliver them; this is a whole different set of skills from those required to use an IT system.

Even once you have easy-to-use IT and competent staff you are not there yet. These people might know what to do and how to do it but you need to ensure that there is time in their day to do it and that it is in their interest to do it. Policy and process only get people to do what you tell them to, not to do it well.

Giving good K&I behaviours the right level of recognition and reward is more likely to influence someone to use the infrastructure and tools you provide them with.

On culture and transforming attitudes

Organisational culture or behaviour is key to KIM. You need an organisation which believes that K&I is a valuable asset. You need this culture to be strong and visible so that new starters are rapidly inculcated into it and for it to be culturally unacceptable to fail to manage and share your knowledge and information as widely as possible. This culture will only really exist in an organisation which has people who exhibit the right behaviours, who are competent to perform the activities and are supported with the right infrastructure.

On measurement, governance and monitoring

Our plan is documented and published; progress is reported through the organisation and discussed on Distillery. IM is well documented and specific processes are being documented but there is no single KM process, just high-level KM and IM policies. For instance, there is detailed guidance on how the shared drive should be used to store technical information, but there is only guidance on how to make best use of a community to steward capability.

We have quantitative metrics of activity for most platforms and systems. Narrative feedback gives qualitative measures. Rarely can you identify how much money or time was saved by something but occasionally you do get this level of detail.

Top-level support and the directive to improve doesn't make the chair any more comfortable to sit in but at least it gives you a peg to hang the hat on and the possibility of support and funding for the things you are trying to achieve.

On the skills and behaviours a KIM professional needs

Patience – nothing moves as fast as you would like.

Perseverance – everything is harder than you would expect or people are less engaged with it than you might like.

Presence – you need to influence a lot of people in person. When you are trying to change an organisation or system or individual process you need to be seen to be a person, not a distant role sending out orders from afar.

On the importance of finding a transformational tool

I probably was not as in favour of the idea of the wiki and social business platforms as I should have been. If I knew then what I know now, I would have been much keener that we actually did it. I was probably more focused on 'Let's get the underpinning IM sorted', and I think I was probably wrong. The guy who drove the two platforms forward was probably right, because they changed people's perceptions and opened an avenue for conversation which we didn't have before. So even though they weren't solving the sort of big underpinning information problem, I think they were transformational.

On the future

Dstl have made great use of internal social media and encouraged social interaction with informal initiatives such as 'Three Word Thursday', where they get people to describe an event in just three words. Here's an abridged version of one such interaction.

Have a thick skin, people won't always like what you need them to do and often no news is good news.

The crux of it is that by 'playing games' on our social platform we actually made people learn how to use the interface by stealth and acclimatised people to the idea that it was an open and authentic forum. In one example, people were asked to describe their biggest mistake in three words. People were very forthcoming about some of their foolish mistakes and it was all done in a very friendly and amusing way.

Dom recognises there is more to do:

There's a whole load of activities we do; we have a new starters' programme within the organisation and we have a lot of lunchtime seminars and talks which are organised on subjects of interest. I think we need to get better about using multimedia to actually make those something which can hit a wider audience than just the people who turn up on the day.

I'm very interested in what could actually be done with the reports catalogue. When you look at it as a very large information repository of free text it is an amazing resource to have. I'm interested in what could be done with it with AI and machine learning and a lot of the other advanced information system techniques.

Mapping the story to the 'KM Chef's Canvas'

Dstl is unique among the KM programmes we have looked at in recognising so vividly that the past informs the future. They don't know what they will need to know so they have focused on developing an effective information architecture to optimise search, while concurrently using social and Web 2.0 collaboration tools to drive dialogue and find expertise.

Technology and infrastructure

The development of a knowledge ecosystem underpinned by an information architecture designed to augment search is at the core of Dstl's efforts to provide scientists with access to relevant content. We found it compelling that Dstl has defined four information types and makes clear the distinction between knowledge and information.

Interaction and internalisation

Dstl is using social enterprise tools (Distillery, CatalyST and wiki) effectively to encourage collaboration and share knowledge. It has helped generate new conversations and locate expertise which previously had been opaque to all but those working in close proximity.

Support

With a complex architecture to navigate it is important that people who access it are fully trained and supported. Dstl have thought of that. A set of how-to guides and induction support programmes helps people to make best use of the extensive tool set.

21

Financial Conduct Authority (FCA), UK: using knowledge to improve detection

NARRATED BY CHRISTINE ASTANIOU, KM LEAD, ENFORCEMENT
AND MARKET OVERSIGHT DIVISION, FCA, UK

> We are knowledge technicians and my job is to ensure that knowledge
> is flowing – that people have got the skills, knowledge and behaviours
> they need to conduct our work effectively, efficiently and consistently.

This is how Christine describes her role. She (and the FCA) are situated
on the edge of what was the venue for the 2012 London Olympic
Games. Her fifth-floor office view, located in a gleaming new building
adjacent to the Olympic Park, takes in the Aquatic Centre and the
Olympic Stadium, now home to West Ham United Football Club.

A glance around the open-plan office reveals two screens, a glass of
water, but little paper, as FCA move to a paperless environment and
an agile mode of working. A laptop is her sole personal possession.

> Wherever we go in the building, we've got full access to Wi-Fi and
> everyone's got Skype for business, so we can work really effectively and
> pull things up in meetings. I'm doing a presentation later which should
> have about 40 people dialling in from home and around the building,
> including from the bank of desks behind me. I'll be sharing slides on the
> screen and doing an online demo on the screen as well.

Christine, who has a legal background, was recruited five years ago to
FCA's Enforcement and Market Oversight Division to do a 'professional
support lawyer' role common in law firms. She takes up the story:

> When I got here I realised they didn't need me to keep up to date with
> legislation and summarise the latest case law, they needed someone to
> embed positive knowledge-sharing behaviours, effect mindset and
> behavioural change and develop a Knowledge Management strategy. I
> quickly adapted, as having been recruited to do one thing I realised that
> what they needed was quite different.

The challenge

When Christine arrived, the FCA was a relatively new organisation, established April 2013 after a restructuring of the UK regulatory environment. As the regulator of the financial services industry in the UK, it aims 'to make markets work well – for individuals, for business, large and small, and for the economy as a whole'.

Its importance to the UK economy cannot be overestimated: UK financial services employ over 2.2 million people and contribute £65.6 billion in tax. If UK markets work well, competitively and fairly they benefit consumers and firms, and maintain public confidence in the UK as a major global financial hub.

Since many of the 76,000 financial services firms it has oversight for work across international borders, the FCA maintains regular dialogue with other international regulators and helps shape legislation in the financial services industry.

> There are three drivers for developing a KM strategy:
>
> First of all, the work we do is really important. In my area, we investigate misconduct in the industry, where our objective is to protect consumers and the markets and promote competition. So, having a joined-up strategy for how we capture, share and access knowledge is really critical to meeting our objectives. If we have a team investigating money laundering and another team on the other side of the floor is investigating the same type of misconduct, they need to be speaking to each other and exchanging tips and ideas.
>
> Second, the work we do is highly visible. While we might have hundreds of different investigators working on cases, often the investigation subjects are represented by the same law firms. So, we need to be consistent in our approach.
>
> Third, the work we do is highly contentious. For example, an appeal went up to the Supreme Court over three words in a notice (we won). The opposition had one of the best law firms representing its case. So, it's really important we are at the top of our game – KM has a key role in making sure that's the case.

Developing and implementing the KM strategy

Christine's arrival coincided with the bedding-in of the new organisation. It was to prove propitious in helping to embed KM change, as she acknowledges:

> Because it was a relatively new organisation, there was a network of change champions throughout the organisation to help with adapting to change. I used them as a key stakeholder group to gain feedback on necessary changes and the plan going forward.

The initial strategy had two foci: 'processes and tools' and 'behaviours and mindsets'.

Processes and tools, behaviours and mindsets.

Christine inherited a number of KM mechanisms, of varying success, that had been established in the FSA to help knowledge flow. She tried to maximise their use to reduce the impact of change while evaluating their effectiveness and value for money. She explains how that worked in one case:

> We have a monthly forum called 'legal round-up' to disseminate information about interesting legal topics. Lawyers were naturally invited to attend, but forensic investigators weren't. That, I discovered, was creating tension. So I simply added forensic investigators to the invitation distribution list. It then meant they felt valued and that all Investigators were current on recent case law.

'Something that can take a nanosecond to introduce can have such a profound impact.'

To address the need to encourage knowledge-sharing behaviours and mindsets, FCA enforcement inserted 'engaging in knowledge-sharing activities' into performance objectives. This could be satisfied, for example, by making contributions to the 'wiki'; presenting at a number of events and round-ups; or championing knowledge sharing across a department.

Over the past five years there have been a number of highlights from the introduction of the Knowledge Sharing Framework (see Figure 21.1) that the strategy became. A few of these are described in the following sections.

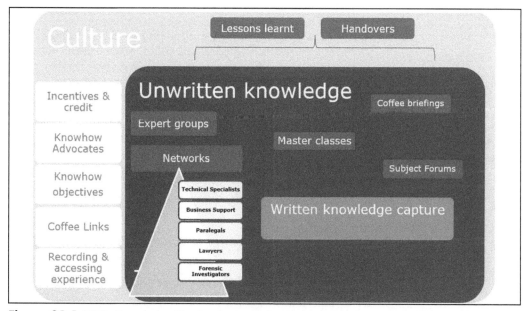

Figure 21.1 FCA's Knowledge Sharing Framework

Using networks to sharpen investigatory technique

Due to the sensitivity of the FCA's investigative work there is an understandable reluctance to publicise the methods and processes they use. However, Christine is able to share one example of how KM facilitated an improvement in investigatory technique:

> Over the last couple of years we've reviewed our approach to interviewing suspects and witnesses. Our forensic investigators' network hosted a number of round tables to support investigators through the changes, to ensure they are being carried out most effectively.
>
> We have 15 expert groups, all focused on pooling knowledge on important aspects of how we investigate. The Interviews Expert Group launched a buddy scheme, where expert members offer to buddy with more junior members of staff. That's good example of where our knowledge-sharing framework kicks into action following a change in strategy to help drive improvements to how we investigate.

A buddy scheme for junior forensic investigators.

KM seizing opportunities to move to the next level

Christine becomes very enthusiastic when talking about the support she gets for KM from the top:

> I'm really lucky, because our directors 'get' Knowledge Management. I know that from the consistent messaging about the value of knowledge sharing and the level of support I receive for my work. Here's an example:
>
> About 2½ years ago our new executive director of enforcement, on landing in post, undertook a big review of how we investigate and conduct cases. One aspect of that review was knowledge, which put KM in the spotlight and gave me a platform to further the KM strategy.
>
> We formed a working group which I led, with representatives from across the business to answer this question: 'Do we have the knowledge to fulfil our objectives and what do we need to do to improve it?' The group ran lots of feedback sessions and came up with recommendations the directors approved. One was that we should take to the next level our approach to 'lessons learned' by embedding it further into our processes, so that discussions about what went well, and what could have been done differently, happened in real time with management and with those who had directly experienced it. The changes also presented a chance to refine our language from 'the lessons-learnt process' to simply 'reflecting', which is much more neutral and less threatening.

Embedding approach to learning from lessons.

Launching the Investigation Academy to bring KM into the centre of learning

Christine is rightly proud of the progress the Knowledge & Learning team has made. Weaving the KM and L&D (learning and development) strategies together is a good example. Building on its work, the Knowledge & Learning Team launched an academy programme for FCA investigators (see Figure 21.2).

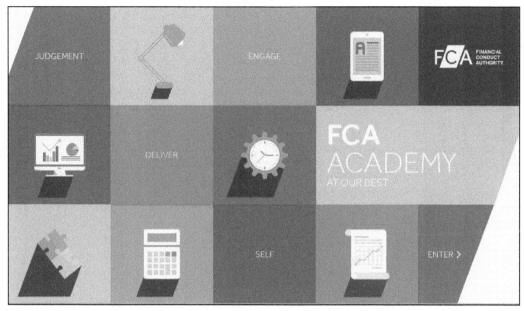

Figure 21.2 *FCA's Learning Academy promotional material*

> Investigators now have a focused learning pathway with three different levels supported by the knowledge-sharing framework. There is also a development scheme where people can access mentoring, action learning and stretch opportunities to gain experience outside their current skill set. There is also a personal portfolio where they can record achievements.

Christine describes how being able to steer the programme and monitor people's progress within the academy has helped her to embed the KM strategy and tie it into the learning strategy:

> We run searches training for investigators, and our forensic investigators' network enhances this by hosting informal round-table sessions for people to talk about their experiences to help keep their skills fresh after the training. This is a good example of how the formal training and KM work together to make us even more effective.

Reflections
On sustainability

Having been a 'lone ranger' for much of her time in FCA, Christine ponders on the scale of what it is possible for one person (plus a junior assistant) to achieve.

People comment on the
breadth and depth of
changes, and mindset
shift, that has been
brought about by one
person.

The size of Enforcement (650 staff) and the fact that I am the only full-time KM person means I have many mindsets to influence. Because I sit in a central part of the division I have a good oversight on what's going on in the business. And I have a network of advocates spread around who are my eyes and ears on the ground.

Originally my role was very much ideas-generator, implementer, deliverer. Now I've moved into more of a consultant space where people come to me for advice on how to go about something in the best way. A success measure attached to my role is how, once I've introduced an idea or tool, others are able to run with it.

Knowledge sometimes
doesn't have a
comfortable home.

We have built up a good amount of momentum, so that to some extent KM is self-sustaining, like a ball running down a hill.

An example of a sustained change is our Paralegal Knowhow Network. This network has been running for a number of years. Members are invited to meet regularly to share knowledge on topical issues – sessions are often standing-room only, and the network is showing no sign of let-up. What has made it a success? Central co-ordination; a network of 'reps' constantly feeding ideas from the ground on what is of interest to the members.

Knowledge-sharing
network meetings that
are standing-room only.

On resisting the 'one-hit wonder'

One of Christine's biggest challenges is sustaining change and resisting the risk of it disappearing after the fanfare of a solution. After all, people move on and KM activity can get lost in the noise of other change. Christine describes it:

> When you have a good idea, you work hard to put it into place. People hear about it and that's good. But before you know it, there is an immediate risk that it will get forgotten about, and the impact and momentum has been lost because people are too busy to do something differently. It's not about launching something, it's about sustaining it.

On the skills needed to run a KM programme

The required set of skills and behaviours would be tenacity, persistence, optimism, high energy and drive.

On how the Knowledge Sharing Framework tools produce tangible outcomes

I am proud of how the different tools and mechanisms of our Knowledge Sharing Framework synergise to help knowledge flow. For example, through our 'Reflections' process, we identified an emerging theme that some case teams had resolved cases creatively without proceeding to a criminal prosecution, thereby saving time and costs. This theme was then disseminated to increase awareness of this tactic, and to encourage others to think creatively, through a Master Class, as part of our Master Class programme.

Mapping the story to the 'KM Chef's Canvas'

FCA's KM activities are a great example of what can be achieved, on limited resources, if aligned to the strategic context of the organisation and with a clear focus on outcomes and targeted at specific business needs.

Strategic context

The arrival of a new Executive Head of Enforcement prompted a root-and-branch review of FCA's approaches and whether they had the right knowledge to meet organisational objectives. As well as leading the embedding of learnings into their investigation process the KM team were able to further refine their KM strategy.

Culture

We liked the fact that FCA used the embryonic structure of transformation and change champions to gather support for KM and that they built on existing networks such as the Paralegal Knowhow Network to share knowledge, rather than introducing new ones.

Support

The establishment of an Investigation Academy reflects FCA's emphasis on knowledge sharing and learning. It provides a learning pathway for staff in the Investigation Department and is especially valuable for new entrants. By monitoring people's progress through the curriculum and how they use the mentoring facility FCA are able to target future training where there is most need.

22

Creating value in Oman: KM in Petroleum Development Oman (PDO)

NARRATED BY HANK MALIK, ENTERPRISE KNOWLEDGE
MANAGEMENT LEAD, PETROLEUM DEVELOPMENT OMAN

> Something is always happening, there's a bit of a buzz. It's worked in
> PDO, now it's got to work across Oman.

This sentence captures the essence of how Hank Malik would like his
time as Knowledge Management Lead at Petroleum Development
Oman (PDO) to be remembered. Hank is an experienced KMer, having
cut his teeth with big consultancy companies including Deloitte and
PWC and industrial groups such as BG and Shell. Add global
experience gained across Europe, America and the Middle East and
it's clear Hank has a good take on what is required to run a successful
KM programme.

Arriving in Oman in the midst of a rare torrential downpour, he was
handed a consultant's report that Hank describes as 'a textbook KM
maturity assessment', which recommended a high-level approach and
a remit on the pilot he was going to implement.

Today, the Enterprise KM team (part of newly named Information
and Digitalisation department) sit in an office surrounded by
recognition awards from his time in Muscat. These include: Shukran
Awards, given as a corporate 'Thank you' for good performance;
Directors' recognition awards; a KM certification and KM Masters
certification; some framed posters of how Hank shaped the KM
programme in PDO; and the roadmap for, and large colourful
screenshots of, some of the applications they've used working closely
with the PDO SharePoint teams. Perhaps most interestingly, there are
posters which create a 'Gemba walk',[1] showing their KM story on a
wall, so people can drop in and see the evolution of the programme
and how it could add value to their own needs.

The challenge

A joint venture (between the Government of Oman, Shell and other stakeholders), PDO plans, oversees and implements energy projects in the Sultanate.

PDO is a limited-liability company, operates on a no-profit, no-loss basis, and is officially revenue neutral. Any profits made after shareholders are paid are invested back into the country. It is helping to build infrastructure projects for the good of the nation, supporting Omani job creation and is forward-thinking in funding new renewable-energy projects, such as solar-power installations.

Implementing a massive investment programme with a succession of major new capital projects coming on stream one after another in its hydrocarbon fields, PDO recognised it needed to learn lessons from past projects more effectively if it was to save money and improve performance.

'You couldn't hit the next stage gate without doing the lessons and looking back.'

Drivers from the board were improved learning, lessons learned, knowledge sharing – not, interestingly enough, communities or the collaboration piece, the enterprise social network. It was actually about the basics of making sure we can capture the learnings, that we apply them and adapt them.

The specific remit was to launch KM in CPD (Central Projects Delivery) in three pilot areas: lessons learned, on-boarding and collaboration.

The evolution of PDO's Knowledge Management – 'Connect, Collaborate, Succeed'

KM was not a totally new concept when Hank arrived. He described PDO as being a 'green canvas' since previous consultants had proposed a set of pilots to test KM and he was brought in to make that happen.

Hank admits he was lucky in having a KM champion at the 'C-Suite' level who was a very knowledgeable and supportive advocate.

'We had an amazing KM champion, a director on the board who was passionate about KM.'

I launched the KM programme in half a day through an envisioning workshop with some of the directors and leads and we had a photograph taken at the end. Dr Suleiman Al Tobi, the former Operations South Director, had it blown up, put on his wall, and placed in our internal PDO Magazine. It was I thought fantastic affirmation.

An important component of the launch of KM was branding. Hank worked with a KM steering group which came up with the 'Connect, Collaborate, Succeed' mantra. They created four simple icons for the building blocks of connecting, knowledge transfer, skills and collaboration. These were turned into posters that people readily embraced and a set of knowledge 'business cards' with a famous quote or saying from a philosopher or knowledge guru (Figure 22.1). On the reverse were the contact details of the KM team. Simple and effective. Widely circulated these became a 'call to action' to share knowledge:

Figure 22.1 *One of PDO's knowledge cards*

> We'd go out to the field with the knowledge cards and put them on tables and leave them in the coffee shops and people started to talk about that and say 'But what is this thing? KM?'

The initial pilots lasted approximately two years; do not believe anyone who tells you they can conduct a pilot in three months, says Hank. In a close working relationship with the SharePoint team, they were creating tools as well as working with the businesses for adoption.

Pilots lasted for two years.

Of critical importance from a governance perspective was the creation of a code of practice, a set of golden rules with the required compliance for KM, which was approved as an official corporate management, numbered document of PDO.

> And when I reflect back now, that was crucial, because there were times when people were questioning the KM function and I was able to refer them back to the officially approved code of practice where it clearly states . . .

The code was written not at the launch of the programme but over the life of the early pilots and so it was able to build on emerging lessons and reflect the culture, the ways of working and the terminology and language of PDO. As an example:

> I remember earlier writing a document of about 100 pages and having to have this reduced greatly in length to be accepted by the KM steering group. It ended up at about 15 pages with graphics and pictures.

Each business function
has a resource
committed to KM.

A core feature of the code based on the key lessons from the pilots is that each PDO business function requires a resource committed to KM. Deciding which model to adopt (a large centralised unit who teach others v. a decentralised unit who provide guidance and support to business located KM resources) was a challenge:

> We created the KM enterprise team and we lead the governance that steers the direction, the guidance, the reporting. I kicked off a KM steering group with core members. This was critical. Sponsored by the KM champion, we would have KM in the business and although there was undoubted enthusiasm to move quickly on the journey it was important to closely monitor and supervise progress.

PDO's KM team is aware that they need to continually refine the messages they give to their organisation. They have 'KM on a page', a 15-second 'elevator pitch' document that is shown to senior executives or new hires that describes what KM is. The team continually does a lot of KM awareness sessions.

PDO's KM services and activities
Lessons-learned model and process guides
PDO believed that a 'Big Bang'[2] approach to KM would not be effective and so they set about creating a set of consistent enterprise tools and techniques that addressed specific business issues. It proved effective, as the businesses, including Well Engineering and Process Safety, soon came calling.

They established a structured 'lessons-learned' process underpinned by an in-house-built 'learnings knowledge base', which now has over 7,000 'learnings' from 120 projects that are beginning to be applied throughout PDO.

Embed learnings into
process.

Surfacing the learnings was not always easy but, as PDO has a formal project evaluation process, based on key shareholder's (Shell's) own variant of the Stage-Gate®[3] process, the KM team were able to use that to facilitate the project close-out and Stage-Gate® review sessions and then assemble teams from different business divisions to help kick off new projects. This process has helped to spawn changes in commissioning specifications and has brought about a number of process improvements – one example being improved cladding for pipes, with different, more efficient, materials, resulting in significant cost avoidance.

The use of learnings does not stop there. Each learning where appropriate needs to be vetted by subject-matter experts, and if they approve, can become a best practice. In addition, learnings are collated by the KM team who create a 'featured learnings card'. Those deemed to have most significance to the business are then disseminated around the organisation.

Learnings knowledge base and learning cards

PDO's knowledge base features a technical taxonomy (a set of metadata tags all linked to the functions' metadata standard), which the engineers in the business bought into. A core philosophy is that everyone should be able to upload learnings for review and that the input process should be intuitive and relevant. Hank feels the knowledge base has been pivotal to their success:

Importance of a technical taxonomy.

> I think you need the killer app even in KM, and that for us was the learnings knowledge base.

The featured learning cards are the consolidated curated outputs of the lessons-learned process. They show the person involved the issue or problem, the response and the benefits. Endorsed by the board, they have proved effective in focusing PDO on the value of KM.

Sharing knowledge through featured learnings.

Equipping Omanis for a KM world

PDO takes its role as a leading Omani organisation seriously. Having trained and certified a number of its own staff as certified knowledge managers (CKMs) from the KM Institute in KM techniques, it is now extending that to include other Omani organisations in both the public and private sectors. Excitingly, it is building up a pan-Oman cohort or community of KM-certified workers to help improve cross-country learning and knowledge sharing, in effect developing potential replacements for the retiring and departing skilled expatriate workforce.

Reflections
On culture

> I have to say, in probably 20 years I've been in this game, this has been the most conducive culture; they're incredibly respectful, an open culture willing to learn; they respect, they listen.

PDO has started to use storytelling as a way of showing the value of KM. It fits with the culture of elders passing on knowledge through

Using storytelling to
illustrate KM value.

stories; people's eyes light up when colleagues start to describe an
event or decision as a story.

The positive aspects of the regional culture are also a barrier. Hank
noted:

> They don't want to criticise heavily. It is not an abrupt culture. We did
> lessons learned and the Westerners will say what worked, what didn't,
> what failed.

On skills

Technical domain expertise and being able to converse in the language
of the business and understand the processes, especially with
experienced, busy engineers, are critical.

'We have trained 30
Omanis in the Certified
Knowledge Management
program of KMI, getting
them ready for the
knowledge economy and
built a community
around that.'

The biggest challenge is resourcing and finding people with the
same vision and passion; equipping an Omani workforce with the basic
KM skills to sustain KM in the long run and avoiding the raft of
distracting technologies that may or may not add value to PDO's KM
programme.

Choosing the right consultant to work alongside is also hugely
important. Hank describes it as equivalent to venturing down a rabbit
hole. Few are versed in the cultural nuances of the region and most
seem to have a differing view of what KM is. He thinks that ultimately
consultants should be phased out as a solid local KM capability is built.

The difficulty of finding
the right consultant.

Hank has high hopes of the recently published ISO KM Standards
to help drive continuity and show what it takes to be a rounded and
blended knowledge manager. Here's how he describes that person:

> A blended proven skill set of people, learning, process and content. Such
> skilled KMers are indeed a rare breed and tend to focus on one area of
> specialism such as communities, information management or SharePoint,
> which is limiting. I particularly value people with skill sets and experience
> from learning, collaboration, change and process management, as they
> bring a wider scope of insights and can often demonstrate real examples
> of 'wrapping' KM methods around existing processes and procedures.

Finally, having a member on the PDO KM team with a deep technical
knowledge of oil and gas (over 20 years' experience) was invaluable
and made the outcomes achieved more believable.

'We estimate the number
is easily in the millions of
cost savings and cost
avoidance that have
been achieved from the
use of the lessons-
learned programme to
date.'

On measurement

Like many organisations, PDO has found putting numbers on the
success of its KM programme challenging. Hank notes:

It's one thing we need to improve on. We did a benchmark before, with a series of health checks and maturity assessments. The reflection would be that we need to go back and do another. We used it to kick-start the programme, with a set of self-assessment questions related to where we were. Where the real success on the project came was in lessons learned. We plan to focus on developing the KM metrics with measurement as we move forward.

Tracking performance through a visual tool (the 'KM dashboard') has helped to bring their many achievements to life.

On creating the learnings knowledge base

Looking back, these aspects stand out for PDO's KM team:

- Spend time getting the metadata terminology right.
- Make uploading of lessons widely available and simple.
- Build on existing structures and processes like Stage-Gate® reviews and close-outs.
- Roll up your sleeves, get out and facilitate lessons-learned workshops and capture the tacit knowledge.
- Curate key lessons and make them available to all.

'Make it easy, make it directly relevant to their engineering disciplines, expertise.'

On communications

PDO was far-sighted in that one of the allocated KM roles was Communications Change Manager.

It's all about selling KM and it's change management, so I think that was a key element of success.

People liked the visualisations. They liked being able to see an expert online. They liked posters of the featured learnings, they liked the culture change piece and they liked the KM branding.

On the biggest contributors to the success of the programme

Four events are significant in PDO's KM journey:

- winning over engineers to share their lessons learned and adopt the learnings knowledge base as the single repository for knowledge sharing
- sending out the featured learning cards and getting board endorsement that 'this is just what Knowledge Management should be doing'

- getting the first real tangible results which meant KM wasn't perceived as being 'fluffy'
- having a senior KM sponsor to champion KM across PDO.

Mapping the story to the 'KM Chef's Canvas'

PDO is a great example of incremental KM: design, test, assess then share.

A clear mandate, a governance framework and clear, consistent messaging underpin the programme. Perhaps of most significance is that it has a well documented approach for feeding learnings back into organisational process and a set of tangible results that evidence cost savings and improvements.

Leadership

PDO's leaders have consistently demonstrated support for the KM programme: from the clear mandate, to the early 'picture on the wall', to the various awards, to making clear what's expected of KM across the organisation.

Governance

The creation of a code of practice and the establishment of a steering group are important indicators that KM is part of PDO's corporate fabric and subject to the same disciplines as all processes.

Codification and curation

PDO's learnings knowledge base is a great example of how an organisation turns lessons identified into lessons learned that have tangible business impact. The featured learning cards are an imaginative approach to sharing critical knowledge that can be applied across the business as well as identifying the source so that others can approach the originator.

Notes

1 'Gemba Walk' Romanised version of genba: The Gemba Walk, much like Management By Walking Around (MBWA), is an activity that takes management to the front lines to look for waste and opportunities to practice Gemba Kaizen, or practical shop floor improvement. [Source: Wikipedia]

2 'Big Bang': Big bang adoption or direct changeover is the adoption type of the instant changeover, when everybody associated with the old system moves to the fully functioning new system on a given date. [Source: Wikipedia]
3 'Stage-Gate': The Stage-Gate® Model is a value-creating business process that, when applied effectively, drives the development and launch of a steady stream of successful new products. It is considered the 'industry standard' and is the world's most widely benchmarked, referenced and implemented innovation management model. [Source: Stage-Gate Inc.]

23

Saudi Aramco, Saudi Arabia: identifying, extracting and regenerating the wells of knowledge

NARRATED BY TONY MELENDEZ, TEAM LEADER, KNOWLEDGE MANAGEMENT GROUP, LEARNING SOLUTIONS & SERVICES, SAUDI ARABIA

Tony Melendez is a long-time oil and gas industry professional whose career has evolved into KM from building customer-facing corporate portals and document management systems. In 2013 he graduated with an MSc in KM from Kent State University USA and has been in Dhahran Saudi Arabia at Saudi Aramco ever since.

He smiles as he points out the artefacts which are the calling card of the KM team when talking to some of the other 200 departments they deal with (Figure 23.1 on the next page).

Tony describes what he found when he arrived to help establish a KM team in the Learning Solutions & Services Department, part of the Training & Development business unit:

> There were people doing KM in pockets, even if they didn't call it that. The knowledge transfer (KT) programme was very mature but little was formal.

The challenge

Saudi Aramco began KM in response to the shift in demographics and a desire to improve operationally. Although it was never formally documented as an organisational process, there were pockets of KM excellence, notably around knowledge transfer in plants and refineries, as far back as 2009.

With the demographic challenge of meeting the employment needs of a changing population – 50% of whom are under 35 – and with diversity now on the agenda, it's easy to see the attraction of using KM

Figure 23.1 *KM 'calling cards' at Saudi Aramco*

as a tool for business continuity. As the process of 'Saudisation' (encouraging in-Kingdom companies to employ Saudis rather than expatriates) gathers pace, so does the importance of knowledge transfer, as specialists exit the business, taking their knowledge and networks with them back to their home country. Tony describes the challenge in more detail:

> Originally, the programmes began quite organically, identifying opportunities and building a programme around them. KT began a decade ago when one department approached us to help them retain some knowledge from a large number of employees who were soon to retire.
>
> However, in an environment where we are trying to do more with less, organisations across the company are feeling pressure to accelerate skills development ('gap closure'), and to mitigate the risks associated with knowledge loss.
>
> In a perfect world, as our late-career staff exit the workforce, the mid-career workforce would naturally fill that void. But the numbers don't line up that way. There are so many early-career employees that some departments need to speed things up to get their staff job-ready.
>
> In addition, education and professional development of its citizens is a core objective of the Saudi Arabian Vision 2030 as it drives towards a knowledge-based economy. Aramco is doing its part to support that vision.

Developing and implementing a KM policy: a formally approved process

It took some time (2017) before KM was formally recognised. A KM policy signed off by Saudi Aramco's CEO became one of only 41 corporate policies, underpinned with dedicated KM functions established in the Training and Development and Engineering business units. These were major milestones in giving KM corporate legitimacy.

Accompanying the KM policy is what Saudi Aramco calls a 'KM General Instruction'. Signed off by all members of the executive team, including the CEO, it is a general guide to implementing KM and includes such approaches as: capturing knowledge, codifying it in accordance with the corporate taxonomy, sharing knowledge online and face to face, as well as KT. The General Instruction is an enforceable document and outlines programme definitions, stakeholders, and roles and responsibilities.

KM organisational structure & governance

While the KM Policy and General Instruction is the documentation that ties KM to corporate standards, governance is executed through a KM board chaired by the Chief Engineer and key stakeholders from the business. Two KM teams participate — Tony explains:

> There are two primary teams within the company. I am a Team Leader within the Knowledge Management Group, Learning Solutions & Services Department, which is under the Training & Development business line. Today we have 13 full-time staff. The second team is within the Engineering business line. They have 12 FTEs. I would say that T&D has a more people focus and Engineering has a more systems focus. We work well together and even though we are in very different parts of the company, we collectively position ourselves as the 'corporate KM team'.

Working with the culture

Culture has a strong impact on how people choose to share knowledge.

Unsurprisingly, given that the majority of employees are Saudi, the culture within Saudi Aramco mirrors that of the country, although more than 100 countries are represented on the payroll. Storytelling is pervasive. Knowledge sharing is more communal that digital. As a result, virtual communities which require written responses in discussion forums are a challenge to sustain.

Family relationships extend into the work environment; trust and respect once gained lasts for a long time and experts are regarded with high esteem and exert strong influence. This is important for the KM team as they set out to identify key influencers.

Like every organisation, irrespective of domicile, it is important that the KM programme is not seen as 'another corporate initiative, here today, gone tomorrow'.

Tony describes how his team work with the culture:

> One very strong corporate cultural dimension is the use of KPIs. We're a number-driven company. KPIs are tracked at the team, department, business line and corporate level. This has resulted in some activity-level metrics. This is fine for young programmes, as it establishes a baseline for qualitative measurements. We view KPIs as a means to an end. It motivates departments to carve out time and resources for KM.

Reflecting the cultural importance of verbal communication and of using the language of the business, the KM team have recently introduced 'conversational cafés' in the technical upstream (oil exploration and production) side of the company. Informed by an instructional video from the founder of the 'knowledge café' approach, David Gurteen, each café of up to 100 attendees begins with an adaptation of Darcy's Law, the equation that determines the flow rate of oil that comes out of the ground (Figure 23.2). Tony illustrates how this works:

What is... Darcy's Law

$$V = -\left(\frac{K}{\mu} \cdot \frac{P}{L}\right)$$

V: Flow velocity; K: Permeability; P: Pressure; μ: Viscosity; L: Length (distance)

Figure 23.2 *Darcy's Law*

Most of these people already know this equation, so it is relatable. We then explain the adaptation to knowledge sharing (Figure 23.3). Oil flow is just like knowledge flow. Changing the variables of the equation can change the flow. Then we pose a challenge statement. How can we increase permeability to sharing knowledge? (Figure 23.4)

The 2019 goal is to deliver this café to all of the upstream business lines. We will draft a report of findings and deliver it to our executive committee. It will be a call to action to build a more complete KM system that supports knowledge sharing.

During the cafés departments bring in the media to capture photos of collaboration.

No one takes pictures of themselves looking at a PowerPoint. When KM is engaging, they want to remember it.

Viscosity
How to reduce the "stickiness" of knowledge?

- Tacit knowledge is very sticky, it doesn't flow naturally
- Explicit knowledge flows better (document sharing, searching, BP/LL)
- Tell Me > Teach Me > Involve Me (OJT, job shadowing)

Pressure
How to increase pressure (or reduce resistance)?

- Rewards and recognitions increase incentive
- KM governance creates "push"
- An easier and better way to access expertise creates "pull" (For example: E-mail vs. Fax)

Length
How to shorten the distance between experts and learners?

- Technical solutions to find skills (expert location)
- Smart repositories (machine learning, chat bots)
- Social collaboration platforms (instant messaging, digital workspaces)

Figure 23.3 *Using Darcy's Law to demonstrate how knowledge flow is like oil flow*

Permeability
Shale formations generally have extremely low permeability: 0.01 to 0.00001 millidarcies. Typical oil reservoir formations range from 100 to 10,000 millidarcies.

Question:

What techniques are used to increase permeability in shale formations?

Fracking our Knowledge Wells
What are the ways we share knowledge to the youth?

How can we increase the permeability to these sharing pathways?

How can we open more pathways and keep them open?

Figure 23.4 *Increasing knowledge permeability*

KM activities

Knowledge transfer (KT) remains at the heart of Saudi Aramco's corporate-wide KM activities. The programme develops competency maps and identifies masters and apprentices. Competency gaps are identified and a structured transfer plan is developed (Figure 23.5).

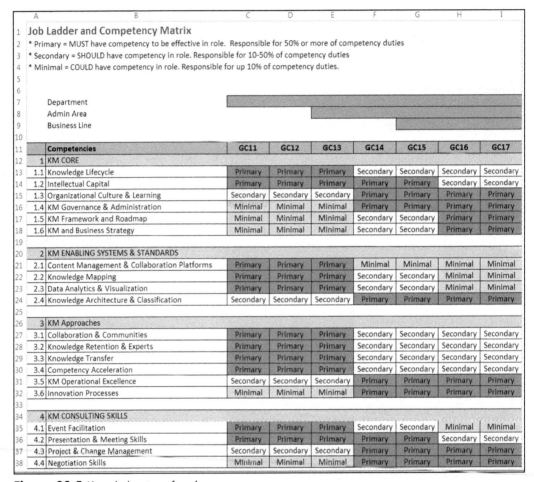

		GC11	GC12	GC13	GC14	GC15	GC16	GC17
	Job Ladder and Competency Matrix							
	* Primary = MUST have competency to be effective in role. Responsible for 50% or more of competency duties							
	* Secondary = SHOULD have competency in role. Responsible for 10-50% of competency duties							
	* Minimal = COULD have competency in role. Responsible for up 10% of competency duties.							
	Department							
	Admin Area							
	Business Line							
	Competencies	GC11	GC12	GC13	GC14	GC15	GC16	GC17
1	**KM CORE**							
1.1	Knowledge Lifecycle	Primary	Primary	Primary	Secondary	Secondary	Secondary	Secondary
1.2	Intellectual Capital	Primary	Primary	Primary	Primary	Primary	Secondary	Secondary
1.3	Organizational Culture & Learning	Secondary	Secondary	Secondary	Primary	Primary	Primary	Primary
1.4	KM Governance & Administration	Minimal	Minimal	Minimal	Primary	Primary	Primary	Primary
1.5	KM Framework and Roadmap	Minimal	Minimal	Minimal	Secondary	Secondary	Primary	Primary
1.6	KM and Business Strategy	Minimal	Minimal	Minimal	Secondary	Secondary	Primary	Primary
2	**KM ENABLING SYSTEMS & STANDARDS**							
2.1	Content Management & Collaboration Platforms	Primary	Primary	Primary	Minimal	Minimal	Minimal	Minimal
2.2	Knowledge Mapping	Primary	Primary	Primary	Secondary	Secondary	Minimal	Minimal
2.3	Data Analytics & Visualization	Primary	Primary	Primary	Secondary	Secondary	Minimal	Minimal
2.4	Knowledge Architecture & Classification	Secondary	Secondary	Secondary	Primary	Primary	Primary	Primary
3	**KM Approaches**							
3.1	Collaboration & Communities	Primary	Primary	Primary	Secondary	Secondary	Secondary	Secondary
3.2	Knowledge Retention & Experts	Primary	Primary	Primary	Secondary	Secondary	Secondary	Secondary
3.3	Knowledge Transfer	Primary	Primary	Primary	Secondary	Secondary	Secondary	Secondary
3.4	Competency Acceleration	Primary	Primary	Primary	Secondary	Secondary	Secondary	Secondary
3.5	KM Operational Excellence	Secondary	Secondary	Secondary	Primary	Primary	Primary	Primary
3.6	Innovation Processes	Minimal	Minimal	Minimal	Primary	Primary	Primary	Primary
4	**KM CONSULTING SKILLS**							
4.1	Event Facilitation	Primary	Primary	Primary	Secondary	Secondary	Minimal	Minimal
4.2	Presentation & Meeting Skills	Primary	Primary	Primary	Primary	Primary	Secondary	Secondary
4.3	Project & Change Management	Secondary	Secondary	Secondary	Primary	Primary	Primary	Primary
4.4	Negotiation Skills	Minimal	Minimal	Minimal	Primary	Primary	Primary	Primary

Figure 23.5 *Knowledge transfer plan*

This is a core process of the corporate operational excellence (OE) programme and is built on a plan-do-check-adjust continuous improvement cycle. The KM Group is part of the OE assessment team, which assesses how effectively departments implement the KT process.

KT participation is built into annual performance goals and so is tied to promotion and compensation. Departments that are big adopters have dedicated, full-time staff to lead locally, usually on annual assignments.

The focus of KT has broadened from the industrial and engineering business line to embrace the professional (main office) workforce. The KM team identify core functions and activities (tasks), determine if those are critical or procedural, identify the subject-matter experts and then determine the potential risk for knowledge loss. Where there is perceived risk, they draw up a transfer plan (which can take up to a year to execute) and appoint a recipient or learner to work with the subject-matter expert to try and plug the competency gap. Tony continues:

Identifying and mitigating the potential loss of critical knowledge.

> To implement, we have adopted a PMO model where the procedures, guidelines, tools and support are managed centrally, but the implementation is distributed. Each department names a 'KT champion' to lead the implementation. We have several courses and workshops to train the champions so that they are equipped to lead it locally. The KT team serve as consultants to ensure a quality implantation and they will conduct interventions when it goes off track. The programme is cyclical, so once the gaps are closed, the programme re-initiates . . . the functions and activities assessment is revisited to look for more risks.
>
> KT is one of the core processes in the corporate operational excellence (OE) framework. OE is built on the EFQM (European Foundation for Quality Management) excellence model. It is one of our critical enablers, as it allows us to implement the programme across all business lines.
>
> The KT programme is our most mature programme. Over half of the company departments are implementing the programme (industrial and professional). The related KPI is 'gap closures' and it is reported to upper management. For some departments, KT is so well embedded that it is now just the normal, expected way of operating. They report that it has shown the most impact in job readiness and builds confidence with supervisors.

Enabling people to transfer across business units based on competency profile.

For those in Saudi Aramco for whom KM is new and unfamiliar, the KM team have a number of innovative 'games' which they use as introductions. They can be seen in the photos of Tony's desk in the Appendices, pp. 256 8. Here he describes how they work.

> We have four photos of people with a bullet list of their unique skills. We cover the skills with that 'Hidden Skills' poster. Each skill is printed on a small card and we ask people to match the skill to the face. Of course, they are just guessing and get most wrong. Then we remove the Hidden Skills poster and reveal their skills. The lesson is that if there were a system where each person listed their skills, especially ones that aren't obvious from their job title, it would be easier to find an expert (KM-speak: expertise location). Yes, we have SharePoint, but this is one of those cases where it isn't the lack of technology, but rather the adoption of it.
>
> We have a poster with a grid of nine different IT systems that serve as knowledge repositories, such as our SharePoint CoPs, our internal video

Find the Expert.

Find the Chocolate.

channel, SAP, network folders, LMS, etc. Each system has a red cup on it and under one cup is a piece of chocolate. We explain to the player that they need to find an important piece of knowledge to complete their task and it resides under one of these systems. We give them three chances to find the chocolate and I would say 90% of the people don't find it. Then we show them the 'KM Portal' poster which has nine cups glued together, side-by-side, on it and explain that in the future there will be a single website that will filter and prioritise content based on their function and role. We ask them to find the chocolate with one attempt, and of course they find it because the cups are glued together! This teaches the merits of a corporate taxonomy, a federated search engine, and integration with an individual's competency map and performance and development goals.

The Knowledge Fish.

This is a lesson in the knowledge lifecycle. We explain how knowledge typically evolves and that each stage is important. We also explain that some people are better at some stages than others are. So, we ask the player to hold out their hand and we place a 'knowledge fish' in their palm. These are called Fortune Teller Miracle Fish. The fish curls up and depending on how it curls up, we determine their knowledge lifecycle specialty. If the head curls, they are a 'knowledge editor' (lifecycle stage: create) and they are good at capturing best practices. If the head and tails curls, they are a 'knowledge librarian' (lifecycle stage: store) and they are organised and are good at managing documents. All these archetypes are positive and even through the curling fish are entertaining, it's interesting to hear their reactions such as, 'Wow, I really am a knowledge editor!'

Measurement and benchmarking

The KM team are fortunate in having moved beyond proving the need to exist. They do not capture return on investment or money or time saved. The only core KPI is around knowledge transfer, where they measure competency and expertise gap closure. This gap analysis takes place at the start of a KT assessment and the progress of a 'learner' is measured throughout the cycle of the KT plan. Tony says their use of stories has 'brought KM to life' for many:

> The success stories that we write about are more about engagement. For example, when we do our KM games with the red cups and fish, it resonates. It's been published in our corporate magazine, in fact. We've even started to look into ways to make a 'kit' out of these games so that other teams can use them for their own lessons.

'We got 10–20 new ideas every single day. It's taken off in our remote locations.'

The future

The KM team have only recently been able to apply both a strategic and an operational perspective on the KM programme. Their remit of the corporate KM team covers the whole organisation and they are able now to identify pockets of excellence and innovation and share those experiences. One such example is the corporate innovation and ideation platform, which has become the home for ideas.

One of the biggest initiatives for 2019 is the KM consultancy programme, which is being developed to address four common concerns frequently raised by the businesses:

- governance – how to comply with KM policy (they are mandated but not yet equipped to respond)
- culture – how to respond to shifting demographics and implement new disruptive technologies
- resources – each department is mandated to have a KM resource and yet KM is not seen as their core business
- value – a one-size KM fits all approach will not work, it has to be based on organisational needs of what is valuable.

Tony explains the rationale:

> To help answer these concerns, we have started with our three KM focus areas.
>
> **Protect corporate knowledge** – Aramco has mandatory retirement at 60. This means that we can anticipate knowledge loss. To protect our knowledge is to capture, retain and institutionalise expertise before it exits the workforce, ensuring resilience and business continuity. This focus area is focused on the older population. KT is a major approach in this area.
> **Develop a quality workforce** – This is looking at the younger workforce. With the volume of workers who need supervision, make occasional mistakes and take more time to complete tasks, this focus areas builds competency through competency maps, job shadowing and other approaches
> **Ensure access to experts** – Between the young and the old are the tools and processes that connect them. Communities of practice (CoPs), expert finders, mentorship programmes and rewards and recognition programmes stimulate a positive sharing culture.
>
> The KM consultancy programme is being designed with the 'agency model' in mind. We will be internal consultants providing KM tools and services to internal customers (departments).
> It begins with an assessment. All the work we've done in 2018 is being reworked to align with the ISO so that it can be benchmarked in the future. The assessment is followed by a report that has identified gaps and improvement opportunities. This will result in a KM solution plan and will be sealed with a formal partnership agreement.
> The solution plan will include services by other service owners. For

example, if the department needs to implement a CoP, they will approach IT to provision a community. If online learning is needed, they will approach our LMS team to develop e-courses. However, other KM-specific solutions will be serviced by the KM Group, such as knowledge transfer and knowledge cafés.

Impact of the ISO KM Standard

'It's flexible enough that we can adapt what we've done and make changes so that it's applicable.'

Saudi Aramco stands out in that it is already shaping much of its future KM approach to reflect ISO 30401. Here's how Tony describes its 'game-changing' impact:

If there is any major course correction, honestly, it is the ISO Standard. We are currently redesigning our KM consultancy model around it – more specifically, the knowledge assessment (KM audit and maturity). The assessment is shaping up to be in line with the standard's tacit and explicit operational dimensions. The reason we are doing this is so that we are able to benchmark with other organisations. So we will be able to adapt and improve over periods of time and show positive trends.

Reflections
On sustainability and scalability

Originally, the KT programme was implemented by the KM Group team members. We would spend lots of time in the departments. We would schedule meetings, do one-on-one training sessions, etc. But it simply did not scale.

We have shifted to a more decentralised implementation approach where we train one of their staff as a KT champion. It was a shift in the RACI (responsibility assignment) matrix and we've since grown the number of departments fivefold.

I would say our successes have a lot to do with our general approach to hold their hands through the process. We offer lots of training workshops and tools to help them to their job.

'Customers are not in our computers – they are people in offices.'

Our customers are not in our computer, they are people in offices in different buildings. We spend a lot of time showing our faces. Be visible. Be vocal. Be helpful.

I would also recommend injecting your message into other presentations. We are constantly in 'Let me introduce our team and services' mode. The KM games are a great way to teach and promote. It's not a boring PowerPoint presentation – and we give them chocolates!

On the skills needed for the role

Equipping people to undertake roles has always been at the core of Saudi Aramco's mission. It can be seen in the training the team gives to those engaged in KM.

Each programme has some roles and responsibilities. Knowledge transfer has the KT champion to implement it. We train them over several multi-day workshops to teach the process and tools.

Another critical role is called the 'knowledge provider', which is the SME transferring down their knowledge to others. We have a workshop for them, since they are required not just to teach but also to assess the developmental progress of the learner (knowledge recipient).

Operationally, the KM Group is expected to be skilled in project management, facilitation and instruction. Most of us have some background in HR management or training. I myself have an MS. in Knowledge Management. Others have KMI certification.

On the advice he'd give to others

We've heard it countless times . . . a successful KM programme depends on executive support. For Aramco, that is with the policy and KM General Instructions. The CEO signatures, and a fair share of 'shall' statements, are powerful for a small KM Group reaching across business lines.

Importance of 'shall' statements from the top.

I have to give a lot of credit to our department manager, Mr Abdullah Ghabbani. As smart as he is in the learning and development discipline, he has given us a real opportunity to lead in design and implementation of KM. While we didn't start from scratch, he pushes us to be more visible, do new things, and not worry about the short-term ROI. Even my direct supervisor, Ms Munmun KC, opens doors to other parts of the company so that we can get our message out. Not all programmes are so lucky.

Role of supportive management.

Mapping the story to the 'KM Chef's Canvas'

As befits one of the largest energy companies in the world, Saudi Aramco's KM programme is well crafted and targeted. The link to operational excellence and process is particularly impressive. We could have selected a number of examples in governance, support and roles to demonstrate how they meet and exceed the KM Chef's Canvas. Here are three we found compelling:

Leadership

Saudi Aramco's CEO signed the Knowledge Management policy, which is one of only 41 corporate policies. This was a major milestone and a major enabler and door-opener. KM is stated within the Training & Development vision and objectives, and is a natural enabler in activities such as e-learning, social collaboration and gamification.

Improvement

Saudi Aramco is using the new ISO KM Standard to remodel its KM consultancy offering, specifically, the knowledge assessment (KM audit and maturity). The assessment is shaping up to be in line with the standard's tacit and explicit operational dimensions. The rationale is to be able to benchmark their activity against other organisations.

Processes

Saudi Aramco's operational excellence model underpins its activities. That KM processes are now ingrained day-to-day behaviour for many, and that they are regularly reviewed, is impressive. We liked the fact that the KM General Instruction acts as a valuable 'how to' and 'shall do' resource and that the KM team have a number of resources to support the active use of tools and techniques, particularly the games that provide an introduction to KM.

24
MAPNA, Iran: the role of KM in designing and implementing world-scale projects

NARRATED BY DR MOHSEN HAMEDI, CHIEF KNOWLEDGE OFFICER, MAPNA GROUP IRAN

> At a recent international KM excellence award, the grand judge, after hearing our case, approached me later and said: 'It is very nice to see that you have been able to implement this stuff.' And I realised that I should be happy with the outcomes rather than being frustrated by the enormous challenges we have encountered.

It's raining (people are happy as a result) as Dr Hamedi reflects on the recent KM excellence award. His ninth-floor office, in one of Tehran's swankier business districts, looks down on a city flanked by snow-capped mountains to the north and a vast urban conurbation of nearly 9 million people to the south, east and west. It bears testimony to a varied and interesting career.

Iran encourages close ties between academia and industry and so, like many senior Iranian executives, he is a practising academic, a professor at the University of Tehran, while heading up MAPNA Group's Research & Development (R&D) function and its Knowledge Management (KM) programme.

A selection of large potted plants, many shelves filled by books, reports, a dozen certificates and awards related to R&D and KM in national and international competitions fill his office. Plus a folder of MAPNA's international patents.

When asked to list his favourite objects, he notes:

> 'I like the potted plants most. A Ficus benjamina and a Russian olive that produce some two-thirds of the oxygen I consume ☺'

> A four-year-old picture of my colleagues and me that all of them have signed. Since some of them have left the company, it has lovely sentimental value.
>
> Another picture showing three generations of gas turbine blades manufactured by MAPNA. It tells me how we have filled 35 years of technology gap with only seven years of R&D work.

My large and lovely whiteboard. It really helps us to understand and formulate complex problems related to organisational problems.

The challenge

MAPNA, founded in 1993, is a multi-division, multi-layered industrial firm employing more than 15,000 people. It is involved in thermal and renewable energy, oil and gas, railway transportation and other industrial projects; and it manufactures the major equipment required for these businesses. The power plants it has constructed and owns provide more than half of Iran's electrical power. Today, the majority of passenger-train locomotives on Iran's rail network have been manufactured by MAPNA.

It has executed 100 projects, together valued at over €30 billion.

'He knew that as we grow in volume and gain knowledge in construction, in manufacturing, in the process knowledge, we have to do something . . . that you can't do R&D without Knowledge Management.'

In 1998 the University of Tehran suggested that MAPNA needed to drive its research and development and take ownership of project and product initiation. Professor Hamedi proposed the establishment of an R&D function. It took the intervention of an international organisational development expert charged with looking at the 'span of control' of the senior executives, before R&D was back on the agenda.

Again, it didn't happen immediately. Seven years after his original proposition Dr Hamedi was invited to assemble evidence to validate the establishment of an R&D unit and report back. Six months later, during Dr Hamedi's presentation, a board member asked whether Knowledge Management would be one of R&D's core functions.

In 2007 KM was established within the embryonic R&D Division. Dr Hamedi recalls:

> One pain-point that made KM appealing to managers was to eliminate the repeated mistakes in execution of the projects. Preventing costly mistakes made KM attractive.
>
> Another was a brain-drain problem in the country, making the organisation worried about know-how leaving the company. Knowledge retention was another appealing feature of KM.
>
> Third, in the last few years there had been accidents that claimed the lives of a couple of workers in a few projects. Besides its high costs, it jeopardised the health, safety and environmental (HSE) credibility of the company. Promoting safety and reducing the environmental impact was a main objective of one of the pilot projects.

'Three people had been killed falling from scaffolding. Our aim was to make sure no accident happened like this again.'

Striving to be a knowledge-oriented organisation

Dr Hamedi and his colleagues, Firoozeh Hadian Dehkordi and Maryam Barikany, lead the Knowledge Management effort within

MAPNA's R&D. They also act as the co-ordinator for many of the KM efforts being pursued by the MAPNA subsidiaries. This is how they formally describe their KM programme:

> It is a continuous strategic programme aligned with business strategies; a catalyst for creating the changes required for organisational growth and increased business performance.
>
> It focuses on knowledge-intensive activities and considers such processes as the collective and systematic creation, acquiring and sharing of knowledge with the intention of identifying, protecting, measuring and reporting the organisation's knowledge assets.
>
> It utilises its processes effectively in order to use key knowledge for reaching organisational goals with reasonable, more predictable and controlled risks.

Over the last ten years MAPNA has built solid foundations for its KM programme. During each phase, it has circled back to the corporate strategy, ensuring that what it describes as 'strategic imperatives' are mapped to specific aspects of the strategy. Each iteration of its KM evolution must conform to its internal quality standards (Figure 24.1).

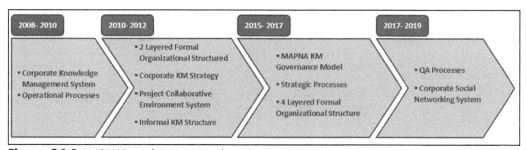

Figure 24.1 *MAPNA's evolving approach to KM*

The importance of quality standards

Quality is ingrained within MAPNA; it is a process-oriented firm. The company processes are underpinned by a quality management system that adheres to ISO standards. All of its processes, procedures, tools and techniques are audited twice a year, once internally and once externally. This requires documentation of all aspects of KM, frequent review and improvement. Accordingly, each KM-related job and the tasks associated with it are documented and reviewed and periodically improved.

It benchmarks its processes by participating in national annual European Foundation for Quality Management (EFQM) organisational excellence awards, which require KM activities to be presented in clear, concise and to-the-point documentation.

Developing MAPNA's own intellectual property creating knowledge assets

As it has grown and projects brought on stream, so MAPNA has shifted away from a reliance on external intellectual property. The knowledge generated is being carefully captured, maintained, stored, organised and made available to inform future projects. Dr Hamedi explains:

> I have a picture in my office of three geometrically identical gas turbine blades made from super alloys. Each 35cm blade is about the price of a car.
>
> The first is 80s technology, for which MAPNA paid millions in technology transfer. The enhancement of the second from the 80s and third from the late 20th/early 21st century was initiated in MAPNA by R&D and developed using the technology labs of local universities working with MAPNA's subsidiaries.
>
> MAPNA captures and stores the process, product knowledge and assessment and acceptance criteria that went into the design and development of the turbine blades. While the blades are the physical assets, the processes and know-how are MAPNA's knowledge assets. Any of our subsidiaries can access these organisational knowledge assets at a couple of minutes' notice.

'If you were to come to MAPNA today and ask anything about a business process you will see that we are able to show you documents, reports and how it's used. This is how process knowledge is growing in importance day by day.'

Harvesting new learnings and ideas, creating new knowledge

The practice of learning before, during and after has become ingrained in the way MAPNA now works. Dr Hamedi explains:

> Experts get together in a meeting to talk about one specific aspect of air-cooled condenser systems and how and where they should assemble the parts: on the ground or on the top where it's higher altitude? They check out their ideas with group experts. This process is captured. It's shown as a new learning and idea which then goes forward for review by the process owner.

This process is best illustrated through a couple of MAPNA's KM pilot projects, in which process improvements from new learnings and ideas are applied across the whole MAPNA Group.

MAPNA's pilot activities

MAPNA did not adopt a 'Big Bang' approach to KM, conscious that to be successful, KM projects involve many infrastructural and cultural changes, results take time to deliver and senior management is always impatient and results-driven.

They sought evidence of the value of KM through carefully selected pilots that addressed real business issues with tangible outcomes. Two are discussed below: 'KCC' and 'Stage-K-Pro'.

The KCC project: learning before to improve safety and efficiency

MAPNA, like most large industrial groups, views safety as a top priority. The firm had a specific concern with safety issues associated with construction of air-cooled condensers (ACCs).

The KM team had been searching for a real business issue, the resolution of which would demonstrate the effectiveness of KM to senior management. So they set up a pilot that they called 'KCC' to attempt to gather lessons from constructing eight cooling systems (in power plants). They surmised that by surfacing new ideas and learnings from experts and engineers they might be able to propose process improvements and methods to improve safety and reliability, eliminate rework and avoid repeating previous mistakes. MAPNA also wanted to reduce cost, make better and faster decisions, increase the level of expertise applied to future projects and apply consistency in construction quality.

The project was kicked off by the KM team working with project managers from the power plants. They identified and assembled experts and operations people from nine power plants to conduct a full day 'peer assist' workshop.

The first workshop in Mashad started early with 50 people who knew nothing about KM. Its aim was to surface learnings and ideas using a KM technique, 'peer assist', that others could adopt whenever they had an issue or were starting a project. The introduction to KM and peer assist took about 90 minutes. Then the KM team split the delegates into seven groups based upon the construction disciplines determined by the project manager and KM team. They invited plant technicians to describe how they did their jobs and the experts drawn from across the country and different industries took notes and asked questions of clarification. The KM Team facilitated the clustering of the ideas.

Running a 'peer assist' to surface learnings and ideas.

By the time they finished eight hours later many new ideas had been surfaced and two further workshops also facilitated by the KM team produced similarly positive results. KM techniques used included: before-action review, during-action review, after-action review, brainstorm and knowledge nomination.

The 121 new learnings and ideas (new knowledge) surfaced were then 'processed' using MAPNA's nine-stage Knowledge Management learning cycle (KMLC – see Appendices, pp. 259-61) and 63 are now informing future projects, as Dr Hamedi explains:

> There has been a dramatic reduction in fatal accidents and other incidents on construction sites and a significant change in the way contracts are drawn up.

The pilot is ongoing and the KM team meets regularly with the power plants to conduct learning reviews and ensure learnings are being applied. It has changed the mindset of people because they see that by discussing the problem together they find solutions emerging in a way and at a rate they could not have envisaged.

'Stage-K-Pro': KM enhancing a new product development (NPD) process

MAPNA uses a formal NPD process to evaluate and implement industrial projects. Their NPD process consists of a set of actions (Stages) and milestones (Gates) a new project has to pass in order to get from an idea (Ideation) to production. R&D act as gatekeeper and custodian of the MAPNA process and manage its extensive R&D investment portfolio.

In January 2014, a group from R&D set out to test whether a core business process, NPD, might benefit from including KM techniques. This is where KM and business process re-engineering come together. MAPNA's NPD process and process maps were examined in detail and an outline of a pilot project focusing on the initial phase of their NPD process developed under the name 'Stage-K-Pro' with this objective: 'undertake better projects by making better decisions, informed by better knowledge'.

The project team formed with defined roles and responsibilities and developed a collaborative system so that team members could record their experiences and suggestions. The pilot team built KM tools and techniques (examples include peer assist, learning reviews, checklists, collaborative knowledge bases) into the new process and trialled this over the next six months. Dr Hamedi notes a couple of issues that emerged:

> The ideation form (a form used to propose new ideas or projects) sets out the questions to be addressed. In the absence of a set of guidelines or a formal checklist, evaluation of the proposal was performed in a manner that reflected the personal style and experience of the officer in R&D.
>
> The original estimate was that it took five months from receipt of the

'Improving, streamlining the previous process and naming it the Stage-K-Pro process to make better use of existing resources and drawing on knowledge of those who have most to contribute'.'

'Learning from doing: adopting a policy of collaboration, upgrading the process, checklists and the templates to reflect good practice.'

'Educating new employees and stakeholders to ensure better transfer of knowledge and hence better decision making.'

ideation form to the signing of a contract for R&D. After pilot-driven brainstorming sessions it emerged that the lapsed time was actually nine months.

The project produced important positive impacts based on four business value metrics: revenues, costs, timings and quality. The results are compelling:

'Mentoring costs to train new entrants show a 75% reduction at mid-manager level and 77% in expert level.'

The cost of processing documents was reduced due to parallel working.
New entrants now get up to speed quicker as a result of the process improvements and documentation.
R&D staff now work on a parallel concurrent process as opposed to a linear consecutive process.
R&D now have a documented process that contains 49 distinct steps.
They are 'learning from doing' and feeding back process improvements from learnings through knowledge nominations.
Lessons learned from this pilot are being applied to other projects.

'Processing time reduced by 1–2 months.'

In human terms the impact has been significant. New entrants are able to 'hit the ground running'. They know who to go to and what is known about a topic. When projects are initiated the best knowledge is applied and perhaps most importantly decisions are made more speedily and are better informed. This is what the team said:

'Documents on the knowledge base are available to all and the work improved.'
'We can undertake projects that we couldn't have before.'
'The quality of submissions to Gates is now much better.'
'There is a standard way of reviewing propositions and a set of checklists and guidelines to facilitate this.'

With project investment often exceeding US$500 million, improved quality and reduced time to make decisions are significant 'wins'.

In presenting findings to senior management, the project team used famous children's characters to describe life as a 'newbie' before and after Stage-K-Pro. It was to prove a highly effective approach, far away from the cultural norm.

As is traditional in Iran, the conclusion of a successful event is marked by the baking of a cake. Bearing the official KM mantra of MAPNA, it was presented by Dr Hamedi to one of the KM pilot teams (Figure 24.2 on the next page).

Figure 24.2 *MAPNA's celebratory cake*

Reflections
On decentralised KM

MAPNA's model relies on having a small core team well versed in KM, able to facilitate others in its use and empowering people in the subsidiaries and business divisions to be able to introduce KM. With more than 40+ subsidiaries, it's an approach that makes sense. Here's an example:

> Rail Construction Company, a MAPNA Group company subsidiary in railway construction projects, approached us and said we want you to establish Knowledge Management in our company. We told them that together we have to do knowledge strengths, weaknesses, opportunities and threats (KSWOT), a change-readiness assessment and a KM maturity assessment. We helped them to complete that task in two months, then presented the strategy to the manager of the company. His feedback was: 'I accept all of these. We could not have done this by ourselves in six months.'

On delegating the KM task

The central KM team of four plus Dr Hamedi cannot be everywhere across such a diverse industrial group. They have three major roles: teaching, coaching and strategy planning, and so require a mix of soft and technological skills to help promote KM across the group. They need to be seen as the ultimate point in answering theoretical, implementation and planning questions around KM. To achieve this, the team needs a robust methodology and relevant tools and techniques, not only to teach them but also to help different organisational units to use them effectively.

The KM team must also take a holistic approach and be able to address alignment with the business strategy, defining the critical success factors and measuring and reporting the KM performance by accurate key performance indicators (KPIs).

On culture and transforming attitudes

MAPNA's cultural characteristics can be defined as 'Individualistic' (focused on individual performance) and 'Results (quick) oriented', based on a centralised structure where in the past senior managers had too many reports and too little time. This resulted in a reluctance to embrace anything not perceived as core to the day-to-day work, a resistance to change and an initial reticence to share in a team environment.

'Convert the persistent challenges to research questions.'

'Use proven and advanced research methodologies for finding the solution.'

> However, the results-oriented culture and increasing organisational self-confidence allied to a 'We-Can-Do-It' spirit are positive aspects.

A great challenge is how through transforming people's attitudes MAPNA can make the necessary behavioural change. The KM team believe this change involves two actions: forming a 'process approach' to KM; and repeating the process several times so that the people can learn and gain by experiencing self-efficacy.

> It's about changing people's attitude from 'KM is extra effort in my work' to 'KM is an important part of my work'.

'Let people talk, listen to them and then innovate to find ways to share what they say.'

On measurement, governance and monitoring

MAPNA measures all activities. At the beginning of each year, KM-related programmes are submitted for review to the Strategy and Planning department. The KM team is charged with executing the programme and producing updates and compliance reports. It's an approach KM-related positions in other business divisions and subsidiaries are required to adopt. These reports are qualitative and incorporate quantitative measures, such as KPIs, that measure and evaluate the performance of all KM activities.

As part of its governance model (see Appendices, pp. 259-61), MAPNA uses a technique called Knowledge-SWOT (KSWOT) to assess its competitive position from a knowledge perspective. It is part of their approach to linking back to the strategic direction of the business.

> What are the weaknesses and strengths in terms of the knowledge content we have, what don't we know and what do we have to do something about? It's something we have embedded in the processes and we have put these activities in the hands of the business divisions. We have told them that they have to do this KSWOT frequently. We have empowered the business divisions to look after the KSWOT and are able to monitor whether they have.

On incentives

'Foster trust as much as you can. It is essential for KS&A.'

The hiring of a new KM team member with an HR background signals the start of an initiative to look at incentives for contributing to KM, as Dr Hamedi is not satisfied that they have got that aspect right yet:

> We need to find the appropriate system of incentive to make sure that people are getting credit for what they do, they are being acknowledged and they are being rewarded.

On communications and stakeholder management

MAPNA is a complex and large enterprise in a developing country. The centralised structure impacts the collaborative environment required for KM to work. MAPNA ticks most boxes, though, when it comes to managing internal communications and stakeholders.

> We developed a KM governance model to address key questions for the people across the firm impacted by KM. This is being implemented. The model gives delegation of each department's KM activities to themselves. Once successfully implemented, it will play a great role in leading the group toward its aim, to be a 'knowledge-driven company'.

In addition, the KM team's goal – 'To identify and valuate the corporation's knowledge assets' – is selected and stipulated by the group CEO. Their objective – 'Increased knowledge sharing in the company' – though modest is aligned directly to the corporate strategy and approved by the KM steering committee, whose members include senior managers and which is overseen by the group CEO.

Top managers are informed about KM in periodic KM seminars. Others are educated in specific workshops and meetings through pilot projects and the EFQM (European Foundation for Quality Management) certification process.

Perhaps of most significance, KM sits within R&D, has a recognised Chief Knowledge Officer and a steering committee presided over by the group CEO.

On the biggest risks MAPNA's KM programme faces

Looking forward Dr. Hamedi wonders aloud:

> Will KM gain enough momentum to percolate irreversibly across the organisation so that it can change the attitudes of the people towards work?
>
> Ours is a verbal culture where people are reluctant to write things down. It makes knowledge codification difficult and costly. MAPNA might need to use other media and tools for knowledge sharing that needs expensive IT tools and equipment. Yet with hardships caused by the economic sanctions, the financial resources to further develop the IT tools are more scarce than ever.

And finally, on the success that's been achieved

Dr Hamedi ends on an upbeat note, proud of the company and his team:

> From zero in 1993 MAPNA has been able to manufacture, modify, improve and even design complex equipment that has taken international firms more than a century of experience to achieve.
>
> We are a new kid in the block in R&D and KM, but given the approach, the methodology and tools and techniques that we use and the outcomes that we have been able to produce, we can see that we have come a long way. The KM outcomes are comparable with institutes from the developed countries with much more available resources and fewer barriers.

Mapping the story to the 'KM Chef's Canvas'

There are so many aspects of MAPNA's approach to KM to admire: from the structured beginnings to the incremental pilot-based approach, the development of roles, skills and techniques, and the adherence to quality standards.

Of great significance are the tangible results achieved from the pilots, the harvesting of new learnings and ideas and the regular evaluation of the programme's alignment with corporate strategic direction.

Strategic context

MAPNA's KM programme maps directly to its corporate and divisional strategies. It uses an evaluation technique called Knowledge-SWOT (strengths, weaknesses, opportunities and threats) to regularly assess how it is aligned with its organisational strategy.

Governance

MAPNA it is a process-oriented firm. It has a governance model approved by the board. The company processes are underpinned by a quality management system that adheres to ISO standards. All of its processes, procedures, tools and techniques are audited twice a year. This requires documentation of all aspects of KM, with frequent review and improvement. Each KM-related job and the tasks that are associated with it are documented, reviewed and periodically improved.

Culture

A code of ethics underpins how MAPNA works and yet it has deployed counter-cultural techniques to demonstrate Knowledge Management's value. We liked the notion of changing the mindset of staff from 'KM is extra effort in my work' to 'KM is a key part of my work'.

25

TechnipFMC, France, UK and USA: agile KM in a newly merged organisation

NARRATED BY KIM GLOVER, DIRECTOR KNOWLEDGE MANAGEMENT, TECHNIPFMC

When businesses are combined, the KM team need to be agile in responding to demand for their services. Following its merger, oil and gas technology and services company TechnipFMC has been redefining what Knowledge Management can do for it.

Here in a short conversation, at Gatwick Airport en route to a meeting in Edinburgh, Kim Glover, who heads up the Global Knowledge Management Team, looks back at the role KM played in bringing the combined business together and takes a glimpse into the future:

> As you begin to mature as a company, which has to happen quickly after a merger, you can pick up synergies and see areas where you could collaborate better to create business outcomes, which is what Knowledge Management is all about.

Here's how she sees the future for her team:

> We connect people or rather, people connect themselves in the moment of need, using whatever it is they need to use to fill that need.
>   What success looks like to me is that we're on speed dial. That we are part of the fabric of work. It's that simple.

TechnipFMC are now looking at ways to optimise talent management, diversity and inclusion, learning and Knowledge Management and improve collaboration. Kim describes her team as 'a high-functioning Knowledge Management team, with a large toolbox and more importantly a suitcase full of soft-skills, who can connect and collaborate with the other back office groups to help them achieve them their own business objectives.'

'Knowledge Management can help fill in the white space between the other back office groups.'

'A large toolbox, and more importantly a suitcase full of soft skills.'

KM in a merger

Prior to the merger of the two businesses in 2017, KM was viewed through very different lenses. One company was organised with 'Knowledge Management and Quality', primarily focused on lessons learned, whilst the other had Knowledge Management embedded across the business with communities of practice, a wiki, Knowledge Management services and workshops, focused on helping to accomplish business outcomes.

> I led the team from one of the companies and we realised as we got to just before the merger that we had a challenge, in that two-thirds of the company were not going to know anything about us – what we do, how we could support integration. We did have some connection to the merger integration streams prior to the merger, but it was limited.

As often happens when corporate leadership and direction changes, there is a vacuum whilst support functions are aligning themselves. In this case the KM team were quickly able to fill this vacuum – particularly as the new learning strategy had highlighted the value of leveraging knowledge and learning. Given that the team were based in Human Resources at the time, they were able to support many of the integration activities of the newly merged company as a result.

The importance of Knowledge Management in a merger.

> We got together as a Knowledge Management team and we had a brainstorming session on all of the services we could provide that support integration. It was quite a long list. We put together a concise piece of collateral, a one-pager, and called it 'Accelerating Integration' (Figure 25.1 opposite); we circulated it through the top 200 managers using our connections. The team has been kept busy, probably 120% utilised, throughout the two years now since the merger, despite not having globally broadcast: 'This is the Knowledge Management team that you have'. In a way, I think it was almost better; it's better for people to have no expectations and then you can just blow their socks off rather than give them a fancy set of taglines and not be able to support or meet expectations.

'You can just blow their socks off.'

Kim details one example of how the team helped with the integration:

> A couple of months after the merger, when we were still making relationships and trying to meet the new leadership, my boss at the time sent me to Paris to help facilitate a workshop for our corporate health safety and environmental (HSE) and quality team. I met the leaders and made relationships – and they are lasting relationships. Departments change, leadership changes, and because of these relationships, we've been able to deploy our team to support them in ways that they wouldn't have expected prior to making those connections.

Accelerating Integration

Quick Start

Knowledge management and facilitation services can help leaders accelerate a new team's effectiveness in areas ranging from business planning to team culture and assimilation. Most services can be either virtual or in-person. The checklist below outlines many actions leaders take as they launch new teams, and lists performance support services from knowledge management resources. Visit *inside.net.fmcti.com/km* to learn more and submit a request for services.

Can be deployed virtually = 🖳
Can be deployed face-to-face = 👥

ESTABLISHING BUSINESS PLANNING AND EXECUTION STRATEGIES		
Defining mission/vision	🖳	👥
Defining objectives / prioritizing opportunities	🖳	👥
Defining risks and issues; developing mitigating strategies	🖳	👥
Supporting change management	🖳	👥
Project reviews, Quarterly Business Reviews, other high-level meetings	🖳	👥

DEFINING AND ALIGNING PROCESSES AND ROLES		
Gathering and sharing existing processes	🖳	👥
Process mapping / process alignment	🖳	👥
Developing RACI matrices	🖳	👥
Facilitating role definitions		👥

CONNECTING EXPERTS AND ENABLING COLLABORATION AND SOCIAL LEARNING	
Facilitating knowledge-sharing events (TED-like talks, webinars, wikithons)	🖳 👥
Building and utilizing a community to connect SME's and practitioners to achieve social learning	🖳
Creating workgroups or team sites to enable global teamwork and collaboration	🖳

DEFINING AND UTILIZING CRITICAL KNOWLEDGE AND CONTENT	
Documenting important reusable knowledge and information	🖳
Collecting existing knowledge solutions	🖳
Building a reference library	🖳
Creating or updating workgroup sites	🖳 🖳 👥
Creation of short "how-to" videos	

ALIGNING THE TEAM		
New Manager Assimilation activities	🖳	👥
Developing team charters	🖳	👥
Planning and execution of "town hall" or "all-hands" meetings	🖳	👥
Hosting teambuilding events / facilitation of building trusted relationships	🖳	👥
Deploying surveys for "culture checks"	🖳	
Awareness and introductory videos	🖳	👥

ADDITIONAL TOOLS AND PROCESSES AVAILABLE
Networks / Communities of Practice: there may already be an applicable discussion forum and wiki community, or you can request a new one.
Survey creation and deployment.
Facilitation Services, including the use of ThinkTank online brainstorming.
Video Production to communicate, capture knowledge, or introduce new leaders or teams.

Figure 25.1 *The 'Accelerating Integration' document*

For example, last fall, 2017, our team facilitated the second-ever health safety and security consortium (HSSC), with our company leading, and with six or seven other world-leading companies involved. It had been done once before and it didn't necessarily meet expectations. We were able to come in for the second one and it was a tremendous success. We helped them facilitate, develop their agenda, keep their attendees happy and do the before and after surveys, basically extract as much knowledge as possible from the meeting that could be captured and acted on. After that we helped them bring it up a level, as they needed a charter. We used our benchmarking network from LinkedIn and all of our personal networks and a set of charters that we gathered, including one from the Houston Knowledge Management oil and gas round table, and created a draft charter for this consortium which we helped to get agreed.

'A couple of weeks ago, the third annual consortium meeting was held and, to quote one of my colleagues, the leader of our HSE was practically doing cartwheels down the hall, because he was so happy with the results.'

Preparing for a bright future . . .

In preparation for the new structure, Kim brought her new KM team together for a week-long workshop. They were conscious of the need to relaunch KM across the whole of the merged company, and took a hard-nosed look at everything they did, asking 'What is the benefit; what are the drawbacks; and how can we do this better?' Kim takes up the story:

We ended up with a list of 34 things or activities that the team of 12 people does. Eight are different types of workshops.

Throughout the week we collected our information. People were thinking about what they wanted to own. On the day, it was time to decide who would be the product manager for what; I left the room and whilst I was gone for the whole morning I let them develop their process to determine it – and it worked!

Each person on the team now owns more than one deliverable platform and is responsible for looking at the business opportunity, understanding the future roadmap. For instance, if it's an external platform like Spigot, when is the next release coming out? How will that affect us? What are other companies doing with it? How can we utilise this for business benefit? If it is something internal, like a workshop, design thinking is one of the kinds of workshops, what are new ways to achieve business outcomes with design thinking? Everyone in the team can execute using any of the platforms or any of the processes.

'I don't believe in the leader making all the decisions. The team is the smart people.'

. . . with documented processes

Embedding KM into the business process management system.

One of the former team members, a physics Master and Six Sigma expert, used his three years in KM to run process definition workshops and then craft processes for each of the 34 KM processes they identified. These now feature in the organisation's business process management system.

When organisations merge or are acquired KM is often a casualty as management seeks to find savings to justify the move. This is a great example of how by being agile and proactive it is possible to combine the best of each KM approach, to re-energise and reposition KM.

Mapping the story to the 'KM Chef's Canvas'

Processes

Creating a team with resources from merging organisations can be difficult, especially when two-thirds of the business's view of what KM is and can do differs. The week-long team retreat to assess KM's products and techniques resulted in a long list of valuable services packaged as 'Accelerating Integration'. In itself that was impressive; what struck us was that those 34 services were then transformed into documented organisational processes.

Endings and beginnings

Congratulations! Sixteen dishes of rich and varied KM experiences consumed in a short time – that's quite an achievement.

As we have written, read and re-read the stories from our 'Chefs', all three of us have been excited, impressed and, at times, humbled by the variety and depth of experience which they have shared.

We hope that we have left you with inspiration rather than indigestion – that our 'food for thought' will be the beginning of new ideas and impact for your KM activities.

The KM Cookbook was conceived over dinner in a restaurant in Lisbon, overlooking the river Tejo – and we celebrated its completion with more Portuguese food in a bistro close to the river Thames in London's Borough Market.

Our website, kmcookbook.com, contains the full story of how the book came into being, including our approach to selecting interviewees, how we structured the interviews, how we collaborated and curated interviewee stories, and how we ultimately navigated our way to completion.

Most satisfying of all, has been the experience of hearing the thoughts of respected peers who kindly reviewed the book for us. In his review, Larry Campbell, Partner in KPMG's Hong Kong office, described exactly what we had hoped to achieve.

Collison, Corney and Eng have taken a would-be dry subject and delved into it in a creative manner, weaving fact and guidance into a narrative that simultaneously informs and entertains. What they have done with this book is a demonstration of a key aspect of knowledge management itself: the use of storytelling to make important knowledge accessible to the average person. Certify that, ISO 30401.

We have learned a tremendous amount in producing this book and are hopeful that our efforts – blended with the tools and tips from our Chefs – make your KM experience satisfying and successful.

Bon appetit!

Chris, Paul and Patricia
July 2019

Appendices
Interview questions

The questions which follow were used as a broad structure for the interviews with each of our 'KM Chefs'.

Orientation

Describe your working environment – what would I see if I was sitting at your desk? (books, views, awards, certificates, artefacts)
    Please explain the background to your KM programme:

Overall aims.
Specific goals and objectives?
Who would know about these?
(Were they documented?)
Position in the organisation. Branding. Team resources.
What leadership support have you had? Has this been continuous or
    sporadic?
Culture of the organisation. Barriers, behaviours, positives to build
    upon?

Execution

What was the starting point? The business need/pain-point/
    imperative?
How did you go about meeting the challenge – tell your story as it
    happened.
What did your plan look like, and how did it change? (Did you have
    to do any course corrections? Why?)
What KM-related roles and competencies are necessary for your
    approach?
How do you measure your success?
What's next? Do you have a continuous improvement approach?
    How would you improve what you are currently doing?

What aspects of your approach to KM are documented? (policy, tools, procedures?)

How do you define and describe your programme to others in your organisation? Do you have a strapline?

Do you have a picture or visualisation you use when describing the programme?

Is there anything you could share with us?

Reflection

On reflection, what was the biggest challenge you faced?

Where did you get lucky?

What are you most proud of?

What's the nicest thing anyone ever said about your programme?

Biggest risk?

What advice would you give to someone facing a similar challenge?

What skills or behaviours would they need in order to repeat your success?

The restaurant critic (Chapter 7)

Preparing for an audit – tips from the field from Patricia Lee Eng

During preparation of this book, we sought out people who have been audited many times over the past three decades and asked them how they prepare for an in-depth audit. Although they have experience with system-wide audits, programme audits and licensing or certification audits, their preparation for each type of audit was the same. This appendix contains their tips and suggestions.

Ideally, staff should work in such a way that what they are doing every day is always auditable. Being ready for an audit, in theory, should be the same as doing the job and doing it well. It helps if key staff keep unofficial current copies of records handy, even if not required to do so, for quick reference when needed, particularly if retrieval normally takes time. All of this assumes that you know about the audit in advance. Even so, if you are subject to a surprise audit you can do some of these things.

The goal is to make it as easy as possible for the audit team to examine your programme and for your staff to assist the audit team. While audits can be stressful, there is value in them. Just as a restaurant critic identifies great service but bad food, the audit team will help you identify programme strengths and weaknesses, ultimately improving the overall programme. Think of it as an assist visit.

1 Before the audit team arrives
Documentation

For audits that are announced ahead of time, the audit team often provides the organisation with a list of documents they wish to review before they arrive on site. Review and compile their requested list of documents and see if you can anticipate additional documents which they may also want to see. Just provide the documents they request but be ready to provide the additional documents as the audit progresses. The organisation should be careful not to appear 'too eager' but being prepared will make the organisation look responsive, which is always appreciated.

If you know the specific area being audited, try to anticipate what records the auditors will want to review. ISO 30401 calls out required documentation. For example, Section 4.3 requires that 'The organisation shall determine the range and applicability of the knowledge management system to establish its scope . . .'. It goes on to provide guidance regarding definition of the KM programme scope, later stating 'The scope shall be available as documented information'. The auditors will want to see this documentation.

Go through the standard and search for combinations of the words 'shall' and 'document', to anticipate what the auditors may want to see. Make sure all official documents are properly reviewed, approved and dispositioned and be prepared to provide copies to the audit team. For brainstorming sessions or workshops, results and follow-on actions should be clearly identified and annotated. This is important, because common audit findings are that document updates and changes are either not reviewed or approved by the appropriate people. Another common audit finding is that the people doing the work do not have the latest revision of the procedure or document. Ensure that documentation reflects what you actually do.

Official documents should be filed appropriately, but it may be helpful to have a copy of pertinent documents readily available during the audit to answer quick questions from the audit team while copies of the 'official' documents are retrieved. In some organisations, it can take a long time to retrieve official copies. Auditors who are waiting for a document will turn their attention to something else to look at while they are waiting. This can result in expansion of the original audit scope into areas with more weaknesses. It is best to get the information that auditors request quickly so that they maintain their focus rather than possibly open another area of enquiry. Auditors can verify later that the copies are identical to the official records, but they should get the information they need quickly.

Some organisations prepare a briefing book for the audit team before their arrival on site so that the team can get started as soon as they arrive. Audit teams are happy to get these briefing books and it reflects well on the audited organisation. The organisation also gets a chance to review its programme and related documentation as it compiles the briefing book – always a good idea when facing an audit.

Management and staff

Hold a meeting of appropriate management and staff and brief them on the upcoming audit. Explain the purpose of the audit, what the auditors will be looking at, how long the audit team will be on site, and what the audit means to the organisation. Is it an internal audit? A pre-

ISO audit? The ISO certification audit? Will there be lots of interviews? Let everyone know what to expect so that they are ready to support the audit team. Executives, appropriate managers, and leads should be present at both the entrance and the exit meetings, therefore schedules should be adjusted to accommodate these meetings.

Identify people whom the audit team may want to interview and make sure they are familiar and conversant with the programme and their individual responsibilities. Suggest that they arrange their schedules to be able to accommodate interviews by the auditors and any demonstration of KM tools during the audit. Where possible select knowledgeable, enthusiastic people who can talk in depth about what they are doing and their roles in the programme. Where a potential interviewee is uncomfortable with being interviewed, it is helpful to pair them with someone with more experience in being questioned to facilitate the exchange of information or assist by providing clarification during the interview if needed.

It may be a good idea to have potential interviewees get together with KM leads and champions to discuss the upcoming audit and to define expectations, so that they all know their roles as they interface with the audit team. Management and staff can also do practice interviews of each other before the audit team arrives. This sort of preparation will make the actual audit go more smoothly.

Identify staff to interface with the audit team and help them navigate through the organisation and the programme. It is helpful to designate a lead person for this function and have them work with the Lead Auditor. This interface team can also gather and track audit team questions and requests to make sure that all their questions are answered before the team leaves the site. Going over these may help determine where the team will look next, so you can anticipate their needs and answer all their questions. Some auditees hold daily internal meetings with programme staff and the affected managers so that all staff know what the audit team is doing.

Regarding audit logistics, think about where to place the audit team. Some organisations set aside a room with ready access to toilets and photocopying machines for the audit team. They also make the organisation's cafeterias and coffee machines available for audit team use. Some organisations prepare lists of local restaurants for visitors. If so, offer the list to the audit team.

2 When the audit team arrives

There will be an entrance meeting where the audit team is introduced to management and the programme principals. At least one senior manager should be present at both the audit entrance and exit meetings. Key programme staff and others who could be interviewed may also attend. At this meeting, the audit team will introduce themselves, define the audit scope, go over the audit schedule and provide an estimate of when to expect the audit report. If there are field or regional offices which the organisation wishes to include in their certification, the audit team may need to visit one or more of those facilities. If there are specific things the team wants to see, they will tell the organisation at this meeting; however, note that the audit team may request more information as the audit progresses.

The organisation should then introduce its staff and, if it has prepared information for the audit team, provide that information at the meeting. If the organisation has questions about the audit, the auditors or the schedule, they should be asked at this time.

The primary organisation contact should then escort the audit team to their work space and offer his or her assistance in arranging to retrieve documents or set up interviews. Once the audit team are in their workspace and provide their initial information requests, the organisation should leave the team alone, so they can get settled. The primary contact in the organisation should make themselves easily available and check in with the team periodically to see if they need anything.

3 During the audit

After looking through the programme documentation, auditors will ask to interview various staff to determine whether the programme is being implemented effectively. They will pay particular attention to the stated programme goals and objectives in the scoping document and look at how the programme enablers described in ISO 30401, Section 4.4.4, impact the knowledge culture of the organisation. In the interviews, auditors will determine what the interviewees know about the programme, its scope, their roles and responsibilities, programme documents and procedures, and if they know who to contact if they have a problem.

While not necessary, it is a nice touch for a manager to periodically check with the Lead Auditor to see if the audit team are getting all the support they need. It reflects well on the organisation. Most organisations request a daily meeting with the audit team to see how the audit is going and to identify any needs the auditors may have. This practice means there are 'no surprises' at the exit meeting.

4 After the audit

There will normally be findings and observations from an audit. Some will be significant, and some will not. In any case, the organisation does not have to wait to address these findings. It can begin remediation immediately or wait to see the audit report; however, when responding to the audit report, the organisation will be in a stronger position if it can describe the corrective actions it has taken or plans to take in response to the findings. In some cases, corrective actions do not have to be complete for the certifying body to accept the programme; it depends on the significance of the finding and the scope and timeliness of the corrective actions. This may be discussed with the certifying body after the audit report has been issued.

In those cases where the organisation disagrees with the finding or believes that the audit team have overstepped the audit scope or made a finding beyond the scope of the ISO standard, the organisation may appeal the finding to the certification body.

The tips described above have been used by organisations for decades. The relationship between auditor and auditee should not be an adversarial one. Please remember that audits are designed to determine if a programme meets a set of defined requirements, in this case, those of ISO 30401. Before deciding whether to seek certification to this standard, it may be a good idea to conduct an internal assessment of your KM programme or to ask an auditor to do a pre-audit assessment. You may find that there are areas which you have not previously thought of which, if pursued, may take your KM programme to the next level. After a period of introspection and programme updates, you will realise that getting certified to the ISO KM standard will be easy. We hope so. Now go do good things!

Knowledge Management in Schlumberger (Chapter 13)

Eureka leader and sponsor roles

Note: in this document the word 'community' means the Eureka community or SIG to which the Sponsor is attached.

The Sponsor of a Eureka community needs to have a strong background or strong interest in the community's technical area. Through virtual or face-to-face meetings with the community leaders, the Sponsor's role is to provide general advice to the leaders and any required liaison with Schlumberger management. There may be one or more individuals recognised as a Sponsor of a Community or SIG.

To facilitate and structure the interaction between the Eureka's advisory activities and management, a Sponsor is tasked with the following responsibilities:

1 Be actively involved with the community leaders, particularly discussing the key goals and objectives the community sets for the year.
2 Ensure that the community is aware of the business vision(s) and management strategy and that the community's goals/objectives are tied to the vision.
3 Help the community provide input to senior management as to technical directions that should be taken and facilitate the dissemination of feedback from senior management in response to the recommendations.
4 Meet regularly with the leaders at least once every 2–3 months, with supplementary offline follow up, and monitor the health of the community.
5 Meet with all the community members via teleconferences, webinars and workshops to receive technical advice from the community and to offer business focus.
6 Engage key business management leaders in the community's activities, particularly by keeping the community informed of business direction and strategy through presentations.
7 Promote Eureka by communicating community achievements.

Eureka leader training structure headings

- Eureka goals
- Communities and Special Interest Groups definitions
- What is your community or SIG?
- What can you expect from your members?
- Who to contact for what
- Your indicators of success
- Leadership roles and planning
- Leader role (community or SIG)
- Sponsor role
- Where do you start?
- Planning activities
- Sample community/SIG activities
- Get members to help
- Ideas for webinars
- Webinars – Skype for Business
- Virtual workshops
- Bulletin boards
- Publications
- Newsletter examples
- Tech/journal/competitor watch
- Patent-watch
- Publication templates on help page
- Communication – upload and post
- Know your members
- Eureka recognition
- How can you get support?

Transport for London (Chapter 17)

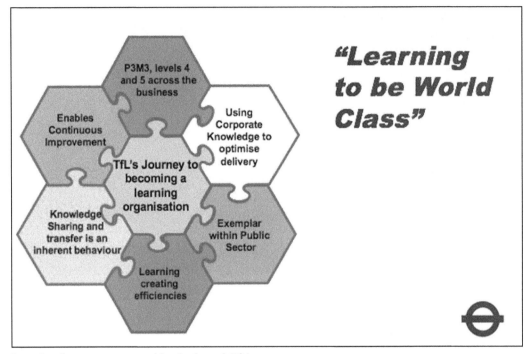

Learning jigsaw as approved by the board (TfL)

Extract from Terms of Reference for Knowledge Sharing SIG

Aims:

To ensure that knowledge-sharing processes, practices and products are effective and consistent across TfL by:

- representing the knowledge requirements of all areas of the business and of key roles
- sharing and pioneering excellent Knowledge Management practice (both within TfL and from outside)
- reviewing information and metrics relating to Knowledge Management (e.g. adoption of lessons learned, analysis of key

themes and systemic issues) and ensuring that issues arising are addressed

- reviewing knowledge-related processes, products, guidance and systems
- acting as champions embedding and communicating improved Knowledge Management practices and supporting the required cultural and capability changes within the wider community of practice
- reviewing the evolving knowledge strategy and programme to ensure this is relevant and achievable across TfL and interfaces with others SIGs and other initiatives are managed.

Saudi Aramco (Chapter 23)

Find the Expert

The player is given some skills, such as storytelling, photography, and instructional design. They are asked to place the skill on the person with the expertise.

The skills are hidden by the 'Hidden Skills' poster, so the player just guesses by looks, and of course gets most of the skills wrong.

We then remove the poster hiding the skills and have a great laugh at how wrong they were. It's interesting how we 'typecast' people. Our Indian friend always gets Excel Macros because they assume he's a technical guy (even though he is!).

The lesson is about expertise location. And how useful it would be if we had a mechanism for finding people based on skill and not job titles.

Find the Chocolate

Today we have many systems (knowledge repositories) and most do not really talk to each other. Systems have their own way of storing and discovering those knowledge assets. We do have a corporate taxonomy, but most applications do not use it.

The player is told that under one of these cups is a piece of chocolate. The chocolate represents some knowledge that they need. And each cup represents a repository of knowledge. We give them three chances to find the chocolate and most do not find it. Hence, knowledge resides in many places and our systems are fragmented.

Then we show a poster of tomorrow. In the future, our knowledge will be linked to the work we do, our functions. By doing this, the knowledge is 'glued' to each other by a common descriptor.

We give the person one chance to find the chocolate. They pick up the handle and of course, since all the cups are attached, they find the chocolate on the first try.

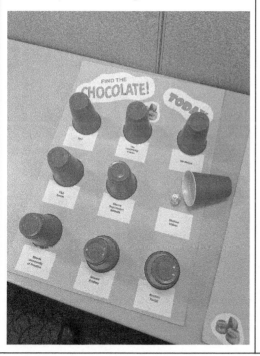

The KM portal is a concept based on a taxonomy of functions (not just disciplines). The idea is to map knowledge assets to the functions of the business, i.e. an e-learning course is linked to the function of 'root cause analysis' instead of just the department disciplines or keywords. If we then map people to the same function, we could essentially deliver content in a more relatable and strategic way.

This is usually followed up with 'When are we getting this?' but that's not the lesson. We're explaining the merits of a smart taxonomy and how it can make finding what you need easier.

MAPNA (Chapter 24)

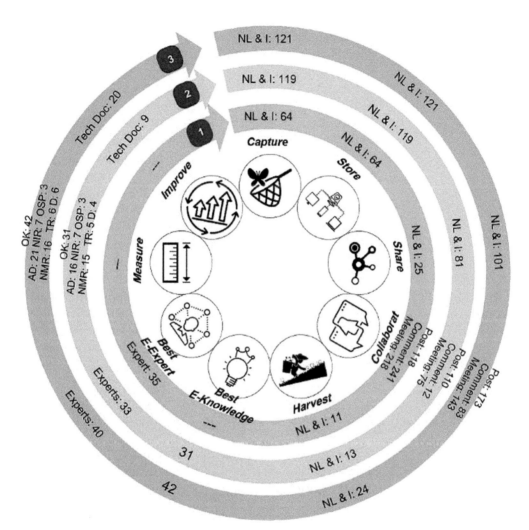

MAPNA's New Learnings & Ideas mapped onto its Knowledge Management Lifecycle (KMLC) model

This illustration displays the statistics on the identified experts, their
new learnings and ideas brought up during the KCC project meetings.
It shows a typical KM lifecycle (KMLC) that has nine stages:
   In the first three stages of the first round, the inner circle, 64 new

learnings and ideas are captured and stored in the workspaces designed for the project so that they can be shared by the project team members.

Then people have collaborated virtually or face to face to start discussion on the validity of each NL&I.

Later in Harvest stage, people register their opinion on each NL&I. In 6th stage, Best E-Knowledge, the validity of each item is verified by the subject-matter experts (SMEs) in the team or across the group if required.

Later the verified knowledge of the 'Best E-experts' is shared between the project team for their utilisation.

In the 'Measure' stage, the results of the expert's interaction on each NL&I are reviewed and the content change is measured.

Finally, in the 'Improve stage' the registered knowledge again is improved and enriched based on the experts' opinions. The most important decision is made at this stage: what business processes and their relevant documents, forms, etc. should be changed to address the new learnings and ideas?

This nine-stage cycle is repeated several times so that knowledge embedding of the pertaining processes are ascertained.

In KCC project this cycle was repeated for three rounds, each one depicted in one circle. In the first round, 64 items were captured where all of them were stored in the workspace. From the 25 NL&I that were shared, 11 NL&I succeeded to the harvest stage.

Meantime a total of 35 experts were identified to further contribute to the project. With their contribution, the quantity and quality of the NL&I items in the second and third rounds improved dramatically and increased to 121 at the final stage. Out of these, 20 ended up with changing the technical documents, 42 are approved for changing the business processes and the rest are being further processed.

The figure is a clear display of the fact that in KM pilot projects, the team have to be loyal to the methodology and follow it so that they can reap the rewards.

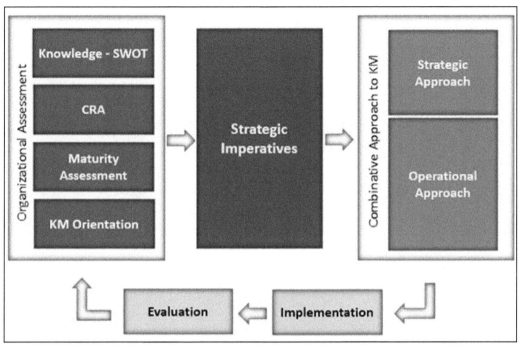

How MAPNA's KM activities are linked to strategy and continue to evolve

Index